WARTIME MEMORIES
OF A CHESTER LAD

WARTIME MEMORIES
OF A CHESTER LAD

by Peter Rowland

Preface

The seeds of this book were sown by Jenny and Bob Joinson, the family now living at 5 Northway, the house where I was born on the 21st December 1931. Some years ago I inherited from my brother-in-law my sister's old cardboard box which had long been forgotten in their loft. In it were various documents relating to the search and purchase of land, plans, building of the house and those lovely old bill heads.

From time to time I would drag out the old cardboard box and reminisce of Mum and Dad, dear sister Mary, relatives and friends. Then it occurred to me that the people whoever they may be at 5 Northway may like to know of the origins of the house. I didn't know their name or full address so they became 'the occupiers' without a postcode; I just hoped they had a friendly postman. A letter was soon on its way and in anticipation of their reply I now had a purpose to delve through what was of interest to keep. I started with my notes of memory or explanation. All sorted, parcelled and ready to post. The Joinson's post code CH4 8BB.

They have now become friends and kindly invited me and my wife Chris back into the house where I was born. It is from the documents of the past along with my notes, letters and discussions with Jenny that she put to me that I had experienced many changes in Chester and that I may care to share them with a local history group. Why not? I am retired supposedly with days to fill, so what could the answer be but 'Yes,' and I did rather like the idea of writing a book.

Within days the reality of the situation was all too clear. The days aren't endless at all, the weeks too short, months fly past - where did time go? I suppose that is the reason I was asked to write this book as time is change.

The Early Years

Change is usually associated with inventions, products, buildings, materialistic things. My memories are of people and how I can relate the changes of today to them, who they were, what was their work, where they worked and where they lived. Most of them were characters and they all came to 5 Northway when I was a boy.

The first person to call on a daily basis was the milkman 'Charlie,' a young cheerful happy man always whistling but still managing the time for passing pleasantries of the day. He would arrive in his horse drawn milk float with several large metal tankards of milk. The whistling would stop and then the usual knock on the back door before opening it. "Good morning Annie - what milk today?" he would shout through from the back kitchen. He knew where the large white milk jug was kept and this he would take back to his cart and ladle out our milk for the day. I remember for a treat we had milk from a Jersey cow at weekends. Not every weekend - just now and again. Cream would settle on the top which we would have poured over jelly. The milk was kept on a cold slab in the pantry and whatever remained in the jug the following morning had 'gone off' overnight, so Mum either made it into scones, which I loved - and still prefer to cakes to this day, but they never quite come up to her standard. Maybe it was the sour milk.

Now the alternative was a concoction called 'Junket' which was usually strawberry-flavoured and it was absolutely disgusting, far worse than even semolina or tapioca pudding. I can only liken it to a variation of yogurt but more watery with unpleasant lumps in. But for some reason Mum, Dad and my sister Mary preferred the Junket to scones so I lost out.

Charlie worked for my great grandparents, the Johnson's at Five Ashes Farm on the Wrexham Road, a dairy and poultry farm. He always seemed to wear the same things - a light brown milking jacket with the odd tear or two which Mum would stitch up for him; and a well worn grey trilby hat with a curly brim. As well as delivering milk he looked after the cows and would do whatever came his way, a most amicable man. He would bring Grandmother Johnson on occasional visits to see Mum. Being a rather large elderly lady she would remain seated in the milk float while we gathered around her, and in the comfort of the house Charlie took time out to enjoy a pot of tea and did considerable damage to the stock of scones. Charlie was just Charlie, I never knew him by any other name and he never spoke of family. I think he may have arrived at the farm from an orphanage.

The land from Wrexham Road to facing Hough Green I was told belonged to their farm. On the right were well established houses, on the left, allotments; a field and a couple of houses on the corner of Cliveden Road. One of the fields had a nice big pond where my best pal Arthur and I always managed to find enough wood to make a raft. Fastening it all together was always the problem as there never seemed to be a length of rope or string at hand. Somehow we achieved a launch which invariably sank, but most times managing dry land before getting too wet. I did however recall one occasion of two oil drums and an assortment of timber completely disintegrating and being submerged into several feet of water and mud. Land seemed far away but was eventually found. The walk across the fields to the gate onto Hough Green seemed endless; with clothes still as wet as when I left the pond, I had the bright idea that removing my trousers and swinging them around over my head by the braces would have dried them by the time I reached home. Then of course my Mum would be none the wiser of my mishap and I would be home for tea. Arthur didn't seem to think it a good idea.

Regardless of this, so off with the trousers now waving frantically over my head we progressed down Hough Green passing the allotments, Arthur following very cautiously some distance to the rear. I had almost reached my crossover point at Selkirk Road, and although I had stopped waving my trousers around I had attracted the attention of the local bobby on his bicycle.

There, who amongst several others to step off the bus, was Inspector Lockley, who lived down Park Road West; a lengthy conversation followed between the pair 'that will be all constable' - what a relief, followed by 'I shall see this young man safely home.' I was going to get home safely anyway, dry, in time for tea, and no one would have been any the wiser. Now I was slightly less wet, 'the world loves a trier' or so they say, and to be accompanied down our path by none other than Inspector Lockley resplendent in his uniform, complete with medal ribbons and carrying his silver topped black cane. The disgrace, the shame of it, in full view of the neighbours! On reflection it could have been worse as Chief Constable Griffiths lived on the corner of Selkirk Road and Park Road West. Inspector Lockley left our house and without going into detail I found that 'the world loves a trier' was completely ill founded.

Around dinner time the bread man would call with an assortment of loaves in a large basket, the more sophisticated items like buns, scones, cakes and pies remained in his cart out of sight as they were seldom called for. I can never recall Mum buying anything but bread as she made all he had to offer herself, and of course any left over stale bread was made into bread pudding. He always wore fawn cord breeches with leather gaiters and brown boots. A long light brown coat with an array of pencils in his top pocket and over his shoulder a large leather bag full of money which noisily yet rhythmically, bounced around as he ran up the path frantically holding the top down in case anything was lost.

He always seemed to be in a hurry. A rather large and elderly man to be dashing about and he never seemed dressed for speed. I never knew the bread man by name. His cart had four wheels, high sides, roof and two doors at the back, all painted green and sign-written in gold and black - 'Griffiths, Bakers and Confectioners, Lower Bridge Street, Chester.' Across the road was the Falcon Tea Rooms and from there as far down as Castle Street was busily used by Crosville buses bound for North Wales. On the corner of Lower Bridge Street with Grosvenor Street was the milk bar and on a small island facing this was a below-street-level gents toilet – and nowhere near as grand as the ones below the Town Hall Square. The bus drivers seemed to have great difficulty negotiating the tight turn left with hardly room for a bus, not to mention the additional hazard of pedestrians after a coffee too many, as I don't recall such a convenience in the milk bar.

I have seen people come and go as I have seen change but one person wouldn't believe the change that I now see in my shopping. His name was Sam Lee. He also came to 5 Northway with his horse and cart which had open sides with neatly tied back canvas curtains. Four rubber-tyred wheels which I suppose had seen better days on a motor car. We knew him as the 'veg. man.' He would knock on the door and shout 'any greens today?' Its winter and he has some cabbage, sprouts, turnip and potatoes. Mr. Lee's produce was purely seasonal.

I take a pause from my writings to see what we have in the kitchen. I find more choice; a pack of washed watercress, spinach and rocket salad from the U.K., Kenya, Portugal, Italy and the USA. Radish from Israel, spring onions from Mexico, cucumber from Spain, peppers from Portugal and tomatoes from the Canary Islands. A very unseasonable salad in January and we have some raspberries to follow - from Morocco.

I can't be positive as to where Mr. Lee operated from but can suggest an area in Saltney. Part way down Mount Pleasant on the left hand side was a break in the housing; through and to the right was a yard with outbuildings. An enclosed passage way provided access to some houses on an unmade road down to Chester Street.

I cannot leave the frequent visitors to No. 5 without what I found the most happy and friendly band of men, affectionately known as the 'Dustmen'; now known as 'Refuse Collection Operatives' as they are no longer 'dusty'. But dusty they were, well and truly, as most of the content of our dustbin was ash from the living room range.

The only other form of heat in the house was the 'Valor' paraffin oil stove which would appear in the hall, but only on the very coldest of winter days. The stove was tall and round. The word 'Valor' was set against a red piece of celluloid and decorative perforations in the stove projected dancing images around the walls and ceiling, which I would sit and watch after dark. Amusement was simple before television.

The Dustmen, of which there were about five, came each week on a Friday morning, the dust cart pulled by a large shire horse, always adorned in brightly coloured rosettes, ribbons and well polished brasses. The man who looked after the horse was Mr. Dodd who also appeared to be in charge of the men. He would bring the horse to a halt outside our house and see to its food in a horse bag and filled a bucket from our tap. This signalled dinner time for all. Mum always provided them with a large jug of freshly brewed tea which must have been absolute nectar to those men.

All the Dustmen wore brown overalls, jacket and trouser style, and carried large baskets, aptly named swill baskets. This would be carried - arm outstretched to hold the substantial rim, the opposite edge supported on the hip. If there wasn't much in your bin then it would be tipped into the swill basket which saved the Dustman a trip to bring back the empty bin. It wasn't usual to have a full bin as everyone had a coal fire and a compost heap which took care of most household waste. Whatever was left in the grate after a day's burning was riddled to separate the cinders from the ash, cinders were saved to go back on the fire.

Other less frequent visitors to No. 5, like Mr. Davies, would arrive by bicycle - he worked for the Prudential Insurance. I don't think he was referred to as 'the Pru man.' Then the 'tea man' who had an enormous tea pot on the roof of his van. The Kleen-ezee man - they never change. The Corona lorry would arrive at the corner of The Green laden with bottles of pop; known as 'the Pop man' he wore a brown coat with a green collar and may even have had a hat. He would arrive at our back door with a selection of four in a wooden crate. I can't recall Mum ever or very rarely buying anything from him. I think he got fed up and stopped calling. The Pop Works were on the left hand side going up Queens Park Road from Handbridge, opposite a piece of land which became a builders merchants yard, Moore and Brocks. Now the coal man I remember had 'Charles Randal' lettered on his lorry. His coal yard was in Boundary Lane, Saltney.

Vast railway sidings stretched both sides of the main road, the crossing gates being constantly opened and closed as Great Western pannier shunting engines moved wagons of coal. Lines went through as far as the river and to the right a good half a mile alongside the river.

They also branched left to the back of Crightons, the Ship Builders. I recall this being a large brick building with a corrugated roof and rather neglected.

Dad and I on a walk one day found an open door through what we discovered to be an empty shell of a building with plans of steamships scattered about the floor. There were landing stages along the riverside though rather decayed. While putting together my memories of Crightons I discovered that the Chester shipyards had quite a reputation - they built ships for the Royal Navy - and in 1810 it was noted that more ships were being built than at Liverpool. The speed and manoeuvrability of Nelson's ships were attributed to the underside of the hull being clad in Swansea copper. The steamship 'Royal Charter' wrecked near Holyhead on 26th October 1859 when many lives were lost was built on the River Dee a few miles below Chester. I wonder if this was Crighton's shipyard in Saltney? At the time of the shipyards, the lead works also contributed to the city's wealth and the still- remaining shot tower, built in 1800, is probably the oldest in Britain.

Beyond Crightons was what I only knew as 'Dobbins Knackers Yard,' what I think now would be an animal rendering plant. My pal Arthur and I would go there for maggots to go eel fishing. A horrible, smelly place, we always had to help ourselves but they were free and the eels seemed to prefer them to worms. Between Boundary Lane and the railway bridge was the Rustproof Metal Window Company.

In the summer months probably only one visit. A man differently dressed than most, sporting a black beret, would call, pushing a bicycle strewn with strings of onions. Mum said that he had come all the way from Brittany in France to sell his onions. This was all a bit of a mystery to me when Mr. Lee only had to bring them from Saltney.

Then of course there were the 'Gypsies', not now I am told, politically correct. They would surprise you any time of any week and they always came in numbers and far too often for Mum to feel comfortable with, with their artificial flowers, boot laces, ribbons, whatever. Of course they would tell your fortune if you crossed their palm with silver, which Mum always did, in case of a curse being left on the house. Rest assured Jenny and Bob she never let you down. Our hall was always graced with a polished brass jug full of their hand crafted artificial flowers.

There was a very large area of land which has changed beyond belief and a piece of this was where Mr. Lee's horse was put out to grass in the summer. From the roundabout in Selkirk Road, the through road to the large houses in Curzon Park was no more than a pot- holed cinder track and marginally any better continuing to the old Dingle footbridge. All the fields to the right of the roundabout belonged to the Hunter family of Redland House, Hough Green. I never thought that one day I would find my way to this very grand house, now The Redland Hotel, to spend our wedding night before motoring on to Ireland.

There were stables at the rear of their garden and further outbuildings across the road which we knew as 'the Backs.' There were always people around when I was in the backs or feeding the hens and it seemed to be run as a smallholding. There were several large poultry houses and pens facing Selkirk Road with fields running alongside and behind with a few cows and sheep, horses being in the top field. To the left of the roundabout was a field fronting Selkirk Road. Alongside this and progressing up the cinder track were fields and allotments, and the field where Sam Lee put his horse out to graze. The land at the top was Browns of Chester sports ground. Fronting the rather nice pavilion was the football and hockey field and alongside the road was a red shale tennis court and a bowling green. Brown's football team of course played in their corporate colours of gold and rich brown. Although I watched from time to time I can't remember whether they played Wednesday afternoons or Saturday. I think Wednesday, as all the shops in Chester would close at dinner time. The lads would be at a loose end and the distraction of television, daytime drinking and DIY had yet to come.

There was a further field beyond the hockey field through to Curzon Park South.

The roads to the rear of Selkirk Road, Rothesay Road, Argyll Avenue and Garrick Road were there, some in an unmade state, with houses scattered about, leaving plenty of open land. The more consistent housing was on Garrick Road from the Earlsway End.

The callers to 5 Northway taken care of, brings me to my Dad, and he leaves No. 5 on a daily basis. All seven days of the week. His life was his shop, and lay preaching on a Sunday. On week days he would bus into Town each morning to open his hardware shop in Foregate Street by nine o'clock sharp. He never had a watch but there was a large standard clock in the middle of the road directly outside the shop.

This regulated Dad's day, and at times of anticipated refreshment, dinner and tea, Dad would commence his visitations to the window constantly checking the time. Refreshment would either be tea in what he called 'the back room' or occasionally, Mr. Williamson from the Park Café next door would ask Dad to come round for tea and a toasted tea cake while Clarence looked after the shop. The key would be turned in the door at 12.30 p.m. when Dad came home and we all sat down to a cooked dinner. In the evening it was six or half past and home for tea.

I always looked upon Clarence as being a very fortunate man as he had the option of either of the two shop bikes to go out on deliveries. One bike had a carrier and basket over the front wheel which was much smaller than the one at the back. It also had a stand that folded away under the carrier. But my favourite was the big three-wheeler. Two wheels to the front and one at the back and only ever used for the heavy deliveries.

Between the front wheels was a cavernous box, big enough for me to play in and on a sprung axle. It had everything, two top doors to lock, handbrakes and a double roller bell. As I haven't seen a cycle bell of this kind to this day I think that I should try to describe it. It was very different and louder than the traditional cycle bell which had a domed top sitting on the mechanism and operated by a thumb lever. Now picture this bell turned on its side with another top added to what was the underside of the mechanism. Unlike the traditional bell it had no thumb lever. The two domes were made to freely rotate and were activated by rolling them with the flat of your hand - hence the name 'double roller.'

I can't deny people knew when you were coming but the sound was both melodious and exciting. It was a musical instrument and I would play it whenever I could much to the annoyance of whoever was in the shop, and Dad wouldn't be too far away to stop the fun. Over the back wheel was for me a rather oversized coil sprung leather saddle with tool box and housed under this was the lever of the parking brake, for when you left the bike unattended. Lamps would be fitted for the dark evenings and I think Dad tried both oil and carbide, but I do remember filling them with oil, trimming wicks and frequently having to clean black from the thick magnifying glass before Clarence had the honour to take her out on the late afternoon run. Although I don't suppose he saw it the way I did, going home was more likely to be on his mind. Marston's had a cycle shop in Bridge Street and this was where the three-wheeler was taken whenever it needed attention, which I remember to Dad's dismay was all too frequent; I longed to ride this fantastic machine.

On the opposite side of the street was their motor cycle showroom, which I think was divided by the steps up to St Michael's Arcade. It was below street level, as most premises were on this side of Bridge Street. Access was by a ramp. It always seemed a busy area and I recall out-front displays of Castrol oils and a petrol pump. They had a third shop in the same street selling radios, which we never had in the early years. Our sole entertainment was a wind-up gramophone and a piano.

Now the clock, as I remember, stood on a small island at the corner of City Road with Foregate Street; an unassuming sort of clock, nowhere near as grand as the Eastgate. I am told that it was financed by a Mr. Rowcliffe, a local man of some wealth and a benefactor of good causes.

On the same corner was the Ring o' Bells public house where some time each day, whatever the weather, this man would appear with his bag of newspapers. He wore a shabby jacket on which was pinned his medal ribbons. He had lost a leg and was on crutches. He would prop himself up against the pub wall as he sold his papers. It was always a very busy area as there was a bus stop directly outside Dad's shop. I don't think he ever had any papers left at the end of the day. After the Ring o' Bells was Gerrards, the tobacconists. They sold everything a smoker could possibly wish for, and the air wafting through the doorway was absolute perfume.

Then comes ' H. Rowland' Dad's hardware and ironmongers shop:

everything for house and home, and always the smell of carbolic soap and firelighters; not quite as exotic as Mr.Gerrards. Then there was the 'Park Café' which was over the bakers and confectioners shop and that smelled of loaves, fresh from the oven. The last shop on the block was Bradley's mens and boys outfitters, a very large shop which also had a shoe department around the corner into Seller Street. This was always known as 'Bradley's Corner.' It occurs to me that every shop then had a very distinctive smell about it which your nose recognised as soon as you opened the door and in some cases before.

I suppose that I should also mention the other two who left No. 5 each day for school - me and my sister Mary - she went to Love Street on the bus and had a book of tickets bought in advance so she got an extra ticket for free. I always had the feeling that Mary rather liked school, after which she usually walked to Dad's shop just down the road. There she would spend an hour or so doing jobs or homework before they got the bus together for home.

Somewhere in the middle of all this 'the early years,' I remember very clearly my first day at primary school on the Lache Estate. It seemed an endless walk with Mum down Hough Green and Cliveden Road. I was left at the school gate and was told to join in with the multitude of boys and girls running around the playground. I found this rather difficult as friends so far had only come in ones and twos. A large lady with grey hair who reminded me of my grandmother was soon to appear, vigorously swinging a bell. The running around ceased and everyone formed a line as if by magic except for me. The silence that followed was soon broken. "Name? You must be the new boy. Go to the back of the line" was rasped out to these sensitive ears. I was always told to say 'please' but thought it best not to mention.

We went into the building and through to a room where we hung

19

our coats, which I thought I might never be able to find again. Then we went into a big cold room, where everything seemed to be extra loud. We were all given a flowered smock to wear even the boys, and a roll of corrugated cardboard which we had to lie on in complete silence for what seemed ages. It gave me time to think things through, and I felt vulnerable and frightened.

This wasn't for me, and after this enforced rest period, I was set on leaving for home. I carefully retraced my way back to the playground. At last through the gate I ran till I could run no longer. How it was to be free of such a place. I managed several successful escapes in the first few weeks after which I was excused the wearing of the smock and the roll of corrugated cardboard, but the memory has always remained.

The early years, the innocent years, whatever one cares to know them by, are coming to an end. Mary has left school and she has her first job in the office of Henry Dodd, Farmers and Butchers in the Market Hall. Out of her first week's wages she gives me my first pocket money - thruppence. All mine to spend.

I well remember the illuminations which I think were in 1938 but I cannot recall why they had them that year, but I do remember walking from our house with Mum, and Mr. Ball with Wilfred. Wilfred was a bit older than me and was called up in the later war years and served in the Irish Guards. I was very envious of this and desperately wished I was eighteen.

The Ball's lived at 15 Northway and next door at 16 lived the Mostyn's. Both Mr. Ball and Mr. Mostyn worked at what was then known as the 'lunatic asylum' on Liverpool Road. Mr. Mostyn unfortunately had lost an arm in the 1914-18 war and never ceased to impress me with his ability to ride a bicycle which he did on a daily basis to and from work. Witnessing his stopping of this machine in front of number 16 would certainly have justified a round of applause. While braking slightly he managed to cock a leg over the saddle and to run alongside the bike before coming to rest at the kerb.

The illuminations were very impressive. We walked through Handbridge and over the Old Dee Bridge, everywhere was bathed in coloured lights. All along the City Walls, through the Groves, the bandstand, suspension bridge, and the Snuff Mill - the island below the weir was full of fountains floodlit in colours of the rainbow.

We crossed the suspension bridge which was exciting as it really swayed by the number of people to-ing and fro-ing. All along the river were so many small boats and motor launches all covered in coloured lights. Across from The Meadows on Dee Banks a huge outline of an ocean-going liner in what must have been hundreds of light bulbs. To me as a small boy I thought it must have been life size. I suppose they were the most tasteful of illuminations but then it was 1938 and it was Chester. So what else would one expect? On the way back, crossing the suspension bridge, we were told that Grosvenor Park was also lit up, but we were tired and set for home. Some we hadn't seen but it was a walk in the dark, which I will always remember. We seemed to walk everywhere then or run and always with an old worn tennis ball in your pocket.

Some Saturday mornings I would set off early for Dad's shop, having fun with a ball all along the rough road through Curzon Park and down to The Dingle Bridge. The walk through Town was an adventure and whatever time I got to the shop it always seemed time for me to make tea. This we had in the back room, Dad with a cigarette and if I was lucky I'd be given a penny to go for a jam pasty from the cake shop next door. They were by far the largest of his cakes. My thoughts were of being grown up and having a telephone and cigarettes, not that we have a telephone at home but we have at the shop. It stood on Dad's desk where he did all the bookkeeping. It was tall and black on a round base with a white disc displaying our number, which I never knew.

The big Browns of Chester where Arthur's, my best friend's Dad, worked as an upholsterer was number one in the telephone directory. On the top of the telephone was to me what looked like a chopped off ear trumpet which old men used in comics. This you spoke down but first you had to lift off the ear piece hanging from a clip with its long tangled cable. As soon as this was held to your ear, as if by magic a lady's voice comes down the cable. "Number please"; quickly I say "Sorry you have been troubled," and put it back on the hook; but only when Dad was in the shop.

I love the telephone and when it rings it's always someone wanting Dad. Dad says things are about to change with the telephone as it's going automatic, which seems even more magic, as they won't need all those nice ladies anymore. All the equipment is going into a big new building on the corner of Little St. John Street with St. John Street, opposite the convent school. Here's another even bigger building being built for the Army opposite The Groves between the suspension bridge and the Snuff Mill - Western Command - sounds very important.

I looked forward to Dad coming home from the shop each night with his newspaper, which had usually been well read by this time, and after he's hung his coat in the hall it's passed over to me to look for the page where I can find the next adventure of Rupert Bear.

Dad isn't himself tonight as he passes the paper over to Mum which she reads in silence. Dad goes into the back kitchen and I hear the kettle being filled and the 'pop' of the gas hob being lit. We are going

22

to have a pot of tea, though no one has asked. It's not the usual end of day home coming and I feel that I have to remain silent.

After a while Mum speaks, but very slowly 'Dear God, those poor sailors!' Dad comes in with the tea and has found some digestive biscuits. Mum folds the paper up on her knee and I listen intently as they talk about news in the paper of a submarine gone missing in the Irish Sea. It was 'The Thetis' built at Cammel Laird's shipyard, Birkenhead. It was undergoing sea trials in the Irish Sea before being handed over to the Admiralty and had failed to resurface from a dive. There was a full crew on board and engineers from the shipyard. They seem to have lost communication with the submarine but know of her location being in fairly shallow water in Liverpool Bay. A rescue operation was underway with salvage vessels and the big floating crane from Liverpool. I don't know where the paper went so I never got to read Rupert Bear. Maybe I will find it in the morning if it hasn't been used for lighting the fire.

All we talked about at school for most of the morning was 'The Thetis' and looking at a big map of England hanging over the blackboard. We can see North Wales and where they think 'The Thetis' will be somewhere out into the Irish Sea, this particular area being called Liverpool Bay. Even on the map it seemed a long way to go from Birkenhead and Liverpool.

When I get home at dinner time, Mr. Dye our next door neighbour who comes from North Wales, has a wireless and he thought Mum would be worrying about the sailors, so he had gone round and set her mind at ease. The good news is that they have located the submarine, all of the salvage vessels are there, and that weather permitting, the floating crane 'Goliath' is confident of a lift. Deep sea divers have gone down surveying the situation. Mr. Dye knowing North Wales thinks that on a good day you should be able to see it quite clearly from the top of the Great Orme at Llandudno.

Afternoon school was back to usual lessons and hoping all the time for some news of the trapped sailors. Some of us get into trouble for not paying attention and have to leave the room and stand in the hall. If you're spotted by the Headmistress, then that's real trouble. I manage to get home without too much grief and when Dad comes in he hangs his coat in the hall. I get the paper to catch up with Rupert Bear, yesterday's going to light the fire. All of this because of Mr. Dye's news from the wireless re-told by Mum which is way ahead of Dad's morning paper. Mr. Dye calls round later with news that some of the crew have managed to leave the submarine by the Davey escape apparatus and are safely on board one of the rescue vessels. The divers have had response from knocking on the hull and are attempting to secure lifting chains. The news is absolute joy and we talk of nothing else through tea and well into the night.

Dad seems to think that we should be taking the train to Llandudno on Saturday, and if it isn't too far out to sea, the possibility of seeing the salvage operation and the rescue of the crew. It all goes quiet; its time for bed. Saturday comes and with Dad I get the bus for the General Station in City Road. Dad buys his usual packet of 'Park Drive' cigarettes and a 'Daily Express.' All aboard the train for Holyhead in a smoker, whistle blown and we're on our way to Llandudno. I spend all of my time looking out of the window as the carriage rocks its way over the maze of points leaving Chester station. So many things to see, places I know. The Roodee, the river, how soon Saltney passes by, and I look around our carriage and all of the passengers including Dad are hiding behind their newspapers, apart from when they struggle to turn pages over, then I get an occasional glance which makes me feel that I shouldn't be there.

After a while I get a bit fed up looking out of the window, field after field, some with cows in - seeing the sea through the far window. It seems ages ago since we left Chester. I wonder if we are ever going to get to Llandudno.

Dad folds up his newspaper before passing it over to me, takes down his leather attaché case from the rack. He's never parted from his case, which soon reveals a couple of sandwiches, cake, some biscuits, a thermos flask of tea and a small corked medicine bottle of milk, all being laid out on the seat between us. What a feast we enjoyed and much to the envy of our fellow passengers.

"Not long now son" as we leave Colwyn Bay. Rhyl is as far as I've ever been before and Dad was right - it's not too long before we are in Llandudno and asking our way to where we get the train that takes us up the Great Orme, which, I'm told is very exciting, as it's a mountain railway and that Mary and Mum would have wished they were here. I wasn't so sure, as they didn't seem too excited about it last night.

Llandudno was cool, grey and windy as we found our way to the train; more a carriage without an engine to pull it. I didn't know whether we were pulled by cog wheels or cable but we made it to the top, or not quite I seem to remember; we had a bit of a walk. I do know it was very high up and we were hoping to have a good view of a rescue and everyone safe and sound on dry land.

It was very windy; rain was in the air when we were off the train, just a few of us. I've never seen so many seagulls most of them on the ground, some that were flying, being blown about are making a shrieking call, it was frightening, haunting. I didn't like being there and I could only think of those poor sailors trapped in their submarine down in that cold dark sea. There weren't many people there with us and as we huddled together in the cold wind, Dad pointed way out to sea on the horizon, what looked like a ship and the tail-end of what we thought must have been 'The Thetis.' It all seemed so small. To come all that way - we had seen it, but weren't sure. It was all just too far away and we hadn't and couldn't have seen anyone rescued. I just felt very, very sad and I think Dad did. Without a word we left the place for our journey home.

Whatever is talked about sooner or later a man by the name of Adolf Hitler crops up. Dad always says "He's a warmonger and we should have finished them off in 1918." I remember thinking it a funny name which I mentioned to Mum. No more than our next door neighbour Mr. Hiram Irlam, who I then thought must also be a German. He managed the Co-op boot and shoe repair shop at the top end of Grosvenor Street opposite Cuppin Street - that lovely smell of leather when you opened the door.

One of my friends at school was Jean Lanceley; she lived on Selkirk Road. They had a car which I thought rather special and when I questioned this with Mum it was explained to me that Jean was an only child and that I had a sister, which was very special compared with a car. How right she was! The Lanceley's did however own a sweet factory making all sorts of boiled sweets. Jean and I would go there after school and watch huge cauldrons of boiling sugar, so many flavours, so many colours, being poured into equally large shallow metal trays to half cool before being wound through a mangle like metal roller press, coming out as hundreds of pear shapes but still all in one piece and back once more into the metal tray to cool before being broken up into individual sweets, dusted with sugar and put into big glass jars ready for the shops.

We would wander off and explore this big fairy tale of a place.

Where they made the sweets was very busy with lots of people and very, very hot, but there seemed so much emptiness to get lost in. One day, exploring, we found lots of cards hanging on a wall with packets of chewing gum stuck on, all in different colours, and we thought, different flavours like the sweets. They were all wrapped in little packets of clear cellophane and looked very nice. It said 'Wrigleys' on the card. We filled our pockets without anyone knowing. Jean said that her Dad wouldn't mind.

A few days after out visit, Jean mentioned that it had been noticed that some display samples of Wrigley's new line in flavoured chewing gum were missing, and that her Dad was most concerned as to what might happen to any poor soul tempted to eat this imitation of the real thing. I thought of a sad story Mum had told me of a little girl buried in the old cemetery and on her gravestone the inscription read, 'chewing gum, chewing gum made of wax has sent me to my grave at last.' We were very quiet for a few days and we never went there again after school.

Lanceley's sweet factory was known as 'Bebbingtons' and was on St. Werburghs Street, across the road from what was the back entrance of Woolworths, now no longer there and Bebbington's is now 'The Living Room Restaurant.'

As youngsters, getting up to mischief was knocking on doors and Mount Pleasant was the usual target as there wasn't the problem of front gardens and gates. Carving your initials on trees - mine could still be on a sycamore tree on The Green across the road from number 5, or was I frightened off by Mrs. Irlam before I could finish it?

Going down the entry into Mount Pleasant and then the path down, passing the tip to the railway line where Arthur and I would scramble up the bank and carefully put ha'pennies on the line before the Great

Western 'castle class' came through for Paddington. Our plan was that after the train had passed over them we might be able to pass them on as pennies, size about right for a penny, but no longer looked like a coin of the realm and too bent about to go in a slot machine. Was our mischief, which sounds quite innocent, what we know today as 'vandalism?'

It wasn't unusual for the Paddington Express to have to stop before the run into Chester Station. Usually on the Gas Works viaduct by Paradise Street, where the kids from the street would shout for pennies to be thrown down; they were seldom disappointed. I happened to be there a couple of times and came home with pennies in my pocket. One time it was our lucky day - they came down in handfuls and were dropped as fast as we could pick them up - our fingers burnt and sore. Unfortunately for us it was the restaurant car that had come to a standstill over the street and we became the victims of a mischievous chef, who was heating them up in a frying pan.

The houses I remember in Paradise Street stood three storeys high, looking rather grand in a continual terrace from the viaduct to almost the Watergate and only on the one side of the street overlooking the Roodee - prime viewing on race days.

Whatever Mum and Dad are talking about I have a listen. The building of the new telephone exchange has been stopped and all the equipment is being sent overseas, most of it to a telephone exchange in Malta which quite surprises Dad, and, he doesn't seem at all happy about the lack of glassware at the shop, mainly globes and funnels for gas and oil lamps from Poland - all to do with what's going on in Europe with that man Hitler and the war, which keeps cropping up.

Mum tells me that they have been talking about my schooling and what were my thoughts about going to Wirral House on the corner of

Selkirk Road with Hough Green. I had no idea what it would be like but I knew what it was like where I was, and I didn't like it. It was the short walk that appealed to me and a school uniform which I hadn't had before. I remember a new cap and tie bought from the 'Etonian'; the blazer, a hand me down from a boy that had left the school. I loved that blazer. It was maroon with silky black edging and the top pocket where we kept our pencils was embroidered with the school badge. All this change going on, and they are having a trial run testing the 'lights' for the illuminations; something to look forward to after school. Unfortunately all the talk of war over the last few months becomes reality and we are at war with Germany - 3rd September 1939, and the illuminations cancelled.

Christmas 1939

Our first Christmas of the war doesn't seem much different to any other, but this Christmas dinner, for a treat, we are having a 'capon', which Dad tells me is a very big chicken. I always remember we had a big chicken at Christmas from Great Grandma's farm. It seemed to last for days and this one's going to be even bigger. Paper decorations some of which I made at school, hang from each corner of the room across to the light and where we usually have a rather faded looking aspidistra in a polished copper pot, stands the Christmas tree. This is in our living room and according to Dad it is the engine room of the house. It is where the coal fired iron range is that heats the room, the back boiler heats the water; it has an oven and a place to dry wood. How I loved toasting bread by that fire and on a Saturday we would have light cakes to toast from old Mrs. Campbell's shop in Northgate Street Row. They were very special; a recipe that died with the old lady.

The living room was the only warm room in the house. It was the room where we lived. We never used the sitting room, our best room with the 'Buoyant' three piece suite, but on Christmas day morning Dad would insist that we all went into the back kitchen and stayed there until he said otherwise. Then after a lot of noise from the dining room he would appear at speed through the door, holding at arms length a shovel full of glowing red hot coals from the range fire and, filling the house with smoke whilst uttering "Stay back, stay back." The hot coals come to rest in the empty fireplace in the sitting room. I am sent out to the coal house for a bucket of coal. The best coal 'Holly Lane.' I supposed the name of the colliery. We soon have the luxury of a nice warm fire and a big soft comfortable settee to look forward to after Christmas dinner. I had a read of my 'Rupert Annual' and a game of draughts with Mary and Dad, which I always loose.

Into the war years, the usual callers still came, but I notice Charlie no longer calls with the milk. I liked Charlie, he was always happy and I never knew what happened to him. I suppose he volunteered for the Army. After Great Grandmother Johnson died her two sons, my Great Uncles Norman and Albert, didn't have the same interest in farming and they eventually gave up the tenancy of the farm to a Mr. Dodd and they moved to his small holding in Browns Lane in Handbridge. I suppose a convenient swap.

So Uncle Norman, every bit as happy as Charlie comes with the milk. I think it's still from the old farm in Wrexham Road, but it's in bottles and we no longer get the top of the milk from the Jersey cow to put on our jelly.

Dad is finding it difficult to get stock for his shop and can't see it getting any better, and he tells me that I won't be seeing Clarence any more as he has left the shop, which makes me feel very sad. - I suppose to go in the Army. But I feel very grown up that I now have some of his jobs to do at the shop after school, and have been given a book of penny bus tickets just like Mary used to have. The bus stop is just across the road from school. I usually get off the bus at St. Werburghs Street as I like the walk through Town, and seeing all those guns and fishing rods on display in Monk's the Gunsmiths which I pass across the road from the Regal Cinema.

At the shop my school satchel goes in the office where I make Dad a cup of tea, then I am on the way to Musgrave's timber yard in St. John Street just past the Blossoms Hotel, for of all things, a bucket of sawdust. It seemed a regular thing at Musgrave's. There were always a few butchers, bakers and grocers all there for their buckets of sawdust. I suppose most of the shopkeepers had floors that were brushed and mopped each night after closing - few shops were carpeted. Dad would always add water to the sawdust to dampen it before scattering it all over the floor, as he reckoned it kept the dust down when brushing. I usually did this as Dad didn't trust me with the mop and bucket.

Dad tells me that he has had a good day, so before he dampens the bucket of sawdust he adds more than a drop or two of disinfectant to the water. That lovely smell of pine and it's nice to see him happy. He has had a delivery of crockery from the Potteries, all packed with straw in a large wooden crate, waiting in the warehouse across the cobbled yard at the back of the shop to be unpacked in the morning. But that's another day and after mopping we go home together on the bus. Dad doesn't have to pay for me as I have a ticket.

Most of what Dad sold in his shop was brought by horse and cart from the railway goods yard and went into Dad's warehouse by an access lane from Seller Street. Some goods came from Crowder's wholesale supplies in Seller Street and Harker's in City Road by the canal bridge. Sometimes Dad and I would carry things back ourselves. I enjoyed this as I had a go in the lift, Crowder's was fully electric. Harker's had only room for the operator who would heave himself up to the desired floor by a thick rope dangling in the corner. A very bumpy ride and once having tried it you opted for the stairs. The back lane as we called the access road always seemed to be busy with shire horses and carts, and I think there may have been a blacksmiths.

The following day after school all the crockery has filled the empty display shelves and the warehouse, with straw everywhere being scattered about by a couple of hens; where they came from I don't know. Amongst the straw I eventually find the saw and hammer to dismantle the crate into lengths, then cut into six inch pieces ready to chop up and wire into bundles. I have a ring to pass them through so as I don't put too much in - kindling wood to sell in the shop. Then maybe a promise of a jam pasty on Saturday!

If Dad wasn't around I would sell the odd thing or two. I could work the till - it was very simple in shape, just a long narrow drawer in a cabinet, on the top a small aperture framed in brass and under this was a roll of paper on which you wrote the item and price. As you pulled the drawer open a bell rang, the money went into the respective compartments. I took out the change and when closing the drawer the paper moved on ready for the next customer. I always had some scrap paper so as I could work out the change as I wasn't as good as Dad. He could work it out in his head, just like that.

A couple of poorly dressed little girls came into the shop asking if we had any wood to spare as they had nothing to burn at home. I thought that whatever there was hasn't cost Dad anything, so I left them some each night at the back of the warehouse. Not cut into bundles it wasn't really sellable and anyway I'd forgotten how to work the till.

It wasn't comfortable being cold, without heat and we haven't any heat worth speaking of other than a couple of Valor paraffin oil stoves in the shop. It's a fair size shop and cold. When paraffin was wanted each day for the stoves I would set off with two big cans to Moriss's paint makers just a short walk further up the street into town.

Morris's was a very gloomy, dark basic sort of place, full of enormous vats painted green, all with highly polished brass taps and under each tap, a tin hanging by a wire to catch the drips. Linseed oil, turpentine, paraffin and creosote all purchased by the pint or gallon if you could afford it, and according to what size jar, bottle or can that you arrived with. A big counter, and behind that shelves with can after can of Morris's own make of paints. They were most helpful men, always having to include in conversation the lasting quality of their lead based paints; and by the look of the sadly sagging shelves, plenty of it.

Some afternoons after school, I would go and see Mary at Dodd's and go into the office where she worked. All the floors were covered in sawdust to prevent drips and bits staining the boards. It was a big shop with about four butchers and always busy. There was a flat area above the shop with access by a ladder fastened to the wall - anything that needed to come down was lowered by a rope. It was up there that they made the black puddings and sausages. One of the butchers who was making sausages, asked if I would like to have a go at making some to take home for tea, so up the ladder we went. He had made all the pork and beef for the day and I was going to make tomato, my favourite, but I'm not sure about the rest of the family, though Mary doesn't seem to mind. I'm going to keep quiet about the whole thing as no one has mentioned paying, coupons came later.

The market was emptying, the shop was closed, shutters down and the men would busy themselves putting all the meat and other perishables into the big walk-in fridge before cleaning their tools and wooden bench blocks where they cut up all the meat. This they did with big double-handed wire brushes before washing them down with buckets of hot water. This looked hard work. Whilst all this was going on, Mary would be quietly busy in her office counting the takings which she entered in the day book before bagging it all ready to be taken to the bank. They were still busy in the shop but we were done and I had a big bag of tomato sausages. What a surprise this was going to be.

If it isn't too late, the ice cream lady, Mrs. Deponeo may be waiting to get rid of the last of her ice cream. There's usually two ice cream carts by the kerb just in front of the 'Dublin Packet,' - Lewis's and Deponeo's. Lewis's wasn't a cart - his was a three-wheeler cycle just like the one Dad has at the shop. Now Deponeo's was a wooden handcart which the poor soul must have pushed or pulled across Chester every day. On one of the shafts was tied a big soft cushion and on it sat this dark, comfortably round, lady. I suppose it was Mrs. Deponeo. Wafers and cornets, nothing else, just wafers and cornets, no flavours, just vanilla, but what happened to wafers?

The lady had a large wooden spoon to scrape round her tub for the ice cream, which was then carefully placed around the top of the cornet. But for the wafer she had a metal gadget, a sort of open topped, shallow box with a handle underneath, and in this went the wafer biscuit, the ice cream was then spooned in and levelled off to take another wafer biscuit. A little lever concealed in the handle was pushed up and out of the box came the ice cream wafer. It looked great when it came out but was soon dripping all over the place and the wafer biscuits went soggy with the licking, trying to cope with the dripping. We never knew whether you got more ice cream in a cornet or a wafer, but at the end of the day when there was ice cream to get rid of, and she never charged us for it, we would, without hesitation, go for the cornet. Of course, when we got home for tea I had to promise Mary that I didn't mention to Mum that Mrs. Deponeo had given us both enormous ice cream cornets. But then I was never asked.

The racecourse which I always knew as 'the big' Roodee was completely covered with bell tents and larger mess tents for the troops evacuated from Dunkirk. However big the Roodee it couldn't cope and our house, like many others, was visited by an Army billeting officer and sergeant clutching a clip board to his chest. The first time I had seen real soldiers and I was in awe of them.

They went through every room in the house then sat round the table with Mum asking her all sorts of questions, and suggesting that we could take in two soldiers. They were with us later in the afternoon with all their belongings and a rifle. I can see them now looking uncared for and tired. Arnold and Bert - I never knew their surnames. The kettle was soon on and although we hadn't much food Mum found something for them to eat. They didn't have a great deal to say and aren't Dad and Mary in for a surprise when they get home!

There were other soldiers billeted along the road and some evacuees, two older children, at the Ray-Jones's bungalow across The Green. Brother and sister of an Austrian Jewish family, their parents left behind somewhere. The Carsley's, - my best friend Arthur's house, have a French boy about our age and he wears a dark beret just like the men that came with the onions. I don't suppose we will see them any more.

Arnold and Bert manage more food when we all have our tea. It's rather nice having them and Dad's in his element telling them how it was in France in the 14-18 War when he was on the guns, the Royal Field Artillery. We didn't hear much about their war and they were soon to bed. Mary had lost her bedroom and had to share my single bed in the little back bedroom. The men left the house early next morning and where they went I don't know but they were always home by tea time and would stay in at night. Bert came from a place called Dukinfield which I'd not heard of, and whenever he spoke of it it made me laugh, but he didn't seem to mind. He cleaned his kit every night and let me help.

Dad has bought a wireless set so as he can listen to the news. It came from Mr. Guy's electrical shop, just up the road from our shop, next door to Monks, the Gunsmiths. It doesn't work off a battery, it's electric, and as we have no power points in the house he has fitted a two way light socket in the living room to connect with the wireless. Sometimes it can get a bit complicated.

I can come in from school and ask if I can have the wireless on to listen to 'Nomad,' a man who walks and talks about the countryside. I turn the knob to 'on' but it doesn't come on. Then Mum comes in, gets a chair to stand on so as she can reach the light fitting, operates the switch, still no sound, so on her way out of the room she flicks the light switch on the wall. We have sound and no light. I have missed most of 'Nomad' and wonder if we will have light when it gets dark. But it works. Its plain, made of wood, has three different stations, Home, Light and Forces. It's called a 'utility' model and I have brightened it up by sticking RAF fighter plane markings on it from one of my balsa wood model aircraft kits. It proudly stands on a small table where the aspidistra used to be in the corner by the window. I do love having the wireless but how I hated listening to Gracie Fields.

Our war effort is on the go. We dig up the back lawn for growing potatoes and a few vegetables. Mum likes to keep the front garden for flowers and refuses to give them up for Hitler. Dad plants the flower beds like the Union Jack with red geraniums, white alyssum and blue lobelia. Mr. Dye next door at No. 4 has dug up the front side and back for growing potatoes and vegetables so has Mr. Ball at No. 15 and Mr. Carsley at No. 17, and they have rented an allotment in Hough Green. Across the road from us just by the Greensway sign, a dustbin has arrived with 'swill' painted on it and nailed on the sign is a smaller tin with an open top, painted 'bones'. Two elderly WVS ladies in green uniform came each week with a car and trailer to empty them.

The swill bin soon began to smell, attracted flies and was constantly knocked over with swill all over the place. Dogs went wild with despair throughout the day after the bones. After a few months, it was thought not to be a good idea and disbanded. I'm sure to the relief of the WVS. Where the swill went we never knew, but for a short period it gave the dustmen less to do.

We are getting used to the blackout - there are no street lights. Bicycle, motor cycle and car lights have to be shielded to reduce the light. We don't see many cars, only Mr.Houghton who owns a garage in town and lives at No. 11 Northway, and Mr. Banks, who manages the coal yard in Boundary Lane, and lives in the bungalow across the road from our house, have cars.

If you have to venture out in the dark a torch is a good idea and that has to be masked, but it's better than nothing, so the person in front has the torch followed by whoever wants to join in and you go on your way carefully.

Mum and Dad have their own ideas about blackout for the house. Black linings are made for the curtains in the dining room and the kitchen, a sort of black skirt is made to go round the light in the hall and in the pantry. All this worked very well when lower powered light bulbs were put in the hall and pantry. They were now two very gloomy rooms. The bathroom and lavatory, never called a toilet, Dad made a wooden frame to fit the windows on which he pinned cardboard which came from the shop, and had a rather strong smell of carbolic. Mary thought this was in keeping with the two rooms and was rather amused by the whole thing. They never seemed to work very well and always denied, but we could hear it downstairs. He never swore but would utter 'for strewths sake.' Dad then considered that the priorities had been covered. We had complete blackout in the dining room and kitchen both with the more efficient lighting, other areas of the house being adequate. Now the bedrooms, all the light bulbs were removed as he thought blackout linings were unnecessary and a waste of money. Getting ready for bed was one hilarious experience.

Dad had picked up some information from one of his customers and came home with rolls of brown gummed paper about an inch wide - 'Butterfly tape'. This he licked and stuck on the inside of all the windows in crisscross patterns. It was fun for Mary and me at the start but we soon became feeling rather sick. And we had done all the licking. It looked a real mess but Dad had been told that it was essential as it would prevent glass shattering into the house when the bombs landed. Mum found it impossible to live with and the windows were eventually reinstated to their former high risk status.

Loads of information and forms to do with the war come each day with the post. So much to read and attend to; Dad says that its Town Hall officialdom gone mad. The priority seems to be air raids and probably invasion which Arnold and Bert think more than likely.

A few of the neighbours get together with a man from the ARP and decide to form a fire-watch group. They would be supplied with appliances to put out incendiary bombs. They would be allocated to various households around The Green. Mr. White at No. 1 Northway would have a stirrup pump, bucket and a whistle. No. 5, that's us, to have a coal shovel and scoop, each with a 56 inch handle, bucket, bag of sand and a whistle. Mr. Edwards at No. 10, who incidentally was in the Olympic Games between the two wars and had won a medal playing water polo for England - probably gold, was to have a stirrup pump, bucket and whistle, and so on along Northway and Greensway.

The appliances came with full operational instructions which Dad thought drawn out, over complicated and didn't credit anyone with any 'nouse' whatsoever. He wasn't pleased and made his views known to the appropriate people. Also that some protection for head, eyes and hands should be an essential addition to the kit. Much to Mum's surprise only a day or so later, a man calls with a very large brimmed tin hat in a light shade of grey, not at all like the tin hats Arnold and Bert have, and a rather tasteful sign 'SP' to go on the highest point of our gatepost. We haven't a stirrup pump. He was most insistent that we had, showing Mum his list. He left and I took the SP down the road and gave it to Mrs. White for when Mr. White came home.

It was on the wireless news that London had been bombed and a few days later, Coventry. Of all things, the cathedral was now in ruins. Dad couldn't believe it. It was just a bit too much. Dad likes the wireless news - keeping in touch with the war and all of us are getting used to how to get it working by working the switches, but the wall switch is playing up. All the light switches in the house are made of brass which Mum kept highly polished, but this one, if you fiddled with it a little bit, made fizzing noises and your fingers tingled which Mary and me thought fun. We used to fiddle with it whenever we had the opportunity. Dad didn't recognise the fun value and our fun was short lived. It was soon replaced by an ugly one in dark brown bakelite - brass no longer available. Bakelite and vulcanite was now the in thing.

On the corner of Lache Park Avenue with Cliveden Road, the field is being built on with army huts, a fire station and this is where our air raid siren has been erected on two telegraph poles. We have already had a test run and it's deafening if standing nearby and still really loud at No. 5. In anticipation of an air raid the siren will sound variable, the all clear will sound continuous, and in case of invasion, the church bells will ring.

Every bit of spare land is being taken over by the War Department, and is being built on with either traditional wooden huts and for the new version, the Nissen hut. This may need some explaining. I look in the dictionary - 'Nissen hut, a military shelter of semicircular cross section, made of corrugated steel sheet.' This leaves a lot to the imagination. My memory is probably of the deluxe version of the time before bricks became scarce. So, a concrete base is laid in the shape of an oblong. On the two narrow ends, a semicircle of bricks is laid, the centre point being approx. 7ft 6ins. Sorry 2290mm. This shape continued from front to back in moulded corrugated metal or asbestos sheeting. This was not made in a continuous sheet but in two halves being bolted in the middle. A small dormer window each side of the hut seemed the usual and a front door; the larger the hut the more windows.

Large houses are taken over by the Military as accommodation or administration. The Dale in Liverpool Road is now a military hospital. We soon become familiar with the uniforms of the wounded servicemen as we see them about the Town. Royal blue jacket and trousers, white shirt and bright red tie. We are all in to the national colours and Mum's still there with her planting of the front garden, which was to continue for the duration of the war. Union Jacks were everywhere, proudly fluttering in the breeze.

Riverwood in Curzon Park became army administration, The Firs in Newton Lane, filled with Nissen huts. There is a big army camp at Blacon and at Saighton. Land outside the Castle wall is filled with wooden huts for the army. Some of the houses in Hough Green are taken over by the Army and one of the bungalows across The Green from our house has a couple of Lewis guns erected on stands in the front garden, every night. I'm getting quite good at recognising guns, tanks and aircraft. Both sides, us and the Germans.

There are soldiers everywhere but The Green remained untouched by the Military throughout the war. Land between Earlsway and Curzon Crescent is filled with wooden huts and the ATS (Women's Army) have moved in, most of them working in the big house, 'Riverwood' opposite and at Western Command. Eaton Hall is commandeered by the Royal Navy, Dartmouth, as an Officer Training Unit, army vehicles of all types and Bren gun carriers are parked on both sides of the Duke's drive on the way through to Eccleston.

Dad says that "it's pandemonium in Town." The old tram lines are being taken up, property and gardens are being stripped of iron railings and gates, and at the same time knocking on doors asking if they would part with their metal saucepans and kettles. Even the guns in Grosvenor Park that Arthur and I used to play on have all gone, everything to be melted down for the war effort. They were three trophy guns. Two from Sebastopol and the third from the Boer War presented to the city by the government and placed around the statue of the second Marquis of Westminster.

All over Chester running alongside gutters of the main streets, is a network of massive water pipes and hydrants, and where space permits, vast emergency water storage tanks in preparation of air raids. All painted black, with EWS (Emergency Water Supplies) lettered on the tanks in yellow. Activity and change increases by the day and night. We now have identity cards, ration books, clothing coupons and very little food.

An ARP warden has been appointed for Northway and Greensway. The fire watch group are not pleased - they thought it smacked of officialdom; the Town Hall. Dad says. "They will have forms all over the place, forms to fill in when we have an air raid, when we need a new stirrup pump, more sand for your bucket, and heaven forbid,

Annie, a new pea for your whistle,", which amused Mum.   But it doesn't finish there. The Warden has better kit, more military. He has the same tin hat as Arnold and Bert but his is painted black with a 'W' painted in white on the front and a gas mask just like theirs which they call a respirator. The group don't seem to be miffed by his whistle.

Across the road from the new telephone exchange building there is some land and talk has it that there may be the remains of a large Roman amphitheatre buried there, which will have to wait until after the war, as a large wooden building is being erected by the YMCA as a club and eating place for the armed services at supposedly lower prices than the usual café or milk bar.

The Land Defence Volunteer is formed, sort of part time civilian soldiers, mainly older men from the last war, Dad's war. He talks about it but I don't think it appeals over much. They are eventually going to have the same uniform as the Army but to start with they only have a khaki arm band with LDV (Land Defence Volunteer) lettered in black.

We often hear the siren warning us of an air raid, usually followed a few minutes later by the all clear. I suppose testing or a false alarm but we get used to it and don't quite react the way we should. According to the ARP pamphlet on hearing the siren we should, in an orderly manner, go to the nearest public underground shelter or blast shelter, as quickly as possible. We have neither so we have to stay in the house and take shelter under the stairs for the duration of the raid and venture out only when the all clear sounds. Now that's not as easy as it sounds. You can't get under our stairs from anywhere in the house. Leaving this house by the back door into the garden and to the left is what appears to be another back door. Open it and it's our under stairs where we keep the coal.

On Mr. Randal's advice we have stocked up as the coal yard in Boundary Lane is running low and very little is coming through the sidings from the collieries. Moving about half a ton of coal every time the siren went wasn't met with much enthusiasm and even if it was all of us crammed into the coal house doesn't bear thinking about. But they have thought of an alternative - the kitchen or dining room table. Our kitchen table, which we call the 'posh top' and under this the big iron mangle, two wooden rollers, a drainer and hand wheel; a mass of iron and wood which I operate whenever I have the opportunity. A draw curtain hangs from the top to conceal this launderer's implement when not in use.

So the dining room table it is and whenever the siren blew we just pushed the chairs back and under we went. Usually late at night all three of us would cram ourselves under the table. Dad's outside with Mr. Dye from next door. I thought they looked a right pair in their tin hats, but they never knew.

Arnold and Bert tell Mum that they are being posted and will be leaving Friday. We are all quite tearful as they have become part of the family and we may never see them again. They leave us and only Mum and me are in when they leave, but we all get through the day and when I get home with Dad at tea time, there is another lot of soldier's kit in the hall and we meet Bill and Ken having a cup of tea with Mum. Ken is in the Royal Engineers and Bill with the Pioneer Corps.

Ken was an engineer before the Army. He came from Bristol and often said of himself - "Bristol born Bristol bred; strong in the arm and weak in the head." He bought himself a couple of boxed Meccano sets from Vernon's toy shop in Northgate Street, opposite the entry to the Music Hall Cinema. One of the boxes was in two layers and he

45

made models of all sorts of things at nights on the dining room table.

Bill was a gents' hairdresser before joining the Army and now he is a cook at the camp in Cliveden Road. He regularly brings food home for us for which we were always grateful, and he cuts mine and Dad's hair. I will always remember the night Bill was suffering with a bad cold, a sore throat, and not at all well. Mum was very worried. He went upstairs and returned with a jar of Vick ointment, then asked Mum if he could cut a couple of rounds of bread. These he spread with all of the jar of Vick and to our surprise ate the lot and then decided to go to bed early as he didn't seem at all well. Mum and Dad were convinced it was the Vick and now really worried. He left for duty early the following morning to cook breakfast as perky as ever and none the worse for his medicinal supper. However bad a cold, I have never been tempted.

RAF Sealand built in the Great War, the 1914-18 war, now trains fighter pilots, the majority making up the squadrons for the Battle of Britain.

Mr. Carsley at No. 17, my best friend Arthur's dad, breeds budgerigars, Australian parrots of many colours. We always called them 'budgies.' They had a super aviary built onto the side of the garage. It's big and they have plenty of room to fly around in and places to perch and play with a bell, even a mirror, but this aviary looks special as it has rough tree bark nailed over the wooden framework to make it look posh. There are several small holes in the side of the garage wall for the budgies to get through to their nesting boxes, being in the garage makes it warmer. Lovely though they are, things aren't looking good as they live on millet which comes from India and such far away places, and cuttlefish. It's Arthur's and my job to go to Richards shop in Northgate Street on a Saturday morning, the pet food shop.

The cuttlefish was dry and hard on a shell backing nailed on the wall for the budgies to peck on. Millet was their main food. We would always have to join a big queue outside the shop and most times go home disappointed. We would go out and collect groundsel, chickweed and other weeds; we even tried carrots, but the poor old budgies sadly died which we never forgave the Germans for.

After a while some new birds arrived in the aviary - three hens and a cockerel. Arthur and me rather liked the cockerel. We called him 'Blackie' for obvious reasons. Mr. Carsley seems well pleased as they eat up all the scraps and lay eggs. The Carsley's would always go on a week's summer holiday to New Brighton before the War; not any more, too close to Cammel Laird's shipyards at Birkenhead and the docks at Liverpool, which we all think will be bombed any night. Dad says Chester is on the flight path of the German aircraft which he calls the 'Luftwaffe.' I quite like the name, sort of comical. German seems more in keeping. But then Dad now calls them Nazis.

I remember having a week's summer holiday in a 'chalet.' The bottom half was painted green, the top half cream. It was at Talacre, near Rhyl. There were a lot of huts all the same in a field by sand hills and the sea. That was before the war when I was very small and don't remember it very well. But I remember we had to heat water in a kettle on a primus stove to wash in and I knocked it over and scalded my legs. Mum put lots of butter on the scalds and it felt better. Just Mum, Mary and me; Dad had to stay and look after the shop.

We seem to go out for days now instead of a holiday. We get the Crosville double-decker in Lower Bridge Street that goes to Llangollen. We get return tickets, which Dad has to keep safe for when we come back; if not he has to pay again. Not like the Chester buses. But I am told it's cheaper than buying singles and ours is cheaper still as it's an excursion ticket.

I liked Llangollen. Dad hired a rowing boat on the canal. There were lots of big flies swimming on the water. I'm told they are water boatmen. We have to keep going into the bank to let barges pass being pulled along by horses. Then we went into an old church and a walk round the graveyard. Dad pointed out a gravestone with a photograph of a man on it, and covered with a piece of glass to shelter it from the weather. It looked old and brown with age, and not seen before.

For a very special treat Dad says he will take us to a café. I have never been in one before. I had a choice of beans on toast or Welsh rarebit. I ask and it's cheese, so I have that and an ice cream. We climbed up Dinas Bran to the ruined castle before catching the bus for home. What a lovely day we had.

The Army are building concrete gun emplacements amusingly known as 'pill boxes,' and tank traps along the main roads and as the two main roads into North Wales start at the big roundabout just in front of the gateway to Eaton Hall, another important road; I go down that way when we visit my Uncle Reg who lives at Eccleston in one of the estate houses. He is a plumber at the Hall. Now the pill box they are building on the roundabout isn't like any other. Rather nice looking and very in keeping with the Chester way of building - a building with wooden frame and plaster work, two wooden doors and a nice tiled roof. A sign on one door states 'Ladies' and the other 'Gentlemen,' just to fool the Germans. I think the only signs left are on public lavatories as all the road signs have been taken down long ago.

Bill and Ken leave us and we won't be having any more soldiers as most of the big Army camps have been built and are ready for occupation. I liked having the soldiers in the house and Ken was very kindly giving me his Meccano sets, as he can't play with them where he's going. Mum says they will be better off in their own place. As we will. I will have my bed all to myself and so will Mary. If Bill and Ken were in for the night when we had an air raid we would pull the two leaves out to extend the dining room table, then we could all fit under it. We won't need to do that any more.

Dad thinks having the table extended really wasn't a good idea after all as it halved the thickness of the top and the leaves with no support worth speaking of. A bit more space all around the house really, and under the table is now quite comfortable as the number of cushions and pillows has grown considerably over the weeks, not comfortable enough to fall asleep, too frightened to fall asleep.

Most nights we sit and wait to hear the siren - some nights it doesn't sound but when it does, we always have a hot flask of tea and something to eat ready to take under the table just in case it lasts a long time waiting for the all clear. Every raid we would all crouch in a huddle under the table and without fail, Mum would always ask "give us a song Peter" and I would sing 'Carolina Moon keep shining.' It was the only song I knew as I played it incessantly on our wind-up gramophone. I suppose she thought it took our minds off what was happening.

The worst raid of the War was the night when a land mine exploded. Land mines were dropped by parachute and self detonated whilst in the air to create the most damage. We were told that the Army spotted this one in their searchlights and fired at it. It made one heck of a bang. The house shook and it was a very long night under the table before we came out to go to bed. As we have had an air raid I am allowed to go to school half an hour later in the morning.

The following morning Dad finds his shop windows blown out as are most of the windows in town, and to make matters worse a couple of incendiary bombs have gone through the warehouse roof into loads of straw, cardboard boxes and wood. What with the scarcity of stock for the shop and the future to be getting worse, this was just too much. Shortly after, windows boarded up, the smell of dampened fire in the warehouse, Dad turns the key in the door for the last time. Only days before he had had a delivery of Oxydol washing powder, Sylvan soap flakes, carbolic scrubbing soap, Lifebuoy toilet soap and some donkey stones for whitening front door steps, which, Jenny, Mum always did at No.5 every day without fail.

Some of it we kept ourselves - the majority of it went to friends and neighbours along the road, which they were well pleased with, as all kinds of soaps are getting hard to come by. A couple of things that had been in the shop a long time and wouldn't sell found their way to No. 5. I was over the moon with the tubular steel garden swing that Dad soon put together in the back garden, and a large posh wooden bird house on a pole which didn't go up at the same rate, which may have been something to do with this persistent person - quite a few other odds and ends that no one really wanted.

People only bought things out of necessity, to be useful. I hadn't realised at the time how serious the situation was at Dad's shop. He had let it go on far too long, I suppose hoping it would get better.

A little old lady a Jehovah's Witness, would frequently call in the shop sometimes leaving Dad with a small book, was it called 'The Light of the World?' This he would put on one side by the till to read later, which he always did. They would soon get into a heated discussion without even trying. Just imagine the situation - two devout people in their respective beliefs - a Jehovah's Witness and a Methodist Lay Preacher, and all the time snatching glances through the window in case she might miss her bus. Dad found a brief pause and mentioned that he had to close the shop. The silence was golden as in tears she put her arms round him for the last farewell. She left like no other customer, and come to think of it I don't think she was ever a customer. They just enjoyed the confrontation.

Although the LDV (Local Defence Volunteers) are now kitted out a lot better, the majority seem to have a complete uniform and a rifle and bayonet, but things are changing. The LDV armbands are going and they will now be known as the Home Guard. Their uniform will remain the same as the Army apart from belt and gaiters, which I think may have been black.

Not all young men went into the Armed Forces - some went into the Home Guard - but the majority were older and had been soldiers in the First World War. They were instantly recognisable by their chest full of brightly coloured medal ribbons and usually accompanied by a few stripes or pips on their shoulders.

Young men are conscripted into the Armed Forces and civilians into jobs of national importance, which aren't always found near to where you live, so it means moving and looking for lodgings. Once again Mum has a visit from a billeting officer. I think this one was from the town hall, and we are to have a Mr. Redhead from Chorley. He will be working at Vickers Armstrong's aircraft factory at Broughton.

That's Mary and I back to sharing, but it's not all that bad as Mr. Redhead is going to have the single bed in the back bedroom and although Mum offers him the use of the sitting room, he would prefer to eat with us and to spend the evenings in our company - someone to talk about the war with I suppose.

When I get home from Arthur's they are all busy chatting away with a rather round red-faced man. They all stop and Dad says, "Peter, this is Mr. Redhead. He's a plumber." He was well suited with the name and I already knew he was a plumber as he had the same lovely smell of my Uncle Reg who always told me it was the putty he worked with.

Dad has a job of National Importance

We all got on well together especially Dad and they both left home for the early morning bus to the Broughton factory. They seem to think that with Dad's shop keeping experience he would be well suited in one of the stores, and he comes home looking rather pleased with himself - he has a job as foreman in the wood store.

Two of Mary and Margaret's old school friends are called up for the RAF. Joe Brown is now Sergeant Air Crew Navigator and Des Walsh, Sergeant Air Crew Gunner, Bomber Command. Fighter Pilot Officer Stoddart, son of a Chester vet, flew his Spitfire from RAF Hooton on a mission to fly under the Suspension Bridge. He did and Arthur and I saw him do it. He came in low over the river, just skimming the water, under the bridge and up, a couple of rolls back over the bridge and away. What an experience! - all over and gone in just a few minutes. Whether he was ordered to do it or was it just something he wanted to do? We didn't know we just hoped it didn't get him into trouble.

It boosted people's confidence when morale was low; everyone talked about it, but at this time we didn't know who it was - just a 'Spitfire.' He also shot a Heinkel 111 down over Chester in a daylight raid. It came down in Bumpers Lane, Sealand. I watched the plane as it came down, leaving a trail of smoke beyond the houses on Earlsway.

This is where Mr. Dodd, our Dustman, makes an appearance once again. I think he must have had a small holding in the area around Bumpers Lane where he stabled the Council's dust cart horses. He also kept The Green across the road from No. 5, nice and tidy mowing it each spring and summer, then leaving it lay for a few days before carting it away for the horses winter feed.

How us kids enjoyed that drying out time, making hay stacks and dens, having hay fights every night till late, going home tired, hot, sticky and covered in hay seed and dust; getting into trouble and a telling off from Mr. Dodd for scattering his laid grass all over the place. When they call on Friday to empty the bins and have their jug of tea, he tells Mum the tale that when the plane came down, he and a few others grabbed whatever they could to defend themselves with before running across the field to the burning aircraft where they took the German crew prisoners. I don't think they were met with any resistance while they waited for the military to arrive. Whether it was all the crew - had they baled out or crash landed the burning aircraft? - I don't know.

This daylight raid has given Dad something to worry about as his fire watching group along Northway and Greensway are only able to operate late evenings and nights. None of the group got home before six. Now that Dad, Mr. Redhead and Mr. Crawford are working at Vickers Armstrong they rarely get home before half past eight, which just adds to the problem. They had a fire watch rota all worked out, who was on and who was off and now the Luftwaffe comes early and messes the whole thing up! The unit had a meeting and thought it to be a stray aircraft, a one off.

Top end of Curzon Park, across the road bridge and to the right, was an area of flat land, enough for the Army to have a hut - accommodation for the soldiers who are to be guarding the rail bridge around the clock day and night. There is a sentry box at the top of the footbridge and a sand bagged area with another sentry box at the bottom of the steps on the other side of the river. There were about three soldiers constantly patrolling the bridge with rifles and bayonets at the ready. Soldiers always seem a friendly lot and whenever Arthur and I are out that way they find time to talk with us.

Down the lane, way beyond the soldiers hut is where we go looking for fallen wood to drag home for burning. The farmer down there keeps lots of hens and sheep. He also looks after the golf links. I can't remember his name, but I do remember us meeting him one day and telling us that he once had a sheep with two heads. We didn't believe him, so he asked us into his house and there they were - the heads on the wall in the hall. They did look very real. We didn't much like it and left as soon as we could.

The shortage of coal that we had all anticipated is upon us, and Mr.Randals can only drop off two hundredweight, which has to last us four weeks. We usually have five. He tells Mum that the coal yard is very low and there is very little coming into the sidings. Mr. Dye, our next door neighbour has been to the gas works and seen mountains of coke where you can help yourself. It burns quite well with a bit of coal. I can't remember how much it was, but it was cheap. I liked the idea of that, so as soon as I could I asked Mum for the money, I found a sack and headed off for the gas works on my bike.

Mr. Dye was right - there were mountains of coke with crowds of people filling sacks. Some had wheelbarrows, handcarts and sack trucks just like the one Dad had at the shop. And how I wished I had that three wheeler he once had. Mr. Dye managed with his bike and so will I. A man near me filled his sack then helped me fill mine. With difficulty we managed to get the sack of coke through the frame lying across the pedals. He left with his lying across the handlebars and along the crossbar, pushing his bike. I shall have to do the same, and I was thinking I could ride home.

It seemed a hard and long push on my own along the Roodee path to the footbridge where I met one of the sentries. He seemed very interested in what I was doing and tells me that they have a stove that burns coke in their hut, and if I could manage to get my bike across, he would take the coke. He had trouble getting the coke across and the bike wasn't as easy as it was on the way down. I couldn't have done it on my own and thanked him. When I got home, it went into the coal house and it didn't look much at all. Arthur and I went for coke several times and to The Dingle and river bank collecting firewood. Coal was rationed and sometimes we couldn't get our ration.

What was Crighton's shipyard has been taken over by the Army as a base for the Royal Engineers and the Pioneer Corps. There is always a lot of transport about the place and flat bottomed boats are stacked high in rows on land outside the buildings that are constantly guarded. Ken, the soldier who gave me the Meccano sets, was in the Engineers and he always said that the Pioneers were there to do the donkey work for the Engineers, so I suppose they were the ones that strung all the cables across the river and built all the sand bagged gun emplacements.

They had sunk thick wooden posts into the ground on each side of the river to support a wire cable which almost touched the water at its lowest point. Each post had two additional support cables anchored into the ground which could be wrenched tighter whenever the draped cable dipped too low. These cables spanned the river every few hundred yards to prevent the landing of German sea planes. You get used to seeing how many yards on signs everywhere, so many yards to air raid shelters, water hydrants, anything wanted in an emergency situation had to have a sign; how long will it take to get there!

Mary tells us that the Jackson's are leaving the house in Earlsway, and where they're going to live in Bromborough isn't all that far away, just a bus ride on a Crosville bus from the Market Square. I know Mary's upset and will miss Margaret just being down the road and so will I and Mum. I don't think Margaret knows Dad all that well if at all, as he's usually at work whenever Margaret came round. It's all gone quiet then Mary slaps her hands on her knees as she gets up from her chair saying, "I'm off to see Margaret - do you want to come?" We say our goodbyes to Mum and are on our way.

I've not been to Margaret's house before so have never met her Mum and Dad. I found them to be nice friendly people. Muriel, Margaret's sister, wasn't in when we went round so I had a long chat with Mr. Jackson and I would love to have the things he has when I grow up. He has a car, I think a Morris Eight and it was out on the road. He was wearing a blue silk smoking jacket with an all-over paisley pattern and he was smoking a cigar. Apparently it's something he always changes into when he comes home from work, finding it more comfortable. Apart from the jacket it was the cigar that got me. Dad only smokes them at Christmas but he does smoke a lot of cigarettes all year round and sometimes a pipe when cigarettes get scarce.

Mr. Jackson's a commercial traveller for Angus Watson. The places he has to visit are miles and miles apart and his sales make for a lot of paperwork when he gets home, so he has a corner in the sitting room where he has his desk and telephone. It's a much newer telephone than Dad has at the shop, the ear and mouth piece are all in one. I didn't tell Mr. Jackson but I did prefer the telephone at Dad's shop.

His desk is a most unusual shape. It slopes like a hillside with lots of slatted pieces. Mr. Jackson says "it's very special, it's a roll top" and then he takes hold of a grooved piece on the front edge and rolls up all the slatted cover to reveal his office work, so many little drawers to keep things in, writing paper, envelopes, ink wells, pens and a blotter, a staple machine, paper clips, all sorts of things, what else could you wish for?

You don't need an office when you've got a desk like this, and there are sets of drawers each side of you when you sit down at the desk before you go into the roll top. Operating it is as good as a game really. I draw down the roll top for Mr. Jackson who locks it up for the night, and then I notice on a small table a brass miniature of a ship's telegraph which I'd never seen before. The big ones, the real ones, are in the wheelhouse on the bridge of the ship from where the captain directs his orders to the boiler room, I think. A lever on the top is worked from left to right as a pointer, in line with the lever, passes over markers from slow to full steam ahead and I suppose reverse must be on it somewhere. While all this is going on a bell sounds on the bridge and in the noisy boiler room, the pointer coming to rest. Full steam ahead sounds exciting. Mr. Jackson's miniature hasn't a bell, but it has full steam ahead engraved on it. I'm fascinated and hadn't realised that I'd picked it up.

"Ah!" says Mr. Jackson, "you've spotted my toy," as he puts another cigar into the hole in his toy, operates the lever which he stops at full speed ahead at the same time nipping off the end of his cigar making it ready to smoke. I can't help thinking what a very pleasurable life this man has.

I took it that Mary was up in Margaret's room and thought it was time I went, so I thanked Mr. Jackson for showing me his desk. Then he said "Now wait a minute" as he left me standing in the hall. He was soon back and pushed a brown paper bag into my hand. "Something to take home;" so I thanked him for the second time. Dad always instilled into me that a please and a thank you would never go amiss whenever the opportunity arises.

When I left the Jackson's, their next door neighbour was just coming home from work pushing his bike up the path. It was Mr.

Brookes. He's a guard on the railway. I have quite a long chat with him - and he's another nice friendly man. The few men that I have got to know that work on the railway seem to be very happy at their work, so maybe I should think of working on the railway when I leave school as being happy with your work seems to be a good thing.

On the way home I couldn't help but look inside the brown paper bag and there were two tins of sardines in oil. I didn't know what sardines were but it was a lovely flat shiny tin with an opener attached to it. The flat top of the tin was covered with a paper label printed in full colour taken from an oil painting of an old bearded fisherman wearing a bright yellow sou'wester; the Skipper of Skipper Sardines.

A few days later both tins of sardines were opened and Mum mashed them up with a fork and we had them for tea on hot toast. I toasted the bread on the front of the fire while Mary spread the sardines on the toast which I handed to her before I burnt it to a cinder. They both know how I like my toast on the black side. Oh! but the taste of those sardines. What a very special treat it was. The first time I'd ever had sardines. Thanks to Mr. Jackson and we saved some for Dad.

The army seemed to be everywhere. Even the land we always knew as 'the tip' hasn't gone unnoticed by the army. This bit of land behind the electricity sub station at the top end of Mount Pleasant over towards the railway, the Pioneers have dug trenches along the ridge of the hill. Down at the bottom they have tunnelled into the hill side .

In several places and each time we go in to explore they get deeper. Dark, damp and very smelly places with duck boards to walk on. Then one visit we find that they have put doors on and padlocked. We would love to know what was inside but we still enjoy playing in the trenches and bushes. It's usually 'kick the can' or throwing chunks of hard clay at each other. I remember getting hit in the face with a piece and running down to see Mr. Kennerley, the chemist, in Saltney. When he saw me he came from behind the counter with a few things to clean me up and then he would say "off you go." I remember as a boy I would go and see Mr. Kennerley several times. I never had money to pay, he never asked. He was always there for me whenever I had a need.

At the front of Crighton's ship yard on the sloping ground down to the river where the fishing boats are usually pulled up on to higher ground after a good day's salmon fishing, is where the army do their manoeuvres. Trying to cross the river seems to be the idea and others try to stop them. The area is cordoned off and they don't seem to mind us watching. We have seen a few already and they all seem much the same; they split into two sides all in full kit, the only difference being red or blue armbands.

So the Blue's row themselves across the river to where they have, for the last few days, been digging trenches and building sand-bagged gun emplacements. This area they will defend with what they have brought with them apart from rifles, Bren guns, ammunition boxes and a few lengths of what looks like drain pipes, which is a puzzle. Now, when they are all settled in with camouflage netting all over the dug outs so as they can't be seen from the air. They wait for the others to try and get across. I suppose they are the Germans for this day. More trucks have arrived, so now there are a lot of soldiers in the red side, the goodies. The Red's are getting ready to cross the river with a lot of shouting going on while pontoons by the dozen are being dragged across the mud down to the water. Then there is gun fire from the other side followed by flashes and explosions on the ground and lots of smoke. That's where the drain pipes come in. Just like real mortars they have a very, very big banger called a 'Thunder flash' which they light and drop down the drain pipe. It then blows back out of the pipe in a trail of smoke, across the river, and explodes in the air or amongst the Reds. As well as being shot at they have to find a way of crossing the river. The Red's are now returning fire which doesn't really help the Engineers very much as they try to get as many pontoons as they can in the water. Platforms are laid across the pontoons as soon as the pontoons are positioned so progress is made across to the other side.

The smell, the smoke and the noise but somehow you can still hear the shouting above it all. The Engineers crossing is backed up with infantry and shortly all is quiet as the Blue's have either been wiped out or taken prisoner. The smoke eventually drifts away. It's decidedly less noisy and we can see the other side taken by the goodies.

Pontoons and platforms are put back into storage and the soldiers organise themselves to leave by truck and some into Crightons ship yard, leaving a few patrolling the area for anything that may have been left behind. Arthur and I usually go back to see for a root around without ever finding anything other than spent blank cartridges and thunder flash cases.

I went round for Arthur the following day and Dennis decides to come with us. He's a new friend. His Dad's a Major in the army and they have come to live in the house on the opposite corner of Greensway. Quite a few new people are now living around The Green who had left their homes to get away from the bombing or for work in factories. Dennis hasn't been before and it's all much the same, but Dennis picks up anything he can lay his hands on, every pocket stuffed beyond capacity. Arthur and I don't bother any more.

Dennis has found an old rusty can and is busy tapping out the thunder flash cases and ends up with a fair old amount of charred looking powder. We find an old broken bollard on the quayside where they used to tie the ships up. It has a deep hollow in the middle "Just the place" says Dennis. In goes the powder and he sets about making a slow burning fuse out of dried grass and scraps of paper which he hangs out over the edge of the bollard. He says he knows about these things, with his Dad being a Major in the army and then he produces a couple of matches from his pocket as he has the occasional fag. Then he lights the fuse which burns very well. Arthur and I are soon well away but Dennis didn't seem to be motivated quite the same and hangs about. The flames from the slow burning fuse though burning fiercely seem to have gone out. We both watch as Dennis creeps very slowly back to the bollard, close enough to have a good look inside to see what's going on. Then there is what I can only describe as a damp bang followed by a large cloud of white smoke. Dennis goes running around the bollard a few times as though looking for a way out and, when he comes to rest emerging out of the smoke, he really doesn't look quite the same Dennis - a bit pink but pale at the same time and decidedly odd without his fringe, which had been very long and eyebrows singed.

This we thought would need some explaining to Mr. Kennerley, the Chemist. He did seem to be alright as he got used to how it all went and he decided it would be better just explaining how it happened when he got home. As it happened he didn't have to as he managed to sneak into his house unnoticed and just got into trouble for cutting his fringe off. They knew he never liked it anyway, so half expected it. Yes! He had found a pair of scissors and smartened up the singed ends. I would never have thought up such a good idea to get me out of serious trouble. Well maybe. Some time later we discovered that Major Coates's expertise wasn't in explosives, he was in the Dental Corps.

There's just one shop in Mount Pleasant and that's Mrs. Johnson's shop. She seems to sell anything that comes to mind. It's a very basic sort of shop affectionately known to us all as 'the pop shop.' A couple of counters, quite small and beyond the counters is just space. Unlike other shops there are no display cabinets or shelves but crates and crates of pop stacked high - Corona and Dee Cestrian and Laycock's. In the middle of it all sits Mrs. Johnson, wrapped in her clean floral overall, busy knitting, which kept her occupied for most of the day other than when someone came into the shop. Then she would carefully put her knitting on a convenient crate before leaving her chair to reveal a floral cushion looking much the same as her overall.

A friendly, pleasant lady, there was always somebody in for pop which she sold by the bottle or you could buy it by the glass at tuppence, or a half glass, a penny. For those that didn't want 'fizzy,' cordial was thruppence a glass. In winter she made it with hot water which she boiled in a big kettle on a gas ring. She would always suggest her hot blackcurrant. There were a couple of upended crates for those drinking in or for those wanting to stay for a while to pass the time of day. She was always prepared for a chat provided you let her get on with her knitting, which she did as soon as you had paid for your pop.

There was a cigarette machine on the wall outside the shop which dispensed small packets of two cigarettes and two matches. "De Reske Minors." Their trade mark was a butler in black jacket, white shirt and black bow tie, holding a small silver tray on which was a packet of De Reske Minors - a highly unlikely situation. I can't remember what coins you had to put in this machine which you could without Mrs Johnson seeing as she was always too busy knitting and I have to confess in using it when we could club enough pennies together. A trip up Mount Pleasant to the tip, down the footpath and under the railway bridge where we were usually disappointed as the allocation of matches never seemed sufficient to get a cigarette operational no matter how hard you sucked. Apart from the matches problem there was a fair old wind blowing under that bridge and always a group of men there wearing flat caps and white mufflers. Sometimes they had a couple of greyhounds and I think they were gambling. They were smoking but we never asked them for a match.

Mrs Johnson's shop had previously been Jack Bowdler's shop before he moved to the opposite corner of the street fronting the main road, and his shop was a proper grocer's. He worked in the shop with his wife, an Irish lady with red hair, that was before he was called up into the Royal Marines. At the side of his shop was what Mum called a haberdashery. It was really a house - the shop had been her front room. She, like Mrs Johnson, always wore a floral overall and her hair in a bun - a very small lady not much taller than the top of her counter. I always made it into the shop first, and then she would appear from the back room after my opening the front door, which set off a loud bell. I felt guilty at having disturbed her.

There were heavy net curtains on the window which made it rather gloomy and dark. It smelt musty. But it was a well stocked shop which saved having to go into town. I used to go in quite often for reels of cotton, press studs, hooks and eyes, zips and if Mum was short of a button, I would take one down as a sample and without fail she would find one to match. Anything to do with dress making was always found, after doing quite a bit of rummaging around her shop.

Mum did a lot of sewing, mainly dress making for the Jefferson girls that lived on the far corner of Greensway. They were nearly always wearing dresses that Mum had run off on her Singer sewing machine. I never remember Mum having patterns for sewing, making dresses or recipes for making meals or even weighing scales. She just made things, cooked and baked. The only problem then was getting the materials, the cloth, hunting through drawers, wardrobes and cupboards. Anything found and I would get the job of unpicking. Dad said many times, "that lad has the patience of Job." I never knew of Job. Washed, ironed, worn out bits cut out and it would all be put away in the chest of drawers. Any material Mum could lay her hands on was always put to use. Her words for it were, 'To make do.' But with a few odds and ends from her collection and the little shop in Saltney, she worked miracles.

Thinking my way around the shops, I go into Saltney and the town; they seem to be pleased to see me, so I suppose they must be happy in their job. Even so Mr. Clarke, the fishmonger and grocer in Saltney, complains a bit about being cold when I ask how he is, but then he always has the door open, even in the winter when he's cutting up cold fish out of boxes full of ice. I suppose it's better to have an office job in the winter, like Mary, but even she says she gets cold through as the market's a very cold place, with stone floors and high double doors most of the time left wide open. The wind blows straight through into Mary's office. It's open to the butcher's shop by a hatch through which customers pay for their meat and things, which are mainly sausages, brawn, corned beef and whatever else is available.

Mary's been on about the cold for long enough and I'm sure there may be other things as well that I don't now about, so she thinks it's time to leave Dodd's and look for something different, not in a shop - and has applied for a job that takes her fancy, - a telephonist with Post Office Telephones. But it's a while ago that her application went off and she hasn't heard anything.

The postman drops a brown envelope through the door with

Mary's name on it, and marked 'private.' Mum puts it on the coat stand in the hall so as Mary would see it when she came in from work. Coat hung up and the letter was noticed and slowly carried into the living room where we were waiting excitedly but patiently, Mum having already made a pot of tea. It took so long to open and then read that Mum had to ask, "Well, is it good news?" Mary's not quite with us. Then, 'Oh yes, I've got an interview' at the telephone exchange in St. John Street, just across the road from the YMCA tea rooms.

Mary went for her interview, did very well, and got the job. She was there for ages having a good look round to get familiar with the place. It was very busy, meeting with lots of people and had a brief teach in on the switchboard finding it a bit difficult to reach the top row of numbers with her being on the small side. It sounds a big place with an all glass roof, and in the yard they have under cover bike racks. Going to work on her bike, not having to go on the bus will save her a bob or two. All in all she seems well pleased and tells us that the switchboards are manned entirely by women. At night they are manned by men. Now that sounds right to me.

Mr. Speed at number 8 Northway is a night telephonist and has an artificial leg, being wounded in the last War and gets about with the help of a walking stick. He's a friendly man and welcomes a stop for a chat whenever he sees me, as I do with his next door neighbour, Mr. Bounds, also a casualty of the last War. Now he gets about on crutches at a fair old rate, chatting as he passes. You should seem him go.

Christmas 1940

We are having the school nativity play in St. Mark's Church Hall and I have a part to play - one of the Kings carrying the gift of gold, and have to sing solo which I'm not looking forward to as all the parents will be there. Even if there's only a few I won't be looking forward to it.

The big day came and back stage Church Hall I was dressed up and surprisingly did look like some sort of a king. Mrs. Hill, one of our teachers, was putting on the final touches, make up! I always thought that was for girls. I had no choice but sit there while it all went on, then stepping back she seemed to be quite pleased with it and flashed a mirror at me to have a look. My face and neck were dark brown. "Just your hands and then you're finished and looking like an Arabian King." If no one recognises me then having to sing solo might not be too bad. But it was, though all that sat through it seemed to enjoy it.

Show over we all got out of our costumes. Unfortunately for me Mrs. Hill in her enthusiasm to make me look the part hadn't thought about it coming off. Tissue paper, toilet rolls even handkerchiefs made no impression at all. Listening to what other teachers were saying seemed to be of no help whatsoever as they had only ever used 'Tonette' dark brown polish to put on shoes so there were no instructions to take it off, no need. So I turned a few faces in Saltney on the way back to school where another attempt was made with hot water, soap and flannel, to no avail.

End of term school finished and we were all given some holly off the tree in the school playground to take home. When I got home I was in trouble with Mum as she thought I had taken the holly from someone's garden. I said that I thought it was the make up thing, the shoe polish. I was reassuringly told not to even think about it - a good wash with plenty of soap will soon shift it. It seemed a good idea for me to keep quiet as Mum has other things on her mind like how to manage Christmas, but it's one less for her to think about, as Mr. Redhead is going home to Chorley to spend Christmas with his family.

We haven't got much in the way of paper decorations which I suppose came from somewhere abroad but we have the paper chains that we make ourselves and a little artificial tree to go on the sideboard.

Even though we have been careful with the coal Dad thinks that we won't be having the luxury of spending Christmas in our best room, the sitting room. All through the last few months we have soaked old newspapers in a bucket of water, then page by page, squeezing and shaping into small paper balls to put on the fire to dampen it down.

A farmer's wife on a stall in the Market Hall has hinted to Mum the possibility of a dressed chicken. Mr. Dodd isn't sure about meat but he will have some sausages which are nearly always a choice of pork or beef and sometimes tomato. Now I don't know if tomato is with the pork or beef, but they are my favourite.

Mum manages somehow to make a lovely cake and pudding with a bit of this and a bit of that having little in the way of dried fruit and nuts. The cake looked a bit different not being covered in icing sugar but we had almond paste with some dolly mixtures pushed in to brighten it up.

Even though doubted, the farmer's wife came up trumps with the dressed chicken and we had the works from Mr. Dodd - all three lots of sausage. What an enjoyable time we had. A few bottles of pop from Mrs. Johnson's shop made a change and what was really nice and pleased Mum no end was Christmas cards from the soldiers. They were somewhere safe.

It had paid off dampening down the fire in the living room to save on coal so we did spend Christmas in the sitting room. Even with dampening down the fire it still provides us with a constant supply of seriously hot water, far more than we ever use.

Many a winter's night we would all be watching the fire while we listened to the wireless. Not a word was spoken then around about suppertime, which was usually a round of toast which I would do with a long toasting fork by the fire. Beef dripping on hot toast well sprinkled with salt was my favourite but we don't have it so often any more. Handing the toast to Mary, Mum reminds her to go easy with the butter.

Then we would hear over the wireless a rumbling from upstairs. It was the hot water cylinder in the little bedroom beginning to boil. Dad would get up from his chair and move in some haste to the back kitchen where he would turn the hot water tap fully on and leave it running while we tucked into a round of toast and a cup of tea. Sometimes a cup of cocoa if we had enough milk left over. This happened most nights but there was only ever one night when we could have a bath. Rather than run all that hot water off down the drain, we could have had another bath in the middle of the week, which Mary thought was a good idea. Dad didn't say a word. The rumbling had stopped and he leaves his chair to turn the hot water tap off. Before opening the door, he turns and points a finger in my direction. "Now look here Peter, bath night has always been on a Friday night and always will be. And I don't want to hear any more about it."

I said 'Hello' to all the people living around The Green and have a good chat with most of them, but for some reason or other I never speak to our next door neighbours, Mr.and Mrs. Irlam. Neither does Mum, Dad or Mary and they are the same with us. All I can get out of Mum is that they like keeping to themselves. They don't seem to have any family or friends going to see them and that's when I feel sorry for them as we always have visits from someone or other.

I know when Arthur comes round to see me and we have a play in our back garden it isn't long before Mrs. Irlam shouts through the hedge for us to make less noise and whenever a tennis ball goes over the hedge. Well, we daren't go round to ask for it so we decide to fish through the hedge with the clothes prop, but we soon hear her back door go before she comes down the garden, followed by the loud clatter of the dustbin lid. Yet another bouncy ball lost forever, but we managed to pull back Mum's clothes prop in the nick of time before Mrs. Irlam could get her hands on it. Mary said that they have always been the same with her and her friend Margaret for as long as she can remember.

Whenever Mrs. Irlam is in a grumpy mood with us I would silently rebel by making cartoon-like drawings of her with appropriate captions which I put on display at the highest point of our sitting room window, the side window overlooking their front path - a prime spot. Mary and Margaret knew. Mum and Dad didn't, but they soon found out as Mr.Irlam sent Dad a letter. I didn't get into too much trouble and the family feud goes on much the same, in silence.

I remember before the war there were two very good toy shops in town - they didn't sell anything else but toys. Pollards were in Bridge Street Row but my favourite was Vernon's in Northgate Street opposite the Music Hall passage. It was on two floors and a much larger shop than Pollards. I had a wooden fort and farm from Vernon's and every now and again I would go there to add lead soldiers and farm animals to my collection - sometimes a Dinky toy.

Now the best toy I ever had, or thought was the best toy I had ever had when I first opened the box, was a 'Frog' model aeroplane. It would really fly. The fuselage and tail plane were in one piece, the wings you fixed in place with rubber bands. It had wheels for landing. Rubber bands ran the length of the fuselage to the propeller which you would wind-up in the box by a special key housing in the end of the box. Fully wound you would take it out of the box while holding the propeller, sorting the wings out, all checks made and launching it into flight, which was fast, short and completely uncontrollable. It never landed on its wheels, the majority of flights ended in crash landings until unfortunately it was way beyond repair.

It became very noticeable that the toy shops were emptying of stock just the same as Dad's shop had. Pollards shop in Bridge Street Rows has closed down and the last time I went into Vernon's with Mum, the show cases and shelves were empty apart from some girl's soft toys. Somehow a toy shop looks particularly sad when it's empty. Of course, while all this was going on I had my Meccano sets that Ken left me and I can make all sorts of things, and I suppose I've moved on from pretend wars with toy soldiers and in a real one.

For all that I have been going on quite a bit about having a real looking army rifle as Arthur has one that his Dad's made, but then Mr. Carsley is quite handy with wood, being an upholsterer. Anyhow this hasn't gone unnoticed as the other night after Mr. Redhead had finished his tea he went upstairs to have his shave, thank goodness, and when he returned, he came over to me and produced from behind his back a big 'tommy' gun.

I couldn't believe it, it looked real, it was super and I was so pleased and I'd never thought of a 'tommy' gun. He had made it from scraps of wood, a piece of old broom handle for the barrel and a 'Cardinal' floor polish tin for the magazine, and one of his old belts to sling it over your shoulder. It wasn't painted; he said that would come later, but I didn't mind. I was made up and I couldn't wait to show Arthur.

On the way home from school I take a short cut across Jarman's field on the corner of Selkirk Road with Park Road West, Mrs. Jarman's being the first house in Park Road West. But not today, the field is filled with children all with brown labels tied through their button holes, looking tired and unhappy. There are some grown-ups with them and I recognise some as Salvation Army people. I run home to tell Mum. She gets her coat on and we go back to the field.

Some WVS ladies had arrived in a mobile canteen and along with a few of our neighbours were soon handing around drinks and food. We soon found out that they were evacuees from the bombing, waiting for transport to allocated addresses around Chester. I thought our soldiers looked a sorry sight when they first came to our house, but these children are quite the saddest sight that I have seen so far in this War and we can't seem to do anything about it to make it better for them. Just some pop, a cake or a cup of tea. One of the WVS ladies assures Mum that they all have good homes to go to it's just a matter of getting them there.

Mum decided to go back home to see what she could find to spare from the pantry to take with them. It wasn't much, but when we got back to the field so many of us had done the same, which was nice. Buses had arrived and we were soon sadly waving them goodbye. Just a couple of hours in our day and Jarman's field was empty again once more..

The leather attaché case that Dad always took to the shop each day has been replaced by a brown canvas shoulder bag. He doesn't need to take sandwiches and a flask as they have a good canteen at the factory. Mum's quite pleased about that as it helps our food situation at home. So really, his knapsack, as he calls it, is just for his gas mask

74

with a bit of room to spare, and it blends in with the place which his attaché case never would.

When we were issued with our gas masks they came in brown cardboard boxes with a long cord to put over your shoulder. These soon came to pieces and we all did our own thing and stuffed them into anything handy but you do see some very posh ones especially made for the job.

Odds and ends seem to find their way from the factory to No. 5 via Dad's knapsack. Usually, just scraps of wooden beading and remnants of fabric. The beading lights our fire and Mum always seems well pleased with the fabric even though she says it's a creamy grey and full of starch. She boils it for hours to get it soft and a few shades lighter, then makes it up into pillow cases and if there's enough, a tablecloth.

The scraps of wood almost every night became a bit boring then one night no wood, no fabric, as Dad produced from his knapsack a roll of something a couple of inches wide, brownish that we hadn't seen before. The colour reminded me of the long sticky fly paper that hanged from the dining room ceiling every summer to trap the flies. "You're not far off son; it's very thin, clear and sticky on the underside." Dad's obviously very impressed with it but he couldn't seem to find the end. The only sticky stuff we knew on a roll was brown paper, the one we put on the windows before the air raids or the coloured version to make Christmas decorations with. Everything was lick and stick and most of this was in post offices where they would stamp and tape up parcels. On the counter stood a thick glass containing a round, wet, red, rubber sponge. They couldn't be expected to lick that amount of sticky all day.

This stuff is called self adhesive - it licks itself. When at last we all had had a go at finding the end, it pulled off the roll but kept tearing so you had to look for an end again, but as Dad said it was sticky without having to lick it and you could see through it. All in all we thought it wasn't worth the bother. What finds its way to No. 5 is unwanted, is either ends of or faulty, but are we grateful for it as we have so little available to buy. What I find hard to believe is that this wood, fabric and sticky tape in good condition somehow all goes into the making of the 'Wellington' two-engine light bombers that come out of the Broughton factory.

Little did we then know that long after the War this same tape, though much narrower and smaller rolls, would appear in W.H. Smiths under the name of 'Sellotape' and we would all think, fantastic, in spite of still not being able to find the end.

There are things new floating around high in the skies over Chester - they are called 'barrage balloons' looking like big fat friendly whales. All shiny silver and they travel about from site to site each one moored by a steel cable to a wagon with a winch on its back. The cables are intended to stop low flying German aircraft from machine gunning people in the streets.

The balloons are full of gas which I think sometimes leaks as they go a bit floppy in the wind, then they are brought down for repair or a pump up. The shape is really like a whale and they have three blow-up fins at the back as stabilisers. Now and again one will break loose and eventually comes down. Arthur managed to find quite a big piece of one which Mrs. Carsley made up into gas mask cases for all the family. It was odd material, sort of rubbery silver on the outside with a black cloth backing. I suppose there wasn't much you could do with it really not at all like the aircraft fabric Dad brings home.

You wouldn't believe the other thing I saw just as funny as the barrage balloon, a car driving through town with a big square balloon on the roof held on to the car with ropes. It was bigger than the car. I found out some days later that it was filled with town gas which the car has been converted to run on, but had proved to be expensive as each gas full being the equivalent to a gallon of petrol, and it was bulky making it difficult to drive, particularly in windy weather and I suppose it got a bit floppy when the gas was running out just like the barrage balloon. I never did see that car again. Some funny things do happen in this war and we have a laugh. It's not all doom and gloom.

Mum and Dad talk about the war most nights when Dad comes home from work, what's in the papers, on the wireless. I listen and try to hear, to know what's going on, but it's difficult when I know they are doing their utmost to keep things away from me.

When they talk of Germans I always think of them being far, far away until the siren sounds for an air raid, then they become very real and when there is talk about being invaded by the Germans - now that does frighten me, and makes me realise how safe I felt having our soldiers in the house. The Italians and Russians seem to be on the same side as the Germans, so many to have to fight, it's no wonder Dad's concerned, as he really knows what's going on. My world is home and just around Chester. Other than the seasons I don't have much thought as to what month or year it is but we do seem to have been at war for a long time.

However, this night Dad comes home in good spirit and talks aloud of General Wavell, along with the Australians have taken the Libyan port of Bardia from the Italians and forty five thousand prisoners of war. Surely that can't be right, what do they do with them all? Dad says as fighters they were more or less useless as whenever the going started to get tough they were just too handy at putting their hands up and waving the white flag.

Soon Tobruk is taken, again from the Italians but the bad news is that we made an ill-fated attempt to occupy Greece. The German opposition was just too strong. So we are all gloomy again.

It's all change at home. Mr. Redhead tells Mum that he has found work nearer to home in Chorley and will be leaving. I just get used to all these people and then they go. I quite liked Mr. Redhead and he put new washers on our taps so they don't drip anymore. The bath tap had dripped for so long that it stained the bath. But that wasn't the reason that I liked him. He was a round happy man, a friendly man. I suppose not being a soldier made him a bit different and he had a nasty habit of, when he needed a shave, he would grab me and delight in rubbing his rough face all over my face - and he had a big face. That was something the soldiers never did.

With Mr. Redhead gone it wasn't long before another man comes to take his place - unfortunately he's not a soldier. He works in a job of National Importance, just like Dad. I don't think we are going to have soldiers in the house any more. I met him when I came in from school and I've already decided that I don't like him. He's a big dark skinned man with black hair and a moustache. We have difficulty understanding what he says. None of us can remember his name, not even Dad, who, when talking about him refers to him as 'Iraq' and so do we. Mary feels sorry for him and says 'if everyone learnt to speak Esperanto which is going to be a universal language, and that she is now studying at a night class, then we wouldn't have such problems.'

Iraq tells Mum that he would prefer to eat on his own, so she puts a table and chair for him in our sitting room and has a fire going for when he gets in from work. Dad isn't too pleased about this as we don't get any extra coal from Mr. Randal's.

Iraq has a bike for going to work on. He leaves the house each day much later than Dad, usually around the time that I set off for school, and he's always first back home at tea time, apart from me that is. Even so we don't see much of him other than Mum of course, and he doesn't have much to say to her. As we haven't a shed, he asks Mum if she would mind if he put his bike in the back kitchen overnight. She found it difficult to say 'no.'

Dad's always first up and busying about downstairs, cleaning out the grate, getting the fire going and making himself a rather generous bowl of porridge. When Mum manages to get a tin of golden syrup it doesn't last long. It's not long before he starts to complain about Iraq's bike obstructing his use of the cooker.

It feels strange Iraq being in the sitting room. Before we all had meals together. It's probably just as well as I know Dad doesn't feel at ease with Iraq and has been like that from the very first day he arrived at the house asking for lodgings. The soldiers and Mr. Redhead came with someone else as Dad pointed out, in an 'official capacity.'

My friend Arthur has seen him and thinks he's an Arab, possibly Dad does as well. If he is, then he's a long way from home, and it's about time I headed for home, Mum will be wondering where I am, but I did say I was going to see Arthur. Soon home and find Mum sitting having a quiet moment while waiting for us all to come in, and it's only me - no Mary or Iraq and far too early for Dad.

Mum then starts to tell me what had happened when I was at Arthur's. She had just made a pot of tea when a police car came past our house, turning down Greensway and stopping outside Astbury's bungalow. A police sergeant and a man in civilian clothes got out of the car and walked back towards our house, opening the gate and soon knocking on the front door. She thought something dreadful had happened. On opening the door the sergeant asked about a man lodging with us as they would like a few words with him. As Iraq wasn't in but expected home anytime, they waited for him in the sitting room. Mum had made them a cup of tea along with the last of our digestive biscuits.

It wasn't long before Iraq came home as usual straight into the sitting room. Mum had decided to keep out of the way. Eventually, the sergeant went looking for Mum and knocking on the dining room door. Apologising for the disturbance and thanking her for the tea. They then left with Iraq. He had said nothing and no explanation from the police.

I couldn't wait to tell Mary which I did as soon as she opened the back door. She listened and said I was having her on. Mum's bothered about what the neighbours will think, the police car, the police coming to the house. Mum was just beside herself. Mary looks up at the clock. I think maybe I should make a pot of tea - its Mum's answer for everything. Then Mary says that poor Iraq looked like missing his tea. I suppose really we are all waiting for Dad to come home to share the news of the day and for a change he's going to be outnumbered three to one, the listener.

It seems ages - is he never going to get home? Then he's spotted slowly strolling up Greensway reading the newspaper. 'Hello' as he opens the back door. 'What sort of a day have you had?' Gee wiz! It seems a long time before anything's said and then a few words from Mum. "We have had the police round"- a major event in Curzon Park. Dad calmly replies "Oh! That will be Iraq."

Without a word Mum left to put the kettle on as she's never parted too long from a pot of tea, and then we talk, or should I say we listen to Dad. Apparently, he has been in touch with the police for the last week or so and they have met with him at work as they thought any contact should be distanced from the house while they were dealing with the enquiry. Dad had been sworn to secrecy, which sounded very exciting, and he's convinced Iraq's spying for the Germans. "Whatever made you think that?" asks Mum. "Annie, of all the men I know employed in work of national importance, and that includes Iraq who we were told worked in munitions, all of them work at least two hours overtime most nights of the week and a Sunday working. Iraq never did." And Mary was right, he did miss his tea and his bed wasn't slept in. The police called again the following day to tell Mum that we wouldn't be seeing him again and they left taking his bike and belongings.

I was over at the Coates's house with Robert and Dennis. Major Coates has a batman, Beswick. I suppose that would have been his surname. Soldiers always seem to be known by their surname. A friendly man often found busying about the house as well as looking after the Major and was busy ironing in the kitchen when I came over. Then he pokes his head round the door. "Quick Peter, get yourself back home and tell your Mum that the Germans have invaded Russia." I couldn't believe it and Beswick was as excited as could be. He couldn't get me out of the back door fast enough.

Just like Beswick, Mum couldn't believe it though I think she was more relieved than excited. Dad comes home. I don't think I could say he was excited. Then I have to remember that he knows what it's like as a fighting soldier being in the last war. He thinks that the Germans going into Russia will reduce our being bombed, and the threat of invasion. Hitler has taken on a little more than he can chew and they will come to grief with the Russian winter. Just like Napoleon.

Even with Dad's experience of war I just don't see how Hitler could be compared with Napoleon. I didn't know a great deal about Napoleon, only that he had infantry, artillery and cavalry. Cavalry was a thing of the past and other than that Hitler had everything that Napoleon had, was fully mechanised with transport, tanks and aircraft. And he knows about how Napoleon came to grief. "Mark my words Peter it will be a repeat of the retreat from Moscow." Apart from bath night only on a Friday, I think this was one of the few times that I had questioned what Dad was saying.

Arthur and I are into exploring and decide to take a walk along the Duke's drive. The last time we came, we only managed to look through the gates, as the lodge keeper was around. I think we are allowed to walk the drive but Arthur and I aren't too confident on our own. The grassed areas on both sides of the drive were full of parked army vehicles, Bren gun carriers; lorries all camouflaged and looking abandoned. Way up the drive as far as we could see. He was probably keeping an eye on them as there were no soldiers about. It's much the same, the vehicles are still there and with no one about at the lodge, we go quietly through the gate. We sometimes go to the Dingle but the woods off the Duke's drive are much bigger. The only problem is you can come across men that work for the Duke - then its trouble.

We're passed all the vehicles and not far from the turn off for Eccleston. I know it goes to Eccleston as it's the way I go with Mum when we go and see her brother, my Uncle Reg. He lives at Eccleston and works at the Hall. Then ahead of us we see a huge hole - the road completely gone. We have a good search around in the grass and find some shrapnel and then something I've not got in my collection so far - the fin of an incendiary bomb. Further into the woods we come across pieces of parachute and cord most of it out of reach in trees. The pieces of parachute we stuffed down our coats in case we were seen.

It took us a long time to get back. I suppose we had gone too far and spent too much time around the bomb crater. We thought it best not to risk going past the Overleigh Lodge as we might be searched and probably lose our shrapnel and things so we took a path through the woods and came out into Wrexham Road. Then we were bound for Hough Green and home.

I often wonder if the Germans, the Luftwaffe, dropped the bomb having seen all those army vehicles, and thought it an army convoy or was it a land mine dropped by parachute, or was it just to off load a bomb intended for Liverpool. I never knew, but I did know that the parachute was made of silk and it went into the making of a lovely blouse for Mary.

I was well rewarded for my find, as Mary was so pleased with her posh silk blouse that she knitted me a very colourful fair isle pullover and Mum made me a brown corduroy 'jerkin' which she lined with aircraft fabric intended for a Wellington bomber. Arthur's jerkin has a zip front. Mum couldn't buy a zip so mine has buttons.

I really liked my new clothes. I had something to wear other than my school uniform.

My little two wheeler bike was in a bit of a sorry state before Dad cleaned it up. He says "an oily cloth works wonders." On the can - 'Everyman Lubricating Oil' - this Dad squirts on the wheels and chain. Then all the chrome is cleaned with his oily cloth which he keeps in a screw-topped jar. He's painted the frame red and it looks a lot better. I helped whenever I could adjusting the handlebars and seat which is now up to as high as it will go. I haven't got blow up tyres like Mary's bike and hers has a name on the frame, 'Elswick'. I think mine was 'Triang' before Dad painted over it.

Arthur came round and now has a bike handed down from his older brother Ken who has been bought a new bike after passing the scholarship exam for the King's School. So now we can both go out on bike rides and not be bothered about being home late.

Mum talks of 'Lill' a school friend of hers that married my great Uncle Alf from the Wrexham Road farm. They have their own farm now at Dodleston, Pear Tree Farm. "Where's that Mum?" "Well you know Cliveden Road where you used to go to school - you just keep going down there until you come to Lache Lane, then it's one way to Chester, the other to Balderton, and then on to Dodleston." She wasn't sure about buses to Dodleston. We weren't bothered about buses we were going on our bikes.

On the day we found our way to Lache Lane without too much trouble, then asked a lady which way to Balderton 'just follow the road until you reach a level crossing and a signal box, then on to Dodleston and Kinnerton. I didn't know about Kinnerton. Even on our bikes it took us quite a long time to get to the signal box at Balderton and the crossing gates were closed. We wanted a rest, so we pushed our bikes off the road alongside some railway sidings, big coal trucks and coal bunkers. We laid our bikes down on the grass to have a look around. Alongside the sidings there was a much smaller narrow line with buffers and some small coal trucks. These we played on, running them down the hill from the sidings into the open fields beyond, then the hard work pushing them back again ready for another ride. It went on for ages before we got tired.

The signal man was in his box but he didn't seem at all bothered. He eventually did poke his head out of the window and said it was about time we went home. He said it was a private railway belonging to the Duke of Westminster. The line goes through to Eaton Hall for taking their coal and whatever comes in for them by rail. I said that we had put the trucks back where we had found them. He smiled and said, "Off you go" and we did.

I was asked where I had been when I got home and I said that Arthur and I had gone to see Auntie Lill but had only got as far as Balderton. "I think that was far enough" Mum said. I don't know how Arthur got on.

Every now and again something new appeared in, of all places, the sideboard, not the pantry. These became known as the food supplements and were intended for growing children who were thought to be in need of additional nourishment to their ration of food. It was some Ministry or other that dreamed these things up. There was a Ministry for everything. And it was now and again probably because it wasn't always available or just couldn't afford. Jars of Virol Malt Extract, bottles of cod liver oil and concentrated orange juice; a spoonful before going to school in the morning. I would willingly dodge any of them especially the cod liver oil and the Virol wasn't much better. I even lied about taking the cod liver oil and I knew that Dad rather liked the Virol.

We then had an addition to our milk ration, National Dried Milk, and it comes in big tins. The only thing you can mix it with is water and I suppose it works quite well but then I remember the milk Charlie used to bring from the Jersey cow at Great Grandmother Johnson's farm.

Now something that came later, which could have also been a supplement but maybe not, were Horlicks tablets to be eaten like sweets. They were really nice but I found going on after a couple, of feeling decidedly ill, so they became a one at a time, and a packet lasted ages. They never became a regular thing with me and could never replace sweets, which we don't have any more.

Dinner times were a bowl of soup with a round of bread or toast. The soup was made with hot water and an Oxo cube or if you were lucky enough to have a jar of Bovril then this made a much nicer bowl of soup. Sometimes as a treat we had cheese on toast. Both of these dinners saved on butter.

However difficult Mum always managed to put a hot meal together at tea time. We had a lot of hot pots usually made with mutton and I didn't like mutton - there was always big grey bones left in the hotpot. We didn't always have puddings but when we did, without fail, it would be milk pudding; rice, tapioca or semolina. I hated tapioca; the look of it reminded me of frog spawn. I didn't much care for milk puddings at all, except for the skin on top when it was brown and scraping around the dish it was cooked in was such a treat. We never had a choice of what to eat and many times we would eat things that we didn't particularly like but we knew the alternative was to go hungry. "Didn't like is no excuse" according to Dad, "it was all good food and your Mother works miracles with what she has." And she did.

The nights are drawing in even though we have double British Summertime. Leaves have gone from the trees and are now covering The Green; and I am reminded of bonfire nights before the War. It's that time again and we can't have a bonfire because of the blackout. Sometime we will be able to have a bonfire again and it won't be Guy Fawkes on it. It seems ages ago when we used to rake the leaves up on The Green to have a bonfire in our back garden, making a Guy Fawkes, setting off a few fireworks and Mum would make cinder toffee. Best not to call it Bonfire Night any more but we are very fortunate this November 5th as when Dad was on his way down to his bus for work, as always, calling in to Moulton's newsagents for his cigarettes and newspaper.

Then Mr. Moulton took Dad completely by surprise; "Now what about a box of indoor fireworks?" The box was brought home a few days ago and I'm dying to see what's inside. Dad says for safety reasons the box will stay sealed in the sideboard until he gets home on the night. This will be the first November 5th of the war that we have fireworks and prepared for any disaster having a complete fire fighting kit at No. 5.

Tonight's the night - food finished and table cleared; blackout doubly checked just in case any bright light shows through. We don't want trouble from the Warden on this of all nights. Dad's read and re-read the things to do and not to do and from what he can see it's all about the risk of fire. Maybe just as well the stirrup pump's in the hall. A box of matches at the ready Mum switches off the light and Dad can't see. Mary puts the light on and suggests we light a candle and have the light switched off.

We always have a good stock of candles which we use whenever there is an air raid, and come to think of it we haven't had one for sometime. I hope the siren doesn't go off in the middle of the fireworks to spoil it all.

Dad goes with the candle idea, opens the box and takes out a piece of brown paper, a bit smaller than a post card. There's more to read on the inside of the lid and then he starts carefully folding and creasing along from the edge all the way across to the other side, half way across "We need a cotton reel Annie" who now needs the light back on to look for the cotton reel. Dad's left holding between his finger and thumb what looks like a ladies folded fan. Now with the cotton reel in his free hand, he tries to push one end of the fan into the hole in the cotton reel with difficulty. We all have suggestions to make which don't appear to help. I think the hole isn't big enough. "Scissors please Annie". Dad trims some of the paper off and it now fits in the hole. He fiddles with it, pulling it apart and it is just like an open fan. We all look at it and it doesn't do anything.

Mary has now got the giggles and can't stop, and I can't help myself. Above it all Dad is heard, "Mary, light off please" - all dark, strikes a match and gently touches the top of the fan with the flame. It glows red all along the top in a sort of zigzag and slowly creeps down the fan leaving behind curling white ash, and a lot of smoke. It eventually stops and Mary has the giggles again. A bit of a disappointment really. It didn't fizz or make a bang. I look in the box and we have a few more of those. At this rate it's going to take all night. There are two boxes of Bengal matches that burn a colour and make a bit of a pop when you strike them. After a couple of them we move onto 'the snake.' It looks like round piece of liquorice stuck on a card disc. We have a break before 'the snake' for a few sparklers which were the best so far. Mum decides all this smoke is drying her throat and makes a pot of tea.

Then it's time for 'the Snake.' Mary turns off the light, match struck and rested on the top of the liquorice bit. After a while it starts to grow and Dad hastily takes the match away, 'the snake' keeps going longer and longer - it must have grown at leas twelve inches, then it starts curling around and heads off towards the bookcase, faster and faster. It then curls off in the direction of Mum, then it's off in another direction curling away all over the place. In the candle light it looks black with white bits. It looks fantastic, definitely the best in the box; again no fizz or bang but Wow! It went on for ages. Mary puts the light on the room's full of smoke. It went, eventually, and we all look in wonderment at this big tangled burnt black looking thing in the middle of the table. And then it all starts to disintegrate into ash, falling all over the table. Mum breaks the silence. "Oh! for goodness sake, it's all in the sugar bowl, the milk and just look at my nice white table cloth"

Mary and I just looked at each other and without a word passing our lips we knew silence to be the better option. The tidy up starts with a dustpan and brush which seems to make more mess. The table cloth rolled up, ready for washing. Had we seen the last of the fireworks, even though there were a few left in the box? I don't think we were all that bothered really, and I can't see Dad buying them again, what with Mum's table cloth and our sugar ration gone. How Mr. Moulton fares in the morning when Dad goes in for his paper, I don't know.

Most of the fireworks just smouldered away, apart from a packet of cut out paper shapes when dropped into a bowl of water grew into flowers. No fizzers or bangers like the real outdoor fireworks before the war. We never saw the remaining fireworks and the smell lingered for days. The tablecloth went into the clothes boiler and came out clean along with a few other things - a lot of fuss over nothing.

If I get my timing right from school I quite enjoy helping out with the washing. We have a fair bit of kit for washing clothes and things, a big galvanised boiler with a copper top which Mum keeps polished. It's hinged for filling with water, has a brass tap for draining off which Mum also keeps highly polished. This stands on four cast iron legs just by the mangle.

We have a gas tap next to the gas stove where we can connect the portable gas ring. This is fired up with a loud bang, and burning fiercely, slid under the boiler. Then there is the dolly tub, much the same size as the boiler, both of these big enough for me to stand in and

I can tell you they took some filling, usually done with our biggest saucepan. While the boiler's heating up, the soap powder goes in. Mum likes to go for Oxydol or Rinso from choice which nowadays we don't have - it's what you can get.

It takes ages for the boiler to heat up, so you can get on with your homework or other jobs. The lid starts to rattle when the water boils, then Mum knows how long to let it boil before the gas ring's turned off, then up goes the lid. The whole house is full of steam and we can't see through any of the windows. Mum transfers half of the wash from the boiler to the dolly tub with a large pair of wooden tongs. Water all over the place is soon swept across the tile floor and out of the back door. Our biggest pan then goes under the boiler tap and start to fill the dolly tub until the washing is well covered.

The set of pans Mum has came from Dad's shop. 'Judge' pans, black stove-enamelled with a white inside and a milk pan with pourer, green stove-enamelled with a cream inside. Dad insists they were the best quality that money could buy and just as well as they have to last us until the War's over, and that they are stove enamelled. If they had been aluminium they would have been taken away to help the war effort in the making of Lancaster bombers. I don't think it was compulsory - most everyone willingly parted with them. How they managed after, we don't know.

Now starts the bit I enjoy, the fun bit. Mum has a copper posser and a dollypeg, both looking very strange, probably even comical, an absolute joy to me. I see them, describing them is another thing, but here goes. The dollypeg. Picture a wooden three legged milking stool (have I lost you already?) set in the centre, a spade shaft and through the top a 'T' bar. The dollypeg is lowered feet first into the tub, then holding the 'T' bar firmly at both ends a pull and push action rotates the pegs swishing the washing about; now the posser. Picture it in shining copper as a conical shafted lamp shade about a foot across - on the inside what looks like a small colander attached by the rim. A collar at the neck of the shade held a long broom handle. I think the comical part was also holed but not nearly as many as the inner round piece.

This, like the dolly, was lowered into the tub, up and down up and down making loads of suds; a swishing, sucking noise the faster you did it, the better it got. I was unstoppable at top speed and managed to get rude noises out of the posser which got Mary in hysterics. She encouraged me to go even faster. Swapping over from dolly to posser several times seemed to make for a good wash, then wringing out before going through the mangle then over to the sink for rinsing in three changes of cold water. Mum always insisted on this to get all the soap out. Back to the mangle once more where I was ready to turn the handle while Mum feeds the washing through.

Now and again I'm too fast on the handle and a shirt sleeve end finds its way through the rollers followed by the crunch of a button. Then it's all ready for hanging out if it's a good day. Memories of wash days were of enjoyment and fun which sometimes ended in trouble if I got the best out of the posser; but always of feeling tired and having had enough.

Most nights Dad comes home with his news of the day which we all listen to. He forgets that we have a wireless at home to keep up with the news, but Mum seldom thinks of switching it on. If she did, it wouldn't be for the news as she likes sing-along songs, stories and plays. Even if we were up to date with the news, Dad never asks us and even if he did, I'm sure we would hear it all again.

I don't mind if its factory news, some of the men he works with are spoken of so often that we feel as though we know them. The majority of them we never see except for Mr. Crawford who lives along our road. He used to have a shoe shop in the same street as Dad's before the war where we would go for our shoes. He suggested that I should have 'Startrite' shoes with a wide welt. I remember the Jepson boys who were his near neighbours (and probably given the same advice) christened him, 'Willie wide welt'. Maurice was of Mary's age and had a nick name for most people around The Green.

Anyhow, tonight Dad's busy explaining in great detail how the factory is planned, taking into account air raids, bombing and sabotage. I pricked my ears up - seemed more interesting to me especially after the business with Iraq. I don't think of German spies getting into the aircraft factory with so many security checks on the gates. Dad's going on about how it all relates to his wood store which of course is classed as inflammable. Now this is in the main factory complex with all the other stores except for one.

The dope store which is classed as highly inflammable and because of this is located on the extreme perimeter on the other side of the airfield. I put my hand up, forgetting I wasn't at school, "so every time a plane is ready for doping they have to bring the dope all the way across the airfield and into the main factory?" "Yes" is the answer! "But they can't risk the highly inflammable nature of the dope in the factory, which I can understand, so if some fool in the dope store decides to have a cigarette while the lid's off his tin of dope, then only the dope store goes up and not the whole of Vickers Armstrong." Dad seems to think that's broadly the picture but not quite as I haven't thought it through – "the factory is non-smoking!"

"The problem is when painters, not the dopers Peter, draw quantities beyond what is required for the job so at the end of their shift or day they are left with a surplus. Then what do they do with it?" Dad's asking me and to me it's very obvious, they take it back to the dope store. The answer is "They don't, because at the end of the day it's a long way back to the dope store, they are tired, all they want to do is go home, not filling in returns forms and so on." So as I seem to be the only one interested, "Well what do they do then?" We lost Mum and Mary ages ago.

It would appear there's an obvious and simple solution to the problem - the toilet block in the main factory. This is in use day and night and where the majority of the work force visit before heading for home. "So any dope left over, surplus to requirement," says Dad, "is taken to the toilet block and disposed of in one of the lavatories." We all look at Dad in complete silence and it's left to me again. "Well I suppose that saves him or her the problem of filling in returns forms and that walk across the airfield on a dark and cold winter night?" "Exactly," says Dad, "but someone hadn't flushed the chain after putting a considerable amount of dope thinners in the lavatory. The last of the over-timers are preparing for home when this chap comes along and goes into this particular lavatory for a quiet time, a smoke, and bang! The unfortunate chap was blown through the door."

I kept quiet for a bit, we all did, but then I just couldn't help it, I fell about laughing. I just saw it as in a comic, a big BANG written in a cloud of smoke and the lavatory door flying off its hinges, hotly followed by this chap, wide eyed and surprised in a crouching position, trousers down round his ankles with one hand desperately trying not to lose them altogether, before he makes for a soft landing on the back of an unsuspecting fellow worker washing his hands.

I thought it the funniest thing I'd heard in ages from Dad. The way he told it had something to do with it. I eventually quietened down.

Mary had more than a smile on her face but hadn't laughed about it. I got a good telling off - Dad hadn't intended, or just couldn't see, this serious accident in the least amusing. Maybe it's something to do with growing up, you don't see serious things quite the same as grown-ups. And there is something a bit funny about lavatories. Dad goes on to say that both the men had been taken to the hospital and the man that set the dope thinners off was seriously hurt, which made me feel really bad for laughing.

I suppose as time goes by Mary will get used to Margaret not being just around the corner to go and see whenever she pleases. I would be the same if my best friend Arthur went to live away from Chester. Mary misses her and this I understand but I am sure she had other friends from school days and at the telephone exchange.

They do keep in touch exchanging letters and sometimes Mary shares the news with me and from what Margaret says, it looks like she's going to join the Red Cross to be a nurse and the possibility of working at the Royal Infirmary in Chester. Now that really lifts Mary out of the doldrums and its good news for all of us.

Then some news especially for Peter - 'tell him that Dad has enlisted for the Army as a commissioned officer and will be joining the Green Howards, his old regiment from the last war. This surprised me as I thought that with his ships telegraph and working with Skipper Sardines, he was more of a seafaring man and would be more at home in the Royal Navy. I think Mary's mentioned before that Margaret's sister, Muriel, is also nursing and that Mrs. Jackson had also been a nurse. I suppose before she married Mr. Jackson.

Quite often when in Town you hear in the distance the sound of a military band. Then you don't hang about - it's off to the Market Square as it's some regiment or other having a march through Town which always goes past the Town Hall where the Mayor and senior officers take the salute. It's all very exciting - the sound of marching feet in step, the brass band, the drums and above it all the shouting of commands as they go through the Square. Arthur and I usually march in step at the side. It makes you feel good and safe. Sometimes a tank or a Bren gun carrier follows the march. Members of the Auxiliary Fire Service, St. John's Ambulance Brigade, the Women's Voluntary Service - whoever has time to spare to make numbers up, join a few uniformed folk enthusiastically rattling tins for our contributions to the war effort.

All the armed services have event days when they bring various pieces of equipment to put on shows to raise funds. The RAF had an event for the funding of a Spitfire and had a fuselage of one on a big trailer in Market Square. It was a very impressive display with flags, banners and a marquee where they had photographs and information where you could find out what being in the RAF was like and airmen to talk with.

You weren't allowed to sit in the cockpit but you could go up on a platform and have a good look inside while a pilot officer told you all about the controls. Just by the Spitfire was a big thermometer-like thing and on the top was the cost to make a Spitfire. I couldn't work it out. I'd never seen so many numbers together. It really was a lot of money and the red bit at the bottom had hardly moved. It only showed £'s so my couple of pennies wouldn't have helped a great deal.

The best one we have been on so far was one advertised well before the event. It was for the funding of a tank for the Royal Tank Corps. I think there was also the Royal Armoured Corps and I should know as I collected regimental cap badges and buttons, buying them from Mr. Bounds shop in Grosvenor Street.

They brought a few tanks on transporters through the streets of Chester and onto the Roodee where they'd pitched a few tents and a marquee. They were big tanks - 'Valentines' and 'Matildas.' Demonstrations, mock battles and you could pay a fare to ride in them just like a Corporation bus, only different, very different. Dad took me and Arthur came along. Dad promised to pay for us to go and have a ride on one. But it might be only to watch so don't be disappointed - we didn't know. Off we went telling the sentry on the footbridge all about it. I knew him and he asked me the password, and I said "coke;" He smiled and said in a light hearted way that "The Tank Corps had it soft riding around all day nice and safe in their tank, popping off at a few Germans whenever they had the opportunity. The steel in those tanks is about that thick," (holding his thumb and finger as wide apart as he could).

Dad had gone and we had to run to catch up with him. We were soon across the Roodee where parts of it were roped off for the tank demonstrations. It was a sea of churned up mud by about half a dozen tanks in no time at all. A tannoy system was playing 'Waltzing Matilda' - it played all day long, never stopped, and I still, unknowingly, sing it to myself to this day. It was a super day watching them and when they came to a standstill they would bring the big gun into play and fire off a few blanks, briefly drowning the tannoy.

Arthur and I had had a ride on the top of a 'Matilda' tank hanging on for dear life as it rocked and rolled its way across the Roodee. When it was over we went and had a look inside one which made me feel pleased that we had had our ride on the top.

It was very cramped inside for the few crew which I think were three, small men would be appreciated, and I got to thinking what do you do on the move at full speed over rough country, then a big gun going off every now and again, no singing along with 'Waltzing Matilda' and you want to have a wee. I thought it best not to ask.

We had a fantastic day but how different it would be to be a man in a battle situation in a tank or a Spitfire when one could be killed. For Arthur and I the planes and tanks were big toys. I am finding this war very confusing. Before the war the games I played were with toy soldiers, now I have seen soldiers for real and have enjoyed knowing them. I have said goodbye to them and don't know where they are. I have known bombing and being frightened, heard good news and bad news, and am confused from day to day. It seems to be going on for so long.

No matter how we try to economise with our ration of coal we still have some days in the week when keeping the fire going is difficult. When it's very cold we light up the Valor stove as well as the coal fire, providing I can get some paraffin oil from Morris's. We put it in the hall and it seems to take the cold off that side of the house and some of the warmth drifts to the upstairs. If a cold spell falls on a Friday bath night we take it upstairs to the bathroom whilst we have a bath. Bath night usually lasts longer when we have the stove on.

I thought finding the gas works where I go for the coke and bits of trees that we find was keeping the fire going, which it has, but Mum seems to think that the coke gives off fumes which are affecting our chests, especially Dad who has a cough and Mum feels much the same. Mary and I don't seem to be troubled that way but we do notice a smell though. It doesn't burn as well as coal but it's a lot cheaper and gives us warmth and hot water. Mum is very positive about it, so I shall just, somehow, try and collect more wood. Getting it dry enough to burn is a problem. All we need is an extra sack a month. Maybe it will happen by next year. Mr. Dye next door seems to agree with

Mum about the coke fumes and is trying out putting a bucket of water in front of the fire.

Our postman, who happens to be a lady, tells Mum that they are going to paint the top of her pillar box green and she's not at all happy about it - as long as she can remember, they have always been red. Mum agrees as she thinks they look nice red. I can't help thinking that they might also change the colour of the vans and the telephone kiosks at the same time, though she didn't say so. I can't understand the reasoning as in this war everyone seems to be thinking only of essentials, but then it may be an essential, a camouflage to disguise that they are not Royal Mail to fool the Germans.

Dad hears all about it when he comes home and seems to approve of my thinking that they are going to camouflage the Royal Mail. But then nothing happens for weeks, then one day when I came home from school there had been an addition to the swill bin on The Green across the road. A post with a flat board on top, painted a bright lime green. The man responsible for this had been across to our house and had a word with Mum and it would appear that we were to tell the rest of the people around The Green the reason it's there and its purpose.

From what I can gather there is a connection with the painting of the pillar box tops which the Royal Mail aren't too happy about as some have already been painted. We have as an alternative a post and board so our post lady won't have her pillar box top painted. She may be happy but I have the job of going to every house on our road and Greensway, explaining how the post and board next to the swill bin works which is very clever.

The board is coated in a special paint so when the Luftwaffe comes over to drop bombs which could contain gas, then we would know by looking at the board on the top of the pole by the swill bin as it would change colour to red. We would of course have to leave the safety of being under our dining room table before the all clear had sounded which we were told never to do. When Dad comes home he finds it difficult to understand how the Town Hall could be so stupid, and all this coming about when he is one of the official fire watch units around The Green and he hadn't been aware of the painting of the pillar boxes in the first place - which never happened!

Arthur and I discovered that if we bit a piece off a candle, after a while in our mouth it became soft enough to chew, just like chewing gum. Well perhaps not 'just like' but when you can't buy the real thing. Last summer we collected the sap seeping through an apple tree in Arthur's back garden and had a chew of that, but believe it or not, the candle wax was the better of the two - until we can get some real chewing gum.

Pearl Harbour and Christmas 1941

Programmes were interrupted on the wireless for a news bulletin. Japanese bombers had dropped bombs on the American Naval Base at Pearl Harbour, Hawaii. The surprise attack began at 6.45 a.m. on Sunday morning, December 7th 1941. Seven battleships were sunk or put out of action in two hours of bombing and raking machine gun fire. Over 2,400 people were left dead or missing. We can't believe what has happened. How this had come about as far away as America and why Japan? From what I can gather it seems Dad doesn't care too much for the Japanese neither does it seem that any of my pals Dads think anything different.

The following day we join in with the Americans and declare war on Japan. Dad now makes it very obvious that he doesn't like the Japanese and it's more the Americans war than ours.

Everyone seems to have gone very quiet and our war with the Germans and Italians isn't talked about. Then came the news that Germany and Italy have declared war on the U.S.A. Dad looked around and with a smile on his face said, "Now they're in for it; it's just a pity it took them so long, just like the last one. What a difference this last few days news has made to everyone and with Christmas not far away. You never know, we may have a chicken this year." When Dad says the last one it was the one he was in (1914-18).

Dad seems to think that the Americans (he usually refers to as Yanks) by the time they sort themselves out we should see them here by the end of next summer. I never thought that they intended coming anyway and would have fought the war from their own country. Dad says something about being used as a stepping stone into France. "A mere stepping stone, Peter," pausing between each word followed by a big sigh and a "dear me." But overall he seems very pleased.

Christmas is with us again and a chicken looks unlikely, but Mum is hopeful for a piece of pork or maybe a rabbit which Dad doesn't seem too happy about - this word 'vermin' comes into the conversation. But Mum had made a Christmas pudding. She managed to get a block of compressed dates from Mr. Salsbury, our grocer in Saltney.

Mr. Dye next door gave her a recipe for a Christmas pudding using mainly carrots, so a few of the dates went next door and then a few carrots came from Mr. Dye. He grows them in his back garden and stores them over winter in boxes filled with dry sand. So we have a Christmas pudding, mainly made with carrots, a few dates (which apparently the Yanks provided) and some suet from the butcher, which doesn't look like we're having a chicken.

Presents were few but we had some apples and some sweets. Dad was persuaded to light a fire in the sitting room. The only problem we have with that is that we can't listen to the wireless there so Dad's popping in and out of the dining room to hear the news. We do have a piano in the sitting room but all Dad wants to play is hymns, though he's easily persuaded to play draughts instead. Mary is the one who usually makes the suggestion.

Mum did get a chicken and along with the usual sprouts we had roast parsnips which I hadn't had before. They were really nice and the Christmas pudding was as good as any one before. Well fed and full up Mary and I sat on the thick rug in front of the fire. Mum surprised us again at tea with ham sandwiches. The ham from a tin, again provided by the Yanks, and we had a fruit jelly. I can't remember when we last had a jelly. It wasn't jelly from a packet of jelly cubes, you can't get those any more. Mum had managed to get some loose gelatine from Mr. Kennerley's, the Chemist, which she made up with some bottled plums. So we did have a good Christmas again.

Whenever we have the wireless on it always seems to be the same lady singing the same song. I've heard it that many times that I know it off by heart. 'There'll be blue birds over the white cliffs of Dover, tomorrow just you wait and see.' Mum sings it all the time as she goes about the house, then Mary comes home from work singing it. "Who is it Mum?" - "It's Vera Lynn." Even I like her and she's a lot, lot better than Gracie Fields, but my favourite is 'Deep in the heart of Texas,' I don't know who sings it, it doesn't matter, he was a cowboy.

Mary tells us that there is a good film on in town at the Regal with Errol Flynn – 'Robin Hood and his Merry Men.' Mum appears to know Errol Flynn as though a friend, much the same as she knows Vera Lynn. I suppose it shouldn't surprise me really as Mary knows all the film stars as she read the magazine 'Picturegoer.' It's all about film stars and she goes to the pictures most weeks with one of her friends. I think it's Mary who buys the magazine and then I suppose Mum has the occasional read when she has five minutes for a pot of tea.

Sometimes Dad picks up a magazine along with his morning paper. 'Picture Post' or the 'Everybodys' seem to be to his liking - he says "one for pictures and one for reading." I see what he means but I just look at the pictures in both. Anyhow some way or other Mary has really impressed Dad with the mention of 'Robin Hood' and the next thing we know Dad's offering to take us to the pictures!

After tea we were all ready for our treat to the pictures and soon on the bus. The next stop after St. Werburghs Street saw us just across the road from the Regal and there were hundreds of people queuing from the ticket desk through the doors right down to the bottom of Love Street and round the corner before we could join the queue.

The Commissionaire, a man in a smart uniform with gold braid on his hat, came down the queue assuring us that we would all get comfortably seated well before the next performance began, which everyone seemed very pleased about.

Mary pointed out her old school as we slowly made our way back up Love Street. She was in the same class as her Auntie Maisie. I always thought it a bit odd and none of my pals ever believed me. It came about as Mum was the eldest of thirteen children, Auntie Maisie being the youngest.

Through the doors and then we were in the warmth of the big hall and down to the ticket desk. With tickets in hand Dad gathers us together. Mary knows the way and we tread thick carpet across the inner hall to a few doors each with a smart lady in a uniform. She tears our tickets in half and on returning half to Dad for safe keeping with an "enjoy the show," as she opens the door.

I can't believe how big this place is, even in this light which isn't very bright. It's quite dark really and there's row after row of seats, there must be hundreds. Carpet everywhere and it's so lovely and warm. Another lady dressed just like the one that showed us in comes along and shining a torch so as to see our tickets. "Four centre stalls - follow me please" and she's off pretty quick time down one of the aisles. The floor slopes, still carpeted, so we don't make any noise at all. Right down at the bottom is a huge curtain all lit up with lights but you can't see any lights. It's like nothing I have ever seen before.

We stop part way down and the lady shines her torch down a row of seats past a lot of people and they all stand up to let us through. We get to our seats and we have to pull them down before we can sit on them. When you get off your seat, they fly back up again. They're super, so soft and comfortable with padded armrests and it's nice and warm. At home, Mary and I use the dining chairs or a small sea grass stool to sit on but I think these seats are even better than the easy chairs that Mum and Dad have. I do love this place - it's so exciting and the film hasn't started yet.

Dad tells me that the lady on the door and the one that found our seats were called usherettes and that part way through the performance before showing the big film the lights would go on for a short interval when the usherettes would come round with ice cream. "So behave yourself!" I can't think how anyone could be any other way, I just want to look around and keep quiet. I will have plenty to talk about tomorrow when it's all over.

I keep looking around; it's so big and packed with so many people there must be hundreds of us all waiting to see 'Robin Hood' and I've just noticed behind me there's an upstairs. Dad says that they are the best seats but the ones we have are very comfortable. Looking around there's quite a few doors with light up signs over them, mainly 'exits' and 'ladies and gentlemen.' Then I start to wonder that if I had to go, would I have to ask one of the usherettes, as I would never ever find my way back. Just about to ask Dad and the lights go down except for the lights over doors and some way up in the ceiling – just like being in the blackout. The curtains go back and the show starts. We see a short film about wartime farming, a 'Popeye' cartoon. Then the news and then the lights come on as the curtains close.

Spotlights were directed on to usherettes way down at the front with trays full of ice cream. Dad was off his seat and there was a queue within seconds. It seemed an age before he was on his way back, then he was up and down the aisle several times before the man on the end of our row managed to grab his arm. We thought it a bit of a laugh but Dad thought differently. Vanilla ice cream in a tub with a wooden spoon! A real treat as we don't often have ice cream. Dad said that they ran out of ice cream when there was still a lot of people left in the queue, so we were lucky.

Sitting through the film in Technicolor in this lovely warm cinema in the comfort of a soft armchair was just unbelievable, the films before, the shorts, the news were all in black and white. I never ever thought about seeing colour and it was on for a long time but it all had to come to an end.

Everyone in the cinema stood up to attention as the National Anthem was played, the sprung seats all going up at the same time sounded like a muffled roll on the drums. Most of us were singing and I could hear Dad next to me above the others with his Sunday church voice. He didn't say but I think he was disappointed as he expected to hear an organ being played.

We gathered our coats together and slowly made our way along the seats to the aisle talking excitedly about the big film. It was so late to be going home and all these people. Was it cold when we got outside! The queue for the bus was a whopper. The first bus to arrive was a double-decker for West View that soon filled up and left us no where near the front, so Dad decides that we walk down to the Bars to get on the next bus whilst there are still seats to be had.

We didn't much like the idea of walking down to the Bars but he was right again, the bus came with room for us and we weren't the only ones to have walked down from the Regal. People soon filled the bus and it sailed past the Regal with its queue without stopping, Dad giving us all a searching look.

We were off the bus at Selkirk Road and soon home. Dad had left the fire well banked up with wet slack before we went out so all it needed was blowing up. I'm allowed to do that now and love doing it. I prop the coal shovel up to the front of the grate, draw the damper in the chimney, then hold a whole sheet of newspaper against and around the shovel. Within seconds the fire is roaring away - then you have to move the paper away pretty quickly before that bursts into flames and gets sucked up the chimney. Then you're really in trouble, especially at night time, with the blackout. But it's not happened tonight. Its fun and we are all in a happy mood.

Mum has the kettle on. She says that there's some of the chicken left on the carcase and bones for picking, parsley stuffing and a few cold sausage. I cut some thick chunks off the loaf and we have a feast just like they had in the film.

No sooner was it on the table, the siren sounded. Cushions were thrown under the table followed by the four of us with all that we could carry. A bit different from Robin Hood! But makeshift eating under that table, hands on with fingers to lick and chasing the pickled onions in a jar which Mum had found with more finger licking, whilst waiting for the sound of enemy aircraft or a bomb - Sherwood Forest never compared with this. Then the 'all clear' sounded. I think it must have been a false alarm - Dad seems to think so - just to keep us on our toes.

Early on in the war years we got used to hearing the intermittent drone of the engines on the German aircraft as they came over on their way to bomb Liverpool, and I remember one night Dad had gone outside in a raid whilst we were under the table. It was the same night that our two soldiers Bill and Ken were caught smoking in the bedroom window by the ARP Warden. Luckily Dad knew the Warden and just a few cautionary words were exchanged. After the 'all clear' Dad came back in quite a state. "Do you know Annie I can still see those Germans now as clear as I see you. Their plane was directly over the house, low enough to see the pilot as the sky lit up with gun fire and searchlights." I somehow couldn't see that having happened in quite the same way but who am I to doubt Dad and it most certainly scared him. Bill and Ken never mentioned seeing the Germans but they did pass a few light hearted remarks about our ARP Warden best not intended for his ears. Just as well they were in the house at the time.

Dad has, over the last few months, got a bit slow at going under the table when the siren goes and I can go along with that as the majority of times it's not followed by an air raid. Even though the air raids are less frequent a brick blast shelter with a flat concrete roof has been built on open land part way down Mount Pleasant, on the right hand side where the terraced houses end. It's pitch black inside, damp, cold and airless with slatted wooden benches to sit on. We think we are more at risk going down there than staying at home under the table.

If the Germans decide to have an air raid day time week days we have the perfect underground shelter at school as we are in a big Victorian house with cellars. Down there we have wooden benches and electric light, water, a lavatory and it's quite warm, and most certainly dry. In fact it's more comfortable than being at home under the table. The down side is - its school!

I must get used to saying 'Luftwaffe' not 'Germans.' Though it isn't, it does sound comical. Now that I'm getting more interested in what's going on, I tend to question grown up things which I think sometimes doesn't go down well with Mum and Dad.

They were having a talk about food, the rationing and I suppose really I was only meant to be listening. Then it started to get complicated. Bacon and butter - four ounces per person per week; sugar - twelve ounces - this I could understand though it isn't much when I compare it with the small paper bags of two ounces of dolly mixtures we used to get. Tea, lard, jam and cheese are rationed and we have food points to spend on things like breakfast cereals, biscuits, canned fruit and fish. The priority was usually for the fish as it was more of a meal with some bread or on toast. Biscuits and tinned fruit were treat food. It was all very complicated but Mum was well in control and I suppose I didn't help by questioning.

Now the meat rationing I just about understand as it's not rationed by weight but by how much it costs, which Mum explains as the cut of the meat. I still don't understand. "Well it's like comparing fillet steak with braising steak and lamb cutlets with mutton, which is about the cheapest cut of meat you can get." What a simple explanation and it all became as clear as daylight. I now knew why we so often have those plates of mutton stew with the big grey bones in.

I think the lack of eggs is the worst bit of rationing. We have one egg a fortnight and we all have it at the same meal so as to make it fair or sometimes they go into making cakes. The ration isn't always available as there is a scarcity of eggs and this is another grown up thing I can't understand, but I keep it to myself as sometimes you can look stupid. Surely we must have the same number of hens on the farms that we had before the war or possibly more, so what's happened to the egg? Anyhow, the last few weeks our ration of eggs has come in a waxed brown cardboard box all the way from the United States of America. No shells, all in the form of powder and we are to have one box per person every two months. This is equivalent to twelve eggs.

We also have two types of what they call 'processed' meat in tins. One called 'Spam' and the other 'Corned Beef.' Dad doesn't like any of it and I don't think Mum or Mary thinks much of it either. Almost forgot, we also have tins of powdered milk. I don't think that comes from the Americans somehow - we powder it ourselves. The same thing has happened again - where have all our cows gone?

Dad won't even consider eating the powdered eggs - he says that they are alligator eggs from the Florida swamps. He has nothing to offer about the Spam or the corned beef but he is most insistent that it's all rubbish that the Yanks can't sell in their own country. I have a feeling that Yanks don't rate very highly in Dad's thinking. He seems to harbour memories of them from his war.

I really liked the dried egg. I would mix it up myself in a bowl with some fresh milk having had the frying pan all greased and heating up on the stove. Nicely mixed it went into the pan and I soon turned it to get it lovely and browned on both sides. It only took minutes and it made a really nice thick savoury pancake to have with a slice of bacon, if we had any, or if not, a thin slice or two of Spam in the frying pan turned out rather nice and tasty with some H.P. sauce.

I didn't mind the corned beef either but Dad wasn't for having it. I wonder if he thinks its buffalo. I'm the only one in the family that likes the eggs which gets me thinking that I might have the opportunity of the family ration of four boxes every two months, which would be a box for me every two weeks. This means the equivalent of twelve eggs which would make me a savoury pancake six times a week! - providing Mum hasn't other ideas like maybe a cake, but then I don't think she would like to use it in a cake though I wouldn't mind a cake now and again for a change.

It's nearly always me that goes down to Saltney to Mr. Salsbury's shop on the corner of Curzon Street with the ration books and shopping list for our weekly shop. I often take him any old newspapers not required for lighting the fire, as he always seems short of wrapping paper and paper bags.

Still talking of food in a funny sort of way, when I went round to

Arthur's house his Mum shouts "Spud's here - wants to know if you're going out to play." Arthur says 'It's because they have had a book about cooking potatoes dropped through their door from the Ministry of Food and it's all about a character 'Potato Pete'. Now Uncle Norman calls me 'Spud' so I have a nickname as well as the one from Uncle Roy - he calls me 'Pip' which I prefer.

We get the same book at home as well as the one 'Eat Me I'm Doctor Carrot.' Propaganda figures to encourage us to eat vegetables, especially if you've grown them yourself, which I know Mr. Carsley has as he stores them in a big box of dry sand in his shed. Well I suppose it's really a garage and we haven't either. So for the time being I'm 'Spud' to some people.

It always surprises me that whenever we go into Town Mum always meets someone she knows - usually a friend from school days or a relative. The lady we meet the most is Auntie Abley. I don't think she's a real Auntie, I think she's an old friend and likes to be called 'Auntie.' "Give your Auntie Abley a kiss Peter." She always looks pleasantly surprised as she bends down turning her head so I can give her a kiss on her cheek. It's always the side of the hairy mole. That done she pats me on the head ruffling my hair, and makes quite a performance of rooting around in her handbag to find her purse. "Now let's see if we can find a penny for some sweets." I seem to have been going through this same routine for years and dread having to meet her. Even so she always manages to find me a penny.

We don't talk for too long - it's usually about what shops have got in to buy or what deliveries they are expecting and when. Or there may be a queue at some shop or other that we could join but not today. It's talk of a restaurant just been opened in Upper Northgate Street across the canal in a church hall, of all places. It's called a British

Restaurant and it's intended for workers where they could get a meal at a modest cost. The way she describes it, it sounds very basic, an uncomfortable sort of place. "The day I went, Annie, it was minced beef and carrots. That's the usual dinner, and queue to collect it yourself, no waitresses, and eat off bare trestle tables. Don't go Annie, its rubbish. I won't be seen in there again. You and Peter are best going home." So we did, and we never experienced what a British Restaurant was like. We weren't workers anyway so in all probability we would never have been allowed in - but Mrs. Abley made it!

Mary was the first of the workers home that night and she wasn't her usual happy self even the letter from Margaret didn't seem to cheer her up. We were waiting to hear how things were going - then eventually Mary tells us that Margaret is nursing at the Royal Infirmary and settled in at the nurse's home. Mum doesn't know whether the nurse's home is in the grounds of the Infirmary or one of the streets close by. It doesn't really matter, she will be in Chester, and we suppose for the duration of the war. This good news for us didn't seem to happen for Mary.

It was a few days later when Mary and I had a quiet time together on our own that she shared with me the reason for her being down. "It's because I'm in big trouble with Dad. A few of the girls at work thought it would be fun going to a dance at Clemence's one night. Now Dad doesn't approve of dance halls and most definitely not Clemence's as he says it's frequented by servicemen, mainly Americans, having a night out on the town and in all probability under the influence of having too much to drink; and not a place for respectable young ladies'."

Dad's views on certain things are very cut and dried and he will never be shifted. Drink being number one and it's all to do with being a Methodist. But how did Dad know about Mary going to Clemence's because I didn't. So I asked her. "Well Peter that's because when I got home it was a bit later than I intended and you had long since gone to bed and so knew nothing about it." All this and then being out late as well, I just don't know what to say.

Now I know what it's like inside a picture house. Arthur and I have become regulars at the Odeon's Saturday Morning Club for boys and girls. They put on a few short films, cartoons and a serial which is shown last. Part way through we have a break and have a sing along. As we don't know most of the songs they are projected on to the screen just like the films and a ball bounces along on the top of the words in time with the tune. I suppose it's quite clever really but I don't think any of us particularly enjoy it all that much; just a bit too soppy. Up to now in the serials, we have seen the Lone Ranger who wears a big white hat and a black mask (why I don't know!) with Tonto, a Red Indian, as his sidekick. They both seem to be going around the range on horses, doing good - sort of Robin Hood cowboys.

The other serial is completely different - it's about space ships. The 'goodie' in this one is Buster Crabbe, blonde curly hair and wears a long sleeved vest, tights and has a ray gun: the evil part - Emperor Ming. He wears tight things and a big cloak with a high collar right up the back of his head. All in all whatever the serials are they're always crummy.

The short films are the best. Laurel and Hardy, Old Mother Riley and the Three Stooges are great. Mary tells me that Old Mother Riley is a man. They always play 'God Save the King' when the lights go on at the end, just like after the grown ups films but all our films so far have been in black and white.

Sometimes when we get bored with the film we can get just a bit noisy and then they put the lights on and the manager walks on in front of the screen. He threatens us with closing the cinema if we don't quieten down. This usually does the trick and we've never gone home early as yet.

Saturday mornings on our way to the Odeon we have a look down Watergate Row to see if there's a queue outside Mr. Blake's bakers and cake shop. So with pennies to spare and no queuing to make us late for the pictures we go in for two of his white batches. He bakes lovely bread. I've always loved nice fresh crusty bread but sometimes a loaf from Salsbury's grocers shop in Saltney finds its way into our pantry, not by me. 'Country Maid' from the steam bakery and I don't like it. Anyway today we have some lovely bread to look forward to when we get to the Odeon. Through the crush to get in and seated comfortably amidst all the chaos and noise of the masses, we carefully make a hole in the side of our batch and proceed to pick and eat. This quietly goes on through the morning and by the time they play 'God Save the King' all the soft pickings have gone.

It seems to take longer to get out of the Odeon than it took to get in but once out in the daylight both having our empty batch case, Arthur and I are off for a few chips. He has a few pennies left and as I paid for his batch he pays for the chips from Hignett's in Frodsham Street. We stuff the chips into our empty batch cases and eat on the side of the canal where it's quiet, so no one sees us, as we mustn't be seen eating in the street.

This didn't happen every Saturday after Pictures Club as it really depended on some pocket money saved from the last week or whether I managed to get a bit extra from Mary or met someone like Mrs. Abley (or even Mrs. Abley) and whether Blake's had a batch or most importantly, Hignett's had fat to fry. Most days now they are closed.

Our treat was always a bit too much to expect and even when it happened I would be in trouble for not eating my dinner, and somehow Mum could always smell chips.

Now and again I can't help thinking what we all do to make do. Arthur and I have had a go at all sorts of things to eat or chew instead of sweets, the latest being chewing liquorice root from Mr. Kennerley's the Chemist, and sucking Chivers jelly cubes though almost impossible to get now.

Mum and Mary try all sorts of things making clothes but this week the funniest thing yet - they are making lipstick out of beetroot and they're finding the result more difficult to control than the proper lipstick. It's creeping beyond their lips so they look like a couple of clowns and unable to get it off before Dad comes home. But then he can't talk because I was in the garden with him last weekend when he and Mr. Dye were having a chat over the garden fence about the scarcity of cigarettes which they both miss, even though sometimes they can buy loose tobacco to smoke in pipes which they both have, it's not enough for Mr. Dye. (Dad calls him 'Bob'). I never knew his name was Bob. Mr. Dye tells Dad that his craving for a cigarette is relieved by sucking a button. Dad's tried it so now they both pass the time of day amongst other things, sucking buttons! I ask you, what on earth are we all coming to?

The longer this war goes on and the more Dad talks about it, the more confused I get. When the soldiers were with us we were at war with the Germans and the French were on our side. Then we lost the French as we left Dunkirk. Then the Italians joined in with the Germans and we sorted them out at Tobruk. Then the Germans took over from the Italians and sorted us out at Tobruk. Now somewhere along the line we have the Russians, the Japanese and now the

Americans who thankfully are on our side. I just don't know where I am. I really try to listen when Dad talks about the war, but I can't keep up with him or the war. It doesn't seem to bother Mum or Mary as much, but then they have so many more important things to think about and to do than I have.

Dad's interest in the news over the last few months has been all about the Japanese. "The Japs (as he calls them) have taken Singapore - so that's the whole of Burma in Japanese hands." I can't shift my thinking away from the Germans just across the English Channel and I'm told that on a clear day you can see France from Dover. For all the confusion of news that Dad creates for me he does come up with some funny bits now and again.

The other night, as usual, we were gathered around the fire, the wireless news long gone, I'm just fiddling with the poker scraping ash off the bars of the grate, thinking maybe I should offer to make some toast, as there looks a good red glow for toasting. That's if we have any bread. It's not that it's rationed, it's just sometimes the bread man calls when Mum's out. Dad's reading, so I don't ask about the bread. Lowering his newspaper he speaks to Mum. "By the way Annie I think that the Dandelion and Burdock is off." I stop thinking about the toast at the mention of pop. "You mean flat" says Mum. "Well yes it is flat as well as being off. How long have we had it?" Mum, with a puzzled expression, looks at me and Mary then looks back at Dad. "I ask you Harold, with Peter in the house, how could a bottle of pop last long enough on a shelf to go off?"

I can tell by this time that Dad isn't far from getting annoyed. Dad is up from his chair, newspaper on the floor and heads for the pantry. We all knew that there wasn't a drop of pop in the house and hasn't been since Christmas. Mum was right - it never has a chance to get flat and it's not only me that drinks the pop. In any case, there's a penny when you take an empty back to Mrs. Johnson's shop. Even so, Dad's soon back with a half full bottle. This he holds up for us all to see. He really loves being right. "Now do you believe me," he says.

It seems an age and how quiet it was. I suppose saying something was down to me. "Dad, that's the bottle I take down to Mr. Clarke's shop in Saltney when we want a pint of vinegar." For the first time Dad was lost for words. Then it was Mum's turn to break the silence. "Do you know when I was in the pantry this morning I thought Mr. Clarke must have only given Peter half a pint." I said, "No, I watched him as he measured a pint out in a jug before putting it in that bottle." Dad's gone quiet and looks very bothered as he admits to having drunk a tumbler full of what he thought to be Dandelion and Burdock! We just couldn't believe it - that he managed to drink that much without knowing it was vinegar, even though it said something else on the label. I got the blame for it for not soaking the label off before Mr. Clarke put the vinegar in. I soaked the label off after school the following day when some of the blame was shifted over to Mr. Clarke. We talked about it again and had a laugh before Dad came in from work.

It's strange at home hearing the difference in what's going on in Dad's world, his work when compared with Mary's. Dad's is really all to do with the war - any funny bits are usually what we see as funny, not Dad. Now Mary very seldom brings home talk of the war. It's about the effect the war has on people like when she told Mum about beetroot when she hadn't got any lipstick. Now, as well as a good idea, that was funny. It may be that Mary works in Town meeting with different people, most times ladies, whereas Dad will meet with the same men every day though there are some ladies working there. And they are a long way from any town, way out at Broughton. Well,

Mary's heard from a lady living out at Vicar's Cross that the American Army have taken over a very big house there and erected dozens of Nissen huts in the grounds. She can't wait to tell Dad and Mum, can't believe they've come all that way. I'm off to tell Arthur.

I don't know around there being on the opposite side of town though we do get the Vicar's Cross bus when we visit Uncle Syd and Auntie Audrey. Uncle Syd is Mum's brother. A tall man, six foot six and he has to duck down going through doorways. I think they just live on this side of Vicar's Cross. The Americans must be much further on, out into the countryside where big houses usually are. It could be a Hall like the Duke of Westminster's place.

A few more days go by and we hear stories of them giving away chocolates and sweets and all sorts of things that we can't get. Apparently they come into Chester by the truck load quite late at night, parked up on the Little Roodee. It's not long before Arthur and I find our way up there on our bikes and what seems a long way beyond Uncle Sid's house, way out into the country and then we come across a big gate set back off the road. Not a house or a Nissen hut anywhere to be seen. You just can't see beyond the gate as the area is surrounded by thick woodland.

It's a busy place, a constant coming and going of lorries and cars. All we can see on the other side of the gate is a big hut and a sentry on duty inspecting passes and lifting the gate up to let them in and out. He doesn't look like our soldiers at all except that his uniform is much the same colour. He doesn't have a rifle and bayonet; he has a revolver in a white holster: much like a cowboy. His helmet's white as is his belt and gaiters. He's an MP. It's on his sleeve. We stand there holding our bikes, say "Hello" and he walks towards us slowly, raises his hand and says "Hi". I think it must be American for 'hello'. I notice a nice little car by the hut and he tells us it's his run about to go back and forwards to the big house and into town. A nice little boxy, open topped car , but nothing like a sports car. He never stops chewing, not even when he's talking and goes on to say it's a 'Jeep.' I think it's a nice name and sounds right for the car.

We often go up there on our bikes and it's always busy on the gate so they don't have much time to talk. I suppose they shouldn't talk to us anyway - some do, some don't. We keep on going in the hope that we might be offered some chocolate or chewing gum and we are getting brave enough to talk.

One of the MP's in particular is a nice friendly man. He tells us his name is 'Mazadrie' and he always offers us chewing gum and sometimes candy which we found out were just sweets. I think he enjoys talking with us as he misses his family back home in the States. He shows us photographs of his wife and two boys much the same age as Arthur and I. The other MP's are alright but not the same as Mazadrie, so if he's not on the gate duty we just turn our bikes round and go back home. It's a wasted journey really, so the next time we manage to see Mazadrie we tell him all this and he then thinks he's someone special. Good friends.

Mum says that we shouldn't wear our welcome out as we seem to go there quite a lot, so we never spend too long a time there keeping him company, but before we are about to head for home he asks us to "Hang on guys while I go inside to check the duty roster." He's soon back with us and hands me a slip of paper and written on it are dates and times when we can go up to see him. And this we did with a few changes of rosters throughout the long summer of '42' we kept in touch with his news from home and what his boys had been up to. They knew all about Arthur and me and how their Dad kept us supplied with candy and chocolate when we hadn't any, and how much we enjoyed their Superman and Batman comics sent for us.

Then one Saturday afternoon we went up to see him and he wasn't on the gate. As there's usually two on we waited for him to come out of the hut, but he didn't. There were two MP's we hadn't seen before. I asked about Mazadrie, "Oh yeah. Mazadrie - I knew the guy - he's been posted." We wouldn't ever see him again and I know he will miss us. We didn't bother going there any more.

Arthur and I often go down the tip path and under the railway bridge along past the golf links on our way to 'the cop' (the riverbank). If there's a train signalled we sometimes scramble up the railway bank to watch it go by under full steam, which we were doing this day, when the window in the signal box was slid open and there stood the signal man. We both knew we were in trouble as we were near the railway line and were trespassing. "Do you want to earn a penny, lads?" We both shout "Yes" at the same time. "Come up then" as he slides back the window. We scramble back down the bank and open the gate to what seems a long walk up the path to the signal box, all the time thinking that it's a trick to get us into trouble for trespassing, and that in all probability he has already telephoned for the police.

When we get close to the signal box it seems much larger than when viewed from the road and it only had one door which took some finding, which I nervously knocked on. Then followed a rumbling from above as another window slides open and as we look up we are relieved to see the round smiling face of the signal man. "Come on up lads, the door's not locked. The inside is very dark without windows and just full of very complicated mechanical things. I suppose the working parts for all the points and signals, and of course, it's where he keeps his bicycle.

He met us at the top of the stairs, held a welcoming hand out for me to shake. I felt quite grown up as this hadn't happened before. He said his name was Mr. Brown. I said mine was Peter and this was my best friend Arthur. All shook hands and he takes us down to where he has a bench with a length of carpet on it and an old more comfortable armchair with a cushion. We sat down – Mr. Brown in his armchair - and I can't help thinking that this place is just like a big greenhouse with continuous windows which overlook the railway - and because it's so high we can see for miles. There must have been six lines across from the box, two G.W.R., Great Western Railway, and four L.M.S., London, Midland and Scottish. What with signals and points he had a lot to look after. He was on his own and couldn't find time to get any coal up to keep his stove going. He was hoping Arthur and I might help him out.

We jumped at the chance so he showed us what to do. There was a hoist over the window he had poked his head through and he would lower a bucket down to us that we would fill with coal from the coal bunker; then he would haul it up into the box and into his coal bunker by the stove.

He had a very responsible job and he just couldn't leave the signal box to replenish his coal store. He really needed an assistant but we just loved doing it for him to help. We must have filled twenty or more buckets of coal that day for Mr. Brown and we spent some time talking to keep him company. He made a mug of tea and showed us how to work the points and signals. We weren't strong enough to work some of the levers so he had to do the last bit. He thanked us for getting his coal up into the box and Arthur and I refused being paid and asked if we could help him anytime that we could. He said that there was another signal man and that when he was on again he would be grateful if we would help him out, as it was very difficult on his own. So we had a day to go back, something to look forward to.

We rarely hear the air raid siren any more and when we do the all clear sounds within minutes, yet another false alarm or testing. From what I hear on the news it's the RAF bombing Germany and how many of our aircraft have been shot down and the relief when we hear that none of our aircraft are missing. We hear news of the Free French blowing up railway lines and bridges. It's good to be fighting back and I think that if the Germans did invade we are ready for them.

I've got quite a collection of model aircraft now, all made from wood. I buy the kits from the model shop in George Street. The fuselage, wings and tail comes in pieces of rough cut balsa wood, soft enough to whittle down to a good shape with an old razor blade from Dad and a bit of fine sandpaper, making sure that it's just like the plan before sticking it together with balsa cement , a special clear glue, it's really good. I sometimes get into trouble as Mum says I get it everywhere and that it's a devil of a job getting it out of clothes, nigh impossible, but I think getting it everywhere is a bit of an exaggeration.

I enjoy the finishing off best; the painting, the different camouflage of the German and English planes. The insignia all comes on a sheet of water transfers and fitting the undercarriage can be a bit tricky. Sometimes the kit comes with a stand as though the plane is flying, then you don't have the problem of the undercarriage. I can't help thinking of the tiny bottles of 'dope' that I buy to paint my model aircraft with, and compare it with the hundreds of gallons they must use at Vickers Armstrong's.

It's not only RAF planes that I make there's German and now American planes but never Italian or Japanese, and it's because of a directive from the Government to make kits available for boys to make of planes likely to be seen in our skies to enable us to identify enemy aircraft. I don't think for one minute that the RAF and Army are really relying on us lads to warn them of enemy aircraft and surely the siren will have gone off long before they arrive anyway. Whatever reason I look forward to going in that little shop to spend my pocket money on a Saturday morning. The hours happily spent in making the kit into something special and of seeing it finished. Though sometimes it didn't quite go to plan when I was a bit heavy handed with the sandpaper and the balsa cement.

We were sat at home one Sunday just after dinner time. Mary had gone out. It was just Mum, Dad and me when a car pulls up by our gate. We are all at the window wondering who on earth it could be. The last time this happened it was that business with Iraq and the police but this car was too small, a little Morris Eight. It was parked there for a few minutes before the man gets out and while he was busy stretching a rather fat lady gets out from the other side. They just stand there staring up at our house, exchanging a few words. He's through the gate, and the pair of them are on the way up our path the lady being a bit slow off the mark. Mum and Dad look at each other and Dad looks, what I can only think of as uncomfortable.

They are soon knocking on the front door and Dad goes to answer. It sounds as though Dad has asked them in and they are talking in the hall, but not loud enough for us to make anything of it. "Who do you think it is Mum?" "I have no idea son, perhaps someone your Dad works with. He seems to be taking a long time." Dad eventually finds his way back followed by the two strangers and close up the man looks just as fat as she is. Dad still looks uncomfortable which isn't at all like Dad. "Annie, this is Eddie and Nellie Peacock."

I hang their coats up in the hall while they make themselves comfortable. Mrs. Peacock on one of our dining chairs, as she finds something lower difficult to get up from, and of all things, Mr. Peacock is sitting in Dad's armchair, and, I notice on the floor at the side of the chair, stands a bottle of wine. Sitting in Dad's chair is bad enough but bringing a bottle of wine I just can't believe this happening in No. 5 but it has, and Dad won't approve. I can see it will be mentioned before the afternoon's out. Mr. Peacock breaks the silence. "How long is it now Harold, it must be 25 years or more when we were in the last one together and have I had one hell of a job finding you." The conversation went on.

I picked up now and again of times when they were on the guns together. It sounded as though they had suffered enough in the first one and he was making sure he wouldn't do the same again in this one. "I'm after number one now Harold and I'm working in the right place in a job of national importance - Manchester Docks.

I think he was a car salesman before the war. I really didn't want to listen to all this or to be with them, so when I thought the time was right I asked if I could call round at my pal's house and thankfully Dad said "Off you go then." With Arthur just living at the end of our road I could keep looking out to see if the car had left and only then I left for home. I could tell that Mum and Dad hadn't had a good afternoon. Mary was back home and so was I, and I felt guilty at having left them.

I don't know whether Eddie Peacock was a relative or a long lost friend; was he someone like my Auntie Abley? Dad said that Eddie had been very badly wounded in the last war and that his lower legs were filled with splinter shrapnel - too much and too small to be able to remove, so he had to keep his wounds damped with a liquid he carried around in a bottle. The dressing had to be changed several

124

times throughout the day and was kept moist by being wrapped over with an oilskin bandage. Dad said that Eddie had changed the dressings twice before they left and it had filled the house with the smell of disinfectant.

I felt very sad about it and regretted going out to see Arthur but thankful that I hadn't seen Mr. Peacock's legs, as Dad said that he had attended to them in our living room. Mum says, "Yes, he did," while nodding her head, "he was just full of what they went through in the war and that he was getting all he could out of the docks on the quiet while it lasted. It really wasn't for both your ears, looking at Mary and me. "He's a very bitter man."

Dad has nothing more to say; maybe he needs to be quiet as it's been quite an afternoon for him. I don't know whether he was pleased to see Mr. Peacock or not. Then he says, "Eddie doesn't seem to have changed, he was always a talker and he has nursed those legs of his for a long time, and who knows what that does to a man."

I can't help thinking of that bottle of wine that Mr. Peacock kept within reach and Dad a Methodist. I had dreaded what would happen had Dad spotted it when he was just using a handy bottle to refill with a liquid to dress his legs. Much the same situation as Dad had had with the vinegar in the pop bottle. What if Mr. Peacock had forgotten his bottle, but then Dad would never have a glass from a wine bottle. Dad's motto was "I never taste, touch nor handle." The times I've heard him say that.

It's funny now when you're doing something, it can trigger off you thinking of so many things, one after the other, and this happened again when I was helping Mum pegging out the washing. Mum was holding one end of a sheet, I was on the other end when I thought, there's something missing on the washing line. Fir cones! There was always a couple on a piece of string by the post and they were Mum's weather forecast - when they were open the washing was pegged out, when closed, the rain was on the way and the washing stayed on top of the mangle or draped other the clothes maiden in front of the living room fire. Then all the windows steamed up. Mum liked the washing to have a good blow on the line.

So the fir cones have gone missing, but now we have a wireless Dad listens to the weather forecast after the news, maybe he thinks we don't need them any more. Come to think of it Mum has the wireless on listening to songs as she goes about the home when she used to like playing records on the gramophone that Granddad gave her when he bought a wireless. And that's how we came about getting all those old records - they came with the gramophone. I thought the wireless was terrific when we first got it, but it keeps me in the house and anyway now I prefer going to the pictures.

"Mum, what happened to the fir cones?" "I have no idea; ask your Father when he comes in as he put them there in the first place." When Dad came in and after his tea while reading the paper, I asked what had happened to the fir cones. I sensed it was the wrong time to ask as he repeats, "Fir cones? Well it's not just fir cones, it's Granddad's old gramophone that's gone as well. Best ask your Mother. I've got more important things to think about," as he disappears behind his paper. I liked those fir cones waiting for them to open and close when the weather was on the change, and Dad has been known to complain about the forecasters.

The big surprise came when Dad read in the paper about the landing of allied troops at Dieppe: six thousand in all. British, Canadian and Free French casualties were high, they think nearly a thousand killed or missing with fifteen hundred taken prisoner. We can only hope the remainder got back home safely. According to Dad to even contemplate it was a disaster waiting to happen with such a small landing force, though he wonders if the intention was to test the German defences for bigger things to come. Somehow when there's bad news about, we can't but help thinking about the soldiers we had billeted with us.

Mum's had a letter from Auntie Lill and she says that they are all well and that they have four Italian prisoners of war working on the farm. They are no help at all for Alf, that's my Great Uncle Alf that I have never seen. I must try and get up to see them sometime. She says they are very lazy and he gets no work at all out of them. They keep making holes in their Wellingtons so they have nothing to wear. Alf says we have to feed and oil them twice a day as well as the two guards and do they shift some food.

From what I hear they had a couple of labourers on the farm that volunteered for the Army and now they're not at all happy with the four Italian replacements. Dad seems to understand the situation perfectly and has a lot of sympathy for Uncle Alf. "Annie, the last time that country had a decent army the soldier was a fighter with a capacity for work and that was when they built the wall around this town of ours."

Dad says the Germans are at the gates of Stalingrad and that's as far as they will get. The Russians will hold on in their winter no matter what happens and then we will see the start of the big German retreat. Whenever we talk at home it's always about how the war's going on, something we want to hear, maybe not. Dad tells us about the men at work and production targets and Mum of shopping every morning in the hope of something to make a meal. Friends and family crop up with Mary and me having a say but when we talk of family it's always

Mum's family, never Dad's.

I know his Mum and Dad died before I was born and he just mentions now and again that he had brothers who emigrated to Australia, but where in Australia he doesn't know. Then the other day, straight out of the blue, Dad mentions Effie, a sister of his from Runcorn. Now I have an Auntie Effie and an Uncle Jim that I never knew about and Dad is going to see them on Sunday and yet another sister of his, Martha, who I've never heard of before. I'm going with him, I think on a Crosville bus. Mum always seems to prefer staying at home when I go out with Dad and come to think of it the same happens when I go out with Mum.

Getting off the bus at Runcorn, having a look around and I don't think I like the place. We seem to be walking for a long time down so many streets - all the houses look exactly the same - a front door, a window and there are no front gardens. Dad seems to know the way.

We find the house with a well scrubbed door step, all donkey stoned in white and a shiny brass door knocker which Dad operates as quietly as he can. It's not long before we hear someone coming along the hall to open the door and there stands Auntie Effie in a flowered overall, a rather round old lady with white hair. She asks us in to their dark and gloomy hall and I can't help but notice how she rocks from side to side as she walks, whilst telling us that we are going into the parlour as Jim has lit the fire. The room we call the sitting room. It's just as gloomy as the hall, smells musty with an aspidistra in the window and a caged canary which seems very excited on seeing us. It's more than I can say of Auntie Effie. She doesn't seem at all pleased to see us nor has she much to say other than, "I suppose you would like a cup of tea Harold."

Dad and I sit down, whispering to each other while Auntie Effie is away in the kitchen. The door opens and in comes an old man carrying a tray of tea while puffing away on a pipe trying to cough at the same time, which again rather excites the canary flying around his cage scattering seed all over the parlour carpet. Holding the tray he shouts for Effie who is soon in busying with dustpan and brush and from what she mutters about it's obvious that it's not her canary. Dad tries to help by clearing some space on the table by edging over the aspidistra. I wasn't told but this man must be my Uncle Jim as Auntie Effie mentions his name from time to time in conversation as if I wasn't there. I look at Dad and though he has white hair and not much of it, he doesn't appear to be old. He looks bright and fresh faced with a smile never far away, whereas they don't look at all happy or well. Their faces have a yellowing, nowhere near as bright as the canary! Putty comes to mind and Jim has a cough like I've never heard before.

"It's your sister Martha that concerns us Harold as she's taken to locking herself in the house and never opens the curtains." It's not long before coats are on again and we are back walking much the same streets as before on the way to see Auntie Martha.

Auntie Effie was right; we found the house with curtains drawn. The same sort of house in a street much the same as Auntie Effie's. She didn't knock on the door but kept bending down to call through the letter box, hoping Auntie Martha would hear and let us in. It took ages - then we heard locks and bolts going once Auntie Martha knew who was at her front door. I think the only mention was "Harold is here to see you."

She wasn't like Auntie Effie. She was a thin old lady with white hair, no taller than me and she had trouble walking about the house which we did from room to room downstairs, then upstairs - why we did I don't know. Then we went back into her parlour and sat down; all much the same with an aspidistra but no canary. Auntie Effie made a pot of tea. I'm getting hungry and would like something to eat but don't like asking as I don't really know any of them well enough.

What a strange house this is. Most of the rooms we went in were just store rooms for food whereas we have very little food to spare at home and here. I'm feeling hungry and my Auntie Martha has enough food to fill a shop. Stack after stack of brown cardboard boxes; tins of everything you could think of - soups, meats, fruit and my favourite beans in tomato sauce and that many packets of sugar I couldn't count. She couldn't have got all this on a ration for one.

All of the rooms had the black out curtains drawn and as we left each room Auntie Martha would replace a carefully folded blanket against the bottom of the door. Dad asked her why she did this and left the curtains drawn all day. "Well Harold, it's these Germans and their planes make such a dust it gets everywhere." We didn't stay all that long at Auntie Martha's and left Auntie Effie once we had had another cup of tea.

On the bus home I had loads to ask Dad. He tells me that as soon as there was any hint of a war with the Germans Martha decided to buy in as much keep-able food as she could for when it became scarce or even unobtainable, and now of course she is only hoarding and isn't eating enough. She thinks every plane she hears makes a dust it's not just the Germans. The curtains are always kept drawn to prevent anyone seeing her very desirable hoard of food and of course, keeping doors locked and bolted and not letting anyone in other than Effie or Jim.

Oh, and though difficult I asked about the putty colour of Auntie Effie and Uncle Jim. Come to think of it Martha was much the same colour. "Your Uncle Jim works at Castner Kelners Chemical Works and has done since leaving school and thinks it's something to do with the making of chemicals polluting the atmosphere. The air they breathe constantly also accounts for his bad chest and I don't think smoking that pipe all day long helps. The only time it comes out of his mouth is when he is unable to drink tea at the same time." Dad's obviously very concerned about his sister Martha and without asking, he more or less answers the age thing by telling me that he is the lad of the family - by how much I don't know, and don't ask.

Days and weeks can go by without much happening, then just when we were getting used to it Dad comes in from work and before he could get his hat and coat off was shouting from the hall, "good news from the desert Annie. Monty has sorted out Rommel's Axis army at El Alamein and they're on the run, the lot of them." Our 8th Army commander, General Montgomery, doesn't seem to get his full title any more from Dad. I don't think for one minute that he intends to be disrespectful when he speaks of him as 'Monty' almost as though he was a close friend, one of the lads. So that's the way it is.

Germans, Nazis I know about but 'Axis' is a new one on me. Dad tells me that it's the combined military forces of Nazi Germany and Italy. I know of the Italians - they're the ones we defeated some time ago who can't fight and are now skiving around on Uncle Alf's farm. I'm surprised there's any left to go on a retreat.

The victory is going to be celebrated with the ringing of all the church bells. Since the start of the war the ringing of church bells was to warn us of a German invasion. How things have changed. It was fantastic; the sound of church bells again when just a few years ago we took for granted and in all probability didn't notice they were ringing.

All this happening just before bonfire night and we can't have a bonfire. Arthur and I are dying to make a Guy Fawkes out of Hitler as we know exactly what he looks like. Why couldn't we have had it early straight after school? It would have been well burnt out by air raid time if there was going to be one as they never come early. It was usually after nine. I can't see it happening anyway and there's been no mention of indoor fireworks.

Good news is coming thick and fast as we the allied troops have made a successful landing in Morocco and Algeria. It's good when you have a lot of friends around especially in a war but they take some getting together and the Germans, along with the Italians and Russians, caught us unprepared. Dad calls it 'with our trousers down.' I know now we have a lot of friends with us, our allies, as I see them when I'm in town, wounded soldiers sailors and airmen getting about the best way they can, some on crutches or wheelchairs, some displaying their country of origin, regimental insignia and medal ribbons on their hospital blues. So many nationalities along with our lads, and hopefully their war is over.

Lots of friends around, church bells ringing and Mary seems bright and cheery, even Dad has noticed, and I know why and it's a secret shared with me. She is going to a dance at Clemence's with a friend from the post office telephones, and all I know - his name is Eric. If Mary will tell Mum and Dad, I don't know it might be that she says, 'I'm off to the pictures', which she might have said before being caught out by the late night when she went to Clemence's.

I think Mary sees quite a lot of Eric with them both working for the Post Office Telephones; she does talk a lot about him. Now whether it's Mum and Dad that want to meet him or Mary thinks it's about time they met him, I don't know. I take it that he is coming round this weekend mainly to meet Mum and Dad and if I happen to be in I will meet him as well. So really it's not important if I miss seeing him by being at Arthur's or doing something else.

I still don't know if Dad disapproves of dances and Clemence's or maybe he's got used to it by now, so if I do meet Eric I will just listen to what's going on and only speak when I'm spoken to.

By the time I got back home I knew Eric was already there as his bike was by our back door. I went in as quiet as I could and they all seemed to be talking away as though Eric had been there awhile and getting on quite well. It's always a bit difficult meeting people for the first time and I think more so when you're considered to be the juvenile amongst the adults. I don't like the word 'juvenile.' A real put you down, young lad sounds much friendlier.

I don't know if they had had a cup of tea already; if so Mum got up to make another pot. Now whether it was because I'd just come in and interrupted their conversation I don't know. Anyway that cup of tea and a biscuit was excuse enough for me to keep quiet for a while, whilst they talked about nothing much really until Eric thought it best to be on his way home. I think he was right it must have been a nervous time for him, meeting Mary's parents for the first time. I thought what a relief for him to be on his bike again and heading back home. Mary seems pleased with everything and I'm sure we will be seeing more of Eric as the weeks go by. I wonder if Clemence's was ever mentioned. I never asked.

This business of boy friend meeting parents of the girl friend - I can't get my thinking around. I put it to Mary that I have had a girl friend along the road for months - Sylvia Houghton - and she has met Mum and Dad so many times I've lost count. And never by an arrangement or is it an appointment. This seems to amuse Mary and says, "Yes, but Sylvia is not a serious girl friend whereas Eric is a serious boy friend as I am a serious girl friend. Mum and Dad know this and seem to be quite relaxed about it. The only problem might be is that

Eric is a Catholic." I thought a girl friend was simply just a friend; now Mary's put me right and there are two sorts, and she has a serious one. I don't know if Dad would approve or not of Eric being a Catholic. Now if he likes to have a drink as well as being a Catholic, then it would be a serious problem. Things seem to get so complicated when you're an adult.

It's dark going home from school with long nights in front of a warm fire making toast. Dad can't listen to the wireless or concentrate on his paper as Mary goes up and down to her bedroom singing all the time, which then sets Mum off; 'White Christmas' sung by a man called Bing Crosby who Dad, sounding annoyed, says "can only be a Yank." But according to Mary, who knows about these things, the man who wrote the lyrics, the words, was Irving Berlin. With a name like that you would have thought he'd have kept quiet.

When I was last in Town shopping with Mum on our way to the Market, the Salvation Army Band were playing Christmas carols on the flags fronting the Dublin Packet. I was always told by Mum that it was the Salvation Army that brought me just before Christmas. I suppose a few days later and I could have been christened Noel, but then I wasn't christened as I think different religions made for problems. Weslyan Methodist, Church of England, Welsh Presbyterian; maybe I was just ill and missed it.

As a family we don't make much of a do of birthdays but then I think that's the way birthdays are as my pal Arthur says they are just the same, though this year he did have a party as it was his 10th birthday which his Mum and Dad must have thought was special. Why, he didn't know - neither did I but I was invited and it was a good party.

Christmas 1942
The Germans surrender
at Stalingrad and in Retreat

So the birthdays come and go much the same as any other day and the same with Christmas but that's because of the war. The sort of food we expect at Christmas has gone long ago. No chicken this year but we are having a piece of pork and some sausages, what sort I don't know. A plum pudding with custard and a Christmas cake without almond paste or icing; well without anything on top really. What Mum makes them of I don't know but somehow or other they taste just as good without the proper ingredients. Maybe it's just that we have forgotten what the proper ingredients taste like.

The months after Christmas always seem longer and colder but Dad's interest doesn't seem to be in our winter - it's in the Russian winter and how they are holding out against the Germans. It seems ages ago that Stalingrad was first mentioned and now its come up again on the wireless news, and it's good news. The Germans have surrendered at Stalingrad ending a five month offensive and are in retreat. The cost in lives was 750,000 Russians and 40,000 Germans. There was no mention of prisoners and we assumed the Russian losses included many thousands of civilians. Dad and his Russian winter - he said it would happen just like it had with Napoleon and he keeps reminding us of it over and over again.

Well into the New Year the cold winter months pass by. Peace time seems such a long time ago that my memories are becoming only of war. Has it really been three years? I suppose in that time we have got better at being at war. Some of the things we did years ago at school supposedly to help the war effort was, I think, just to boost our morale. We went at it with enthusiasm in the first spring and summer of the war.

Miss Harrison, not one of my favourite teachers, always had to have something in her hand either a cane or a wooden blackboard pointer.

She told us our task was to bring into school any old towels not wanted at home and even better if we could ask up and down the road. We did rather well, ending up with a lot of old towels.

Back at school we cut the towels into twelve inch squares making sure to dodge any badly worn bits. We carefully hemmed the squares by hand and we had made face flannels. Then we had a spell of stitching edges of grey blankets and making up packs of field dressings. The WVS (Women's Voluntary Service) are always the ones that delivered and collected and we were thanked for our efforts on behalf of the soldiers. I could imagine a soldier being grateful for a thick grey blanket and having a need for the field dressings but some of the pretty towels we made into flannels, he wouldn't have dared to take out of his kit bag in fear of getting his leg pulled.

It wasn't all collecting and making things. We had an allotment at school where we each had a plot just big enough to keep us occupied for an hour or two each week. It's a nice break between lessons. Miss Tuplin, the Headmistress, takes us for gardening. A round, cheerful, approachable lady, but for all that her gardening skill she doesn't compare with my Uncle Ewart. At that time he was still at home, a civilian; now he's away somewhere in the army.

We grew vegetables mostly cabbages, potatoes and in the summer things for salads. After a while on lettuce, spring onions and radish there's nowhere to go and I got a bit bored so I had a word with Uncle Ewart, a keen market gardener, who has a collection of silver cups won at National Shows for growing vegetables. I hadn't realised before just how many cups he has won; they're on the mantelpiece, side board and in other rooms. Auntie Olive says she's sick of cleaning them. He just smiled as we both sat down surrounded by his cups.

"First of all, (he asks), what sort of soil have you in this allotment of yours?" Now I knew it was better soil than we have in the garden at home which Dad says is clay. Now this soil at school is fine and black. The school is a big old house, I think built in Victorian times and had a lovely big lawn at the back before it was taken up as turf and stacked against the wall at the start of the war to make way for our allotment. "If that turf is still there and available, I think you would enjoy growing marrows. You should take some of the grass turf, which I call sods, and lay them grass side down to form a four-wall system about three foot square and a foot high. Then fill it with chopped up grass sods again grass side down, leaving enough room for about three inches of good topsoil, which you seem to have plenty of."

My plot was big enough for marrows and a few other things, sounds good already. I remember being very excited about it all and couldn't thank him enough before I left for home with a packet of marrow seeds with instructions on the back, no end of growing tips from Uncle Ewart and he's put some of his special mix of fertiliser in a bag for me to mix in with the top soil.

Everything went well back at school to do with the marrows that is. The structure alone had caused a lot of interest, a sort of monument within a sea of flat boring plots. Keeping to Uncle Ewart's tips, it's still a bit too early to sow the seeds and I was dying to get on with it. Then came the day the soil was starting to warm up and the seeds were sown; the packet with the picture on proudly displayed on a stick. The well kept secret was out now.

Waiting seemed endless then I have all four plants popping out of the ground. I kept them well watered and the idea was to nip out any unwanted flowers as they appeared so as to concentrate on growing one marrow on each plant and were they performing. In no time at all there they lay in this elevated spot, dwarfing anything else on the school allotment. But for some reason or other it doesn't seem to have gone down too well with any of the others or the teachers and I didn't know why. Maybe it was because I had carved my name on one of the marrows when it was small just to see if it would go any bigger as the marrow grew, and it did, day by day. A way of boasting I suppose, which you can't do quite the same with leafy things. When I thought they couldn't get any bigger, I took my marrows home.

They remained on the shelf in the pantry for a few days, if anything looking even bigger than they had whilst growing in the allotment. Then after Mary and me going on about it so much Mum finally cooked one for dinner and there was more than enough for all four of us, too much really. Come to think of it the soldiers might have been with us then so it would have been six. I decided, there and then first taste, that I did not like marrows. I managed to eat it all as not eating it was not an option as I'd grown it and talked about it for so long, they must have been fed up with marrows before I even got them home.

Looking around the table at their faces I don't think they much liked them either. Knives and forks were put down on their plates to rest and Dad said, "Well done, Peter. I think that's the first marrow we have ever had." My raised bed was demolished and my plot became well raked and flat again, just like the others, with rows of the usual salad things. I never knew what happened to the other marrows and never asked.

Well things have moved on at school. We rarely do things to help with the war effort, if at all. We collect things from time to time but nothing like we used to. I suppose it's with everything getting more organised and used to operating as the war goes on.

We do have, you could say as an alternative, periods out away from school. Dad says it's with not having the threat of air raids, but we could always find an air raid shelter in town and that's where we go on a bus just outside and across the road. This takes you to Bridge Street to Miss Baker's Music Academy in Bridge Street Row just a short walk up from the bus stop on the non-shopping side of the Row. Music Academy sounds a posh sort of place, but it isn't. It's just a big dark empty room with a piano in the corner. Miss Baker teaches music and singing. She is a rather large, not old say middle aged, lady. Not a person or place you look forward to going to and we all think much the same. Come to think of it we don't have any men teaching supposedly because they are all in the forces.

We have about an hour in this place, just gathered around the piano whilst she sits there swaying from side to side to the continuous thumping of the keys with her head turning from time to time to shout - "Louder, louder." We don't have any sheets with words on so she reads them from her sheet music and expects us to remember them, so half the time we don't know what to sing. When we do she can't hear us because of her misguided determination to wreck the piano. People out and about in the street below must be able to hear all this. If only someone would knock on the door to complain about the noise, and it wouldn't be for our singing.

This period out of school can't have anything to do with the war effort. Is it boosting our morale singing around a piano when we have a piano back at school? But there we only sing hymns and here with Miss Baker we sing all rousing Scottish songs about Highland laddies off to fight in wars gone long ago, bring back my bonnie to me and all that and it's because Miss Baker is a Scot.

Over the weeks we see changes made to the all Scottish hour which came about after being constantly questioned by a few of us, led by

Betty Ashton, but the choice still seems intended to boost our morale. We had a whole period of poetry reading - 'Lochinvar' and 'The Charge of the Light Brigade' which we all learned and recited in turn as best we could. I know I didn't do very well - poetry isn't my favourite thing and we still had a Scot around in young Lochinvar.

Then a more colourful sheet of music and song comes to light on the piano. 'Johnnie's got a zero' an American song one of their morale boosters brought in by Betty Ashton. 'Zero' is the name of a Japanese fighter plane. I know because I've made one in balsa wood from a kit, the insignia - a big red spot on fuselage and wings. If one came over I would recognise it straight away, but then it's highly unlikely. Whatever the song is about, this guy, an American fighter pilot has shot down quite a few Zero's and scored yet another.

Now as Miss Baker always sings along with us and also drowns what combined sound we make as a choir, this continues with 'Johnnie's got a Zero' American words just don't sound right in a broad Scottish accent. One by one we all stopped singing as laughter overtook us. Miss Baker, oblivious to it all, continued this rousing American song, as it became a solo performance. Thankfully, she saw the funny side of it and we didn't get into trouble. Miss Baker thanked Betty for bringing in Johnnie Zero. It was taken back with us on the bus and most definitely saw the end of the Scottish hour.

The last visit to the academy cannot pass by without a mention, as it was the one that put Miss Baker in a fluster, a confusion that we hadn't seen before. It was the same as any other time all grouped around the piano, Miss Baker still larger than life and sounding very Scottish, singing along with the songs of her choice, still no sheets of words before we had to sing them. I suppose it was very clever of her. The song was 'The Lass of Richmond Hill'. The piano was getting a thumping and we were quite happily singing away, and I suppose I pricked my ears up just a bit too late and wasn't sure what she said. I got the ' young Mollie who lives at the foot of the hill whose name, or was it fame that every virgin with envy does fill.'

We have a break between songs for discussion as Miss Baker doesn't like being interrupted whilst playing the piano. I mustn't loose the plot by break time. I know that Mollie is the lass with the delicate air, is it just her name or is it fame that the Virgins of Richmond Hill envy?, and it sounds as though there are a lot of them. The only mention of one before has been in Religious Studies and in our nativity play at Christmas. But why should they be envious of Mollie for not being a virgin?

I put this to Miss Baker for discussion and most unlike her there wasn't an instant response. Then all I got from her was, "Peter", followed by another wait while she looked very bothered and a little flushed. You could hear a pin drop, then it came, "You should concentrate on your singing and not let your mind wander while doing so. You are looking for complications that do not exist. Now can we carry on?"

There was very little space given to singing in my school report, just that I had a quiet voice, little sense of rhythm and that I found it difficult co-ordinating words with music. Mary was quite amused by it and that all Dad said was, "Miss Baker you say, now that's strange, a Scot a Baker. I thought Baker's over the border were called Baxter's." That was it - never spoken of again - but I often wondered about my singing of 'Carolina Moon' under the table in the air raids. I must have inflicted more misery on my family than anything the German Luftwaffe could have dropped on us.

Dad surprises me - as an ex-soldier from the last war he seems more interested in the RAF than the Army. I'm sure he's enjoying the war and I suppose it's his involvement at Vickers Armstrong making bombers that provides the interest in the RAF and he's full of news of the bombing of the Mohne and Eder dams; destroyed with bouncing bombs by 617 Squadron of the RAF (now known as the Dambusters). It's in all the papers and I really enjoyed reading about it, how they made the bombs to bounce and how the pilots flew in to drop them on the water to bounce was unbelievable.

Apparently the dams generated power just the same as what we call the hydro plant just by the old Dee Bridge but much, much bigger, enough to produce power for running large factories producing armaments for the German war effort so it was a job well done and something that will be difficult or impossible to rebuild in time to be of any use.

Whilst Dad talks about the war Mum and Mary talk about other things, which made a change. On coming home, Mary could hardly wait to tell us the news about Leslie Howard - he's an actor, a film star. It must be something Mary's read in the 'Picturegoer' or picked up from the girls at work as she never buys a paper. I'm not all that interested but I can't help listening. He was in a film they both went to see at the pictures, 'Gone with the Wind.' I remember when they came home saying it was a very long film and that Dad and I wouldn't have liked it. Neither of us remembered being asked before they went, but I'm sure they were right.

They seem quite upset as the poor man has been killed in a plane shot down by the Germans over the Bay of Biscay, on the way back from Lisbon to Bristol. Mum's head goes slowly from side to side whilst saying, "He was no age at all." I ponder as to what she means by saying that, as they go on talking about what he was doing in

Lisbon. Being in a neutral country we wouldn't have troops there for him to entertain. Dad thinks a comedian would have been a better choice. Was he in a civil aircraft or was it in an RAF plane? which would account for it being shot down. I think after a while Dad got a bit tired of it and made some remark about having gone with the wind, which didn't go down well. I don't think Dad had quite the same interest in film stars as Mum and Mary.

Whenever Arthur and I go down by the railway lines at the top of Mount Pleasant or when we are on the way down to the river, we always stop for a while and wave up at the signal box to see if Mr. Brown's on. We don't see much of him in the summer when he doesn't have his stove going or maybe someone's with him in the box maybe his boss on a visit. I mentioned to Mary about us going to see Mr. Brown and Mary says, "Yes, I know Mr. and Mrs. Brown - they're Joe's Mum and Dad." Joe is one of her old school pals now in the RAF. I just never made the connection. I shall have to tell Mr. Brown next time we see him. So we made a few trips down watching the trains go by and then we were lucky the window slides across and we see the friendly wave of welcome and we are on our way up to his signal box.

It's like a coal yard at the back of the signal box, a sort of stockade made of old railway sleepers heaped up with tons of coal, when we have so little at home. He's never short of coal as it comes by the truck load shunted up the track direct from the coal yard.

The problem is getting it up into his coal bunker as that holds about three hundredweight. We only fill the buckets he hands down.

He's a friendly man and we weren't all that long topping up his bunker before sitting down and having a chat with him, with a mug of tea and sharing his biscuits. I mentioned that we all knew Joe, which came as a surprise and then he tells us that Joe's now a Flight Sergeant

Navigator on Lancaster's and he has dropped a bomb or two on the Germans when its dark.

Whenever we manage to see Mr. Brown he always asks us for our coats which he hangs up in his cupboard. It's not the usual sort of place to hang a coat. It's about three feet square and stands about six feet tall, so size-wise it's pretty big, but it's not a wardrobe, it hasn't got a mirror, it isn't made of wood; it's made of thick sheet steel with slits cut into the top of the door. So I ask Mr. Brown, "Why?" "Oh that's my air raid shelter. You see I can't leave the box unattended to go to the shelter in Mount Pleasant so I have a shelter for one in here. You can't move it - it's that heavy it came on a truck with a crane to lift it up into the box. Go in if you like and have a look inside.

I was in before the invitation was finished. There was a wooden shelf to sit on, an old cushion and a piece of carpet that Mrs. Brown no longer wanted. "All right? Isn't it nice and cosy?" says Mr. Brown, "now what do you say Arthur if we shut the door and pretend as though it's a real air raid? Now make yourself comfortable Peter and after the air raid we can put the kettle on and make another cup of tea."

I sat down on the cushion; it was pitch black inside apart from a bit of light that came in through the slits. Mr. Brown shouts, "Can you hear any German planes yet?" "No," I answer. "Oh! That's because the ARP haven't spotted them, so keep very quiet or else you won't hear the siren first and then you will hear the planes. O.K.? Then there was a wailing sound, not at all like a siren, followed by a very distant droning sound, just like a German plane, even so I knew it was Mr. Brown and I could hear Arthur trying not to laugh.

I was thinking of getting out and found I couldn't. Then there came the most loudest of bangs and crashes like bombs exploding and guns going off. I had my hands over my ears and I still can't stop the noise. After a while it stopped; the door opened; I couldn't see too well in the bright daylight neither could I hear anything. Arthur stood there with a big poker in his hand and Mr. Brown with a coal shovel in his. I knew what they had been up to, laughing their heads off, but I couldn't hear a thing. After a while when it had all quietened down and I could hear again, Mr. Brown says to me, "What about that cup of tea we were promised? It was hard work for Arthur and me while you were sat in the shelter." They were off laughing again and I joined in after a while, though lacking the same enthusiasm. There was only one man on a shift at a time in that signal box and it was a big box.

Demands on his time were continuous and there was no alternative other than to stay in the box in an air raid, but then he couldn't stay in his iron wardrobe in an air raid as bells and telephones seem to be constantly ringing, points and signals to change and all to be entered in a log book. I just cannot see that the whole of the railway network comes to a standstill in an air raid, or even in a false alarm, and believe me we have a few. The poor man would be in and out of that box like a yoyo.

Mr. Brown was always fun and jokingly he called his shelter his iron coffin. I suppose it could have been in an air raid, but somehow, thankfully, we don't see things that way. He loves his job and constantly talks about it as he attends to bells and signals.

"That's the Irish Mail, Shielder Class, the something or other number to Holyhead. I learned that all engines, locomotives had a number, some a name, but all of them on the front of the boiler had a shed number. Through the Saltney box passed the Great Western, the London Midland and Scottish, and if you went to the Northgate Station it was London and North Eastern, and Mr. Brown had found me a hobby - collecting train numbers - train spotting. I already collect stamps but this sounds exciting.

He said there were books to buy, catalogues with all the engine numbers in and you ticked them off when you saw them, where it was and what they were pulling. I decided I would save my pocket money for the GWR and LMS books but in the meantime, Mr. Brown suggests that while saving, I could start train spotting on scrap paper to transfer to the special book later on, which I did and Arthur too. We both enjoyed going down to the railway bridge at Saltney train spotting, and of course seeing Mr. Brown when he was in his signal box.

The news, an airborne force of British, American and Canadian troops have launched the allied invasion of Sicily: a new place for Dad on his wall plan of the war. How things are changing. Most news now seems good news, and of all places the RAF have bombed Rome, avoiding most of the ancient sites and buildings. This is when I saw Dad really annoyed and I'm with him all the way. We cannot understand why our RAF pilots have had instructions not to bomb ancient sites and buildings when the Germans have already bombed Coventry Cathedral, St. Paul's and we think Buckingham Palace and Windsor Castle. "Do you know, Annie, it wouldn't at all surprise me if the Italian Army were sheltered in the Vatican that night," which brought a smile to Mum's face.

Dad thinks the bombing of Rome will put the wind up the Italians and it's not long before we hear of workers striking in factories, unrest and of Partisans. Mussolini is made the scapegoat. I didn't know what that meant. Dad says, "Stripped of his powers, the government overthrown." There were riots, mob rule and anything to do with the Fascists was destroyed. The Mussolini regime collapsed in Rome without resistance.

The Germans soon took control of Rome and Northern Italy. Mussolini was rescued on Hitler's orders and taken somewhere out of the way to become a puppet ruler. It all sounds very good to me but I don't understand what's going on. I listen and hear not just Italians, but Fascists and Partisans. So Dad explains that the Fascists are also Italians but supporters of Mussolini, so the rest of the Italians were suppressed by the Fascists and now the Italian people look like being on the losing side some are coming out of the woodwork and calling themselves 'the Partisans'. "So really, Dad, it's just like the Nazis and the Germans?" "Yes, and if we're lucky, the same thing might happen to Adolf." Dad's back again on Christian names. The Italians get called 'Ities, sometimes 'Wops' you can really get confused.

Then Dad's off again; "What's really surprised me Annie is that the Italians have had the gumption to form the Partisans after all the Germans are still around and they can be a very nasty lot." Then I think, 'here we go again, back to Germans.'

Then Mum has her say. "Peter, you will just have to get used to whatever he likes to call the Italians or the Germans according to which way the wind's blowing." (I think she means, 'the war's going').

Arthur's big brother Ken often talks about the 'Loggerheads' and has been camping there with the school and talks of climbing Moel Fammau. There was a stream, cliffs to climb and some disused mines. This made our minds up - we were going to go. We knew it was a long way and our bikes were a bit small for that so Arthur had the idea of borrowing Ken's for the day. Now that was a super bike. A 'Gazelle' with cable brakes, Sturmey Archer gears, a dynamo and a big saddle bag with side pockets. This idea of Arthur's was never going to happen. But Arthur's sister, Phyllis, rescued our day with the loan of her bike and Mary agreed to let me have hers.

Ken had drawn a plan of the roads with some notes and said that it would take us a whole day, even if we set off very early, but we weren't to be put off. On the day, with sandwiches and a pop bottle of water each, we set off on our sisters' bikes through Saltney and the long road to Broughton. I couldn't quite manage the seat and pedals at the same time, so spent most of the time standing up and only sat on the seat coasting down hills. On most hilly bits we got off our bikes and pushed.

We passed the aircraft factory where Dad works and kept left for Mold, which Ken says is uphill and then it's all down hill to Loggerheads. We managed to find Mold but had asked people the way a few times. It seemed hillier and longer than Ken made it out to be but he is much bigger than Arthur and me put together, and has been at the King's School for a long time.

From Mold it was a bit of a struggle and it was just the last bit down to Loggerheads and the last freewheel. There was a pub at the bottom of the hill and we knew we were there by the name of the pub as there didn't seem anywhere else to go. We asked the man if he would fill our empty bottles with water and were given glasses of lemonade as well, even though he knew we hadn't enough money. He made us promise not to fill our bottles from the stream and thought we were having him on about riding from Chester. We thought it a super place, a stream with loads of fish. We paddled, went on walks, climbed the cliffs and found old mine shafts.

By the bench where we had left our bikes there were slot machines to play all sorts of things with balls. Then there was one a bit different, a few could play at the same time, and looked very simple to operate. The first person was to firmly grasp the handle on the machine, then by holding hands a chain was formed, the last person was to play the game by turning the knob on the machine. A cheap do really for a party of people but as we were only two it was down to Arthur to operate the machine, turning the knob round as far as it would go whilst I held on the other end. The fright it gave us - something you would never do a second time.

As with all slot machines we soon ran out of pennies. Then we found a machine you looked into to see 'What the Butler saw'. The first one was free and we weren't to see the rest without pennies. Arthur said something about being a bit rude. We couldn't see over the high hedge; then we got to a gate and a path to a big wooden pavilion with a veranda belonging to the Crosville Bus Company. There was a clock over the door so we knew the time. Well we thought we did, then realised it wasn't working. The place was empty, all locked up for the duration of the war, with no one to wind the clock or mow the lawns. It happens to so many things.

We catch sight of an old lady in her garden, just by the stream, and go over to ask the time. She had seen us paddling earlier in the day and tells us, it's called the "Leet." We talked for quite a while before we got round to asking the time, and it was about time we set off for home, maybe even a bit late, so we said our goodbyes to the old lady. We finished off what was left of our sandwiches and the water and we were soon pedalling, and more than a bit of walking up the hill from the Loggerheads on our way home after a lovely day.

(Looking back at these times, I can't believe the things we got up to and were allowed to do). This ride to Loggerheads - all we knew was from Ken. Straight through Saltney and when the road forks for Hawarden and Mold, but it might be Buckley. There are no signs anyway so don't go right, go left and just keep going and when you go through Mold or Buckley just keep going on again and you will get to

Loggerheads. You can't miss it. We didn't know road maps existed and all the sign posts had been taken down early on in the war so asking someone was the only way.

We had the bikes and that's all that mattered. We hadn't padlock or chain to lock them up. No puncture outfit or tyre levers, spanners or even a mac. But we did have a pump. Anything going wrong never entered our heads, if it had we would never have gone where we hadn't been before, an explore, an adventure, and that's what made it special for us.

Dad's the one for news on the wireless, whereas Mum, if she has it on at all, prefers to be entertained, so it's not surprising when Dad comes home that we hear all about the war whilst Mum puts the kettle on for a pot of tea. We've already had one when I came in from school, then another when Mary comes home, so you've gathered Mum likes her tea and its always two cups for her to our one.

"The Italians have surrendered, Annie, to our lads and the Americans. It doesn't surprise me, they never had any bottle for a fight but how its all going to work out I can't imagine. As far as I know the Germans are still around and come to think of it we've heard no more of Mussolini." Dad's obviously in some confusion as to what to do with his wall map. It's all to do with battles and flags and doesn't cater for surrenders.

It doesn't seem any time at all. It could have been a few weeks and we hear of the Italians all over again, and much to Dad's amazement, they have declared war on Germany. "What do we do with them now they're on our side? We would be better off without them, Annie, no bones about it as Alf at the farm soon found out they're not worth their salt. Absolutely no use whatsoever as fighters or workers. What a mess they've got us into."

Most happenings in this war - good or bad - come straight out of the blue without warning. Eric is leaving the Post Office telephones to join the RAF and I gather he and Mary are going to get engaged before he goes.

We don't think of being bombed anymore or being invaded and are getting used to the news of our bombing raids over Germany and the possibility of troop landings on the French coast now we have the Americans here. What with the Free French, Polish, Belgian and whatever countries troops managed to find their way across the Channel from Dunkirk, we have them all here in England along with troops from all over the Empire. When you think about it, it's an unbelievable gathering of troops; this little island must be full to capacity, all just waiting for the day.

All the events that changed our day to day living we had no option but to cope with, and it all began to happen well before this outbreak of the war and continued throughout the next couple of years. We didn't like having to make changes but when these adjustments to life became routine they were accepted and we just got on with it and looked forward to the odd treat that may come about by way of good fortune or in some cases, a bit of fiddling the system which we hear about from day to day on what they call 'the black market.'

Black market never seems to touch our family, but occasionally Mum if offered something at Mr. Salsbury's shop from what we now know as, 'from under the counter.' However, not many changes come our way other than war news. Then, out of the blue, comes a change from the normal day-to-day and of all people it's from Granddad, whose been happily digging away for victory, growing vegetables in his back garden in Overleigh Road whilst I've been giving him a hand looking after his front garden, mainly his privet hedge. For some reason or other he needs help with his hedge and I enjoy doing it knowing I can be of help. Granddad's been digging for victory since the early war years when it was thought to be the right thing to do by the Ministry of Food. Now it's all to go at Granddad's as soon as the last of his vegetables have cropped and then Gran is going to keep hens, which really isn't surprising as she was born into a farming family that always kept a lot of hens, so she grew up with them and probably looked after them.

Now why digging was thought to be the way to victory I don't know as someone must have already dug for victory before the vegetables became available at Mr. Clark's shop in Saltney. With so many of us growing our own he can't be too pleased, but then he's a fishmonger as well as a greengrocer, and we, though enthusiastic growers, we are not entirely self sufficient and out of necessity drift back to Mr. Clark's when needs must. I think Mum feels bad about it and so do I when I go down for the shopping.

Digging for victory really caught on, front and back gardens - there's hardly a lawn in sight when you look around the Green. Mr. Irlam next door has kept his rose garden in the front and back, a mass of roses with enough lawn to sit out on. No digging for victory there.

We keep on growing vegetables in the back garden and every summer stick with the patriotic planting of red white and blue at the front. I think the neighbours have come to accept it as normal and would be most disappointed if a change came about. Makes you feel good seeing the colours of the flag set in a nice green lawn.

I wonder why the Council never suggested that we went digging for victory across the road on The Green. It was large enough to provide everyone with a sizeable plot while leaving plenty of grassed areas. There would have been no need to erect the usual sheds found on allotments as everything you needed couldn't have been handier, just across the road, back home. It could all have looked rather nice and more importantly we could all have kept our gardens just as they were. Everyone red, white and blue would have been fantastic.

Granddad, with help from Uncle Ewart, has enclosed all of their back garden in wire netting and built a really good hen house. Both of them being in the building trade they know all about making huts and things. We have been up to see it and it looks great. Inside there's nesting boxes, perches and special containers for water and feeding. The nesting boxes are filled with straw and some already have eggs in. Then Gran tells me they are pot eggs and are to be left where I found them. I can't remember whether they were put in to encourage the hens to lay more or whether it's to kid the hen that there's still one egg left to sit on when in fact all the eggs have gone. They have a couple of cockerels and I think ten hens and it's rather nice walking amongst them while they scratch about pecking the ground.

Mum and Gran are on the path talking about all the red tape they have had to get through to get the hens. I only hear bits of it whenever there's a break in the clucking of hens which never seems to stop. I think Granddad's going to get a bit fed up with it and that's without the cockerel, which I haven't heard up to now.

The Town Hall comes into the conversation and the Ministry of Food. Egg coupons have been removed from both their ration books and Uncle Roy's and Auntie Maisie's, so they won't be able to buy any eggs from the shops. But in exchange for their egg coupons they will be getting coupons for corn for the hens and Gran seems to think that the hens will lay more eggs than the coupons would have provided. I'm sure they will - one person's ration being an egg every other week -sounds funnier if you say half an egg every week.

I like going up to see Gran and Granddad on a Sunday. We always walk up the lane and through Curzon Park, then come home along Hough Green as it's usually dark.

After we have been there an hour or so Gran will say, "I suppose you would like something to eat," as she heads off for the pantry, soon to return with the left-overs from their Sunday dinner. If Gran managed to get a small joint of meat, my favourite is the cold lamb sandwich which she always sprinkles over loads of salt. I think it must be the salt that makes them taste so nice. Then its cold apple pie that's never sweet as sugar is scarce, but then I like it that way with the top of the milk from a little jug. She knows I love it and Granddad always makes a performance about the apples being a bit on the sharp side. He's just like Dad - they both have a sweet tooth.

Mum always takes Granddad some ginger and shortbread biscuits to keep him going through the week which makes a big hole in our rations. It really pleases him. You should see his face when he opens the brown paper bag and picks his way through the biscuits before deciding which one to have with his cup of tea.

Mum always manages to find a bit of something for the hens and if we get any eggs from Gran then we take the shells back for Gran to crush them up to mix with the corn. Gran says they're essential for a healthy hen. Life is a sort of exchange of things, every day all of us helping one another even though we have so little.

I like the weekend, and Friday over, my school blazer goes into the wardrobe along with the cap and tie and my brown corduroy Jerkin comes off the hanger for the weekend wear, and of course Friday night's bath night. Saturday mornings are when I go to do Granddad's garden and his privet hedge if it needs doing. I usually get there when Gran's busy donkey stoning the edges of her steps down to the footpath. Arthur and I got a bit fed up with the films on a Saturday morning at the Odeon, so we don't go any more. Gran must be getting used to seeing me in my Jerkin that I love wearing but she will insist on calling it a 'gherkin.' I keep telling her it's a Jerkin. Arthur has one like mine and so have some of my other pals and they all call them Jerkins. I sometimes think she's like this just to get me going and she knows all the time what my jacket's called and it's not a 'gherkin.' When I get home I tell Mum about it which brings a smile to her face, much the same as Gran and Dad doesn't help by saying, "She just likes to see you getting yourself in a pickle." It seems to amuse everyone, including Granddad.

I don't think Granddad has adjusted to the food we have in the war. I know he has a sweet tooth like Dad but whenever Gran makes us a sandwich he always has to mention the loaf. "Bread's not like it used to be before the war." It's what we call 'the National Loaf.' It's not white, it's a sort of off white, say a shade of grey. I don't mind it, Granddad hates it. But then there's plenty of it and its not rationed. I'm more interested in who bakes it as it does make a difference. Blake's in Watergate Row are on my shopping list when I have the chance to shop in town as are Hawarden's in Newgate Street and of course Griffiths' our man with the horse and cart who still calls. I do love my bread when it's baked by a proper baker.

The more I see of Gran and Granddad's house the more it fascinates me when compared with ours - it's so different in many ways. The first thing you're aware of on going through their front door is looking down a very narrow and dark hall that they call, 'the passage' - just a little square of glass over the door to let the light in. On the left is their only front room, the parlour, which we call the sitting room, and like our sitting room, is very seldom used.

Gran has a lot of framed photographs on the mantelpiece and on the piano that Auntie Maisie plays. There's a large photograph hanging on the wall of Granddad in his army uniform showing off his medals. All of the photographs are brownish and look quite old even though they were much younger when they were taken. They also have an aspidistra in a pot on a bamboo stand. Everyone seems to have an aspidistra.

Back to the passage and on the left where they spend most of the day is a room they call the scullery and this is where it all gets really different. This is where Gran does all the baking and cooking on the coal fired range. Now in this room by way of furniture is a rocking chair where she sits so as she can keep an eye on the fire and what's cooking, as there's always something on the go even if it's just a kettle on the hob for tea. There's a long leather couch that Granddad tends to lie on with his feet up and in arms reach of his wireless. A scrub topped table, six chairs and a sideboard which they call a dresser. I suppose a room similar to the way we use our dining room except Mum doesn't use our range for cooking as we have a back kitchen with a gas cooker, a sink with hot and cold water, a dolly tub, posser and mangle for the washing. Gran hasn't any of this. No water at all in the house. No back kitchen, no bathroom. Granddad has built a wooden lean to over the back door and Uncle Reg has fitted a pot sink with a cold water tap. Before that, Gran had to go down the yard to the wash house to fill a kettle.

Now that's where it all happens in the brick built wash house. Inside, all the walls are white washed and there hangs the big tin bath along with various buckets and tubs, mops and all sorts of brushes. A cold water tap, pot sink with wooden draining boards, a fired boiler and in the corner, a stack of coke and wood ready for wash day or a bath, if you didn't want to be bothered taking it all into the house. A door at the back takes you into the back entry where they keep the dust bin.

Next to the wash house is the separate water closet that we call a lavatory. It doesn't seem to bother them not having a bathroom or lavatory in the house. I don't really mind having to go down their yard though it can be unpleasant in the winter when it's cold and dark, as it's a candle when you get there. It's not like a lavatory, it's just a big wooden board with a hole in the middle and on the wall hangs, by a string, neatly cut pieces of newspaper. I don't think much of 'Bronco' or 'Sanizal' but it's a lot better than the Daily Herald.

When walking back home from Gran's I sometimes ask Mum what it was like living at 74 Overleigh Road when she was a little girl. The answer I always get is that, "Even though your Gran had thirteen children, some of my brothers and sisters died when they were very young, so there were never all that many of us living there at any one time." I never found out what it was like so I took it that Mum, being the eldest, must have had a pretty hard time and really didn't want to talk about it. Then I reasoned it out for myself. I had an Auntie and five Uncles and then I understood why.

Both Mum and Dad have said on several occasions that I'm going to have my birthday and Christmas present together this year as it's something very special. I think they mean it's a lot of money. Mary has hinted that she knows what it is but isn't telling me. When I'm told of this arrangement I never know whether my birthday is going to be late or Christmas early. Present-wise that is. It's nearly always that birthday is late. Well nothing came on my birthday so whatever it is it's going to be at Christmas, as usual.

Christmas 1943

Up early Christmas morning to the coloured paper chains and sprigs of holly in the polished copper jug standing in the hall. As I come down the stairs I can feel the warmth coming from the open door of the sitting room where Mary is busy talking with Mum and Dad by the fire. And there it is, standing against the wall - now I can see what they meant. Not a small present, only one, and what a present, the best one I have ever had and probably ever will have - a grown- up-man-size B.S.A. bicycle. Dad says it's what known as a 'utility model' as it's all painted black because of the war and there weren't many available, it had to be ordered. There are some chrome parts, the chain drive and wheel hubs.

Uncle Roy has brightened the frame up with coloured red white and blue line transfer and silver letters - B.S.A. Above the front forks is a very decorative B.S.A. trade mark of three standing rifles - the Birmingham Small Arms. I suppose they make rifles most of the time and just stopped for a while to make my bike. Best of all its got cable brakes, blow up tyres, (Dad says they are called 'inflatable') a pump and a tool bag where I found a bag of sweets; then Dad gave me the spanners, tyre levers and a puncture repair outfit. I thanked them so many times, Mary as well, as I am sure she helped out.

I ride my bike round The Green a few times before dinner's ready and Gran had done us proud with a chicken. Just as good as the ones we used to have from the farm, if not better, maybe because we helped to feed it up. But what a chicken! I just love the crispy, salty skin and at the end of the day, picking the bones. Mind you that's usually on Boxing Day. I like Christmas in the sitting room, lying on the half moon rug in front of the fire. A white furry rug, thick just like a real polar bear skin, but I know it isn't.

Christmas gone I have a grown-up's bike and not next year but the

Left, Margaret Jackson, me, Joe
Brown, Arthur and Mary.

Left, Mum, me and Mary with Auntie Olive and
Uncle Ewart.

Eric's Dad and Mum far left left Eric and Mary centre, my Mum and Dad far right.

Art school party. I'm the St. Trinian's girl in the Panama hat and plaits.

RAF Wittering 1951-52,
LAC Rowland, P.

Me and Bett.

5 Northway, as it looks today.

Bett, me and my nephew John.

Me, Sarah and Debbie.

Sarah and Debbie at Woodlands Primary School.

Hornsea Pottery 1979.

Sarah, me, Bett and Debbie.

Mary and Eric.

Me and Chris, our wedding day.

Steve and Sarah.

David and Debbie.

Left, with Sarah and Steve's daughters Samantha (Sammie) and Zoë.

With Debbie and David's family, Daniel (Dan), Katherine (Kate) and Lydia (lyd).

In my studio at home and my paintings.

Topiary gardens, Levens Hall, Cumbria.

Dry crossing, Goathland, Yorkshire.

Levens Hall, Cumbria.

Glasson Dock, Lancashire.

year after I will be fourteen. Old enough to leave school and start work, which I've always wanted to do. Granddad thinks I should learn a trade and the one that appeals to me the most is working with wood, making things, a cabinet maker. Then there's a carpenter or a joiner and I don't know how they differ, but I think I will be one or the other. I would really like to be an architect designing buildings like my Uncle Roy but he was good at arithmetic at grammar school and went on to Liverpool University to study architecture. Granddad thinks that I would get on in a trade and who knows one day could be a master builder - the same line of business as my Uncle Roy. It sounds all right to me.

I have a talk with Mum and Dad and Dad says, "that Peter's interests are in history, drawing, creativity, the natural world and very good with his hands, which is not at all bad. But he will never be an academic, as his interests don't lie there." Dad saying this made me feel better about myself.

The other day when I got home from school, right out of the blue Mum said to me, "It was Mr. Carter who suggested that you had your special present on Christmas Day and not on your birthday." I had to think about this one as it's a while past. In fact two punctures past and adjustment to brakes, saddle and lots of polishing.

Now Mr. Carter needs some explaining. I know he's a friendly man. Most days I see him in plus fours riding a rather special drop handlebar Sun Tourer bicycle as he goes to work. He also has a tourer tandem which he uses weekends, his wife taking the back seat when they go off to explore the Cheshire countryside or North Wales. He has a different bike that Dad says is called a 'sit-up-and-beg' when he's in the uniform of a Special Constable or Air Raid Warden. I don't know if he's in the Home Guard. All this isn't at all surprising as he has a shop just selling cycles across the cobbles in Cuppin Street. The name over the door was 'Davies'.

That is where Dad went to talk about the bike I would have for my special present. Mr. Carter was used to better times before the war selling superb racing bikes and now all he had to offer were bikes of a utility nature, so he ordered what was available and thought he could get around Christmas time. I had a birthday four days before. I thought it could possibly be in time for my birthday and it was, so I could have had it as a birthday present. Mr. Carter thought it best to keep the bike in his shop until Christmas Eve. His thinking was that Christmas would have been a bit flat for me after such a fantastic birthday present with nothing to come at Christmas. Even a small present wouldn't look at all anything like after a bike, and he was right.

All seems to have gone quiet on the news of the war, other than bombing raids on Germany which seem to be every night, followed by how many of our aircraft are missing, as if the aircraft were of some importance, the air crew never mentioned.

I think of Joe Brown and ask about him whenever I see his Dad, the signal man, then some news of German troops having entered Hungary. The Germans keep on doing it and I can't help but think that there can't be many more countries left to go to war with. Just as I thought things were changing and I was getting used to the idea that the Germans were the losers. Then they go and have a go at Hungary as if they hadn't had enough. Dad just accepts the situation and shows me where Hungary is on his Daily Express war map. It's on the wall in our living room between the clock and the bookcase. When you see it on a map it does look a lot of wall with German flags, swastikas, on pins everywhere. Dad says that one day it will all end. The one that wins will have to pick up the pieces and God willing, just like the last one, it will be us.

Arthur comes round to tell me that his brother Ken has had his call up papers and is going into the Royal Navy. Arthur seems to be really pleased about it as he's going to have the box bedroom all to himself, as he doesn't think Ken will have any leave spent at home as he will be living on a ship. Now I don't know if you can choose what you go in, but the Navy wouldn't appeal to me. I don't like being on water and even worse, the thought of being in a submarine. I really want to be away from school to start work or join the R.A.F. It's the R.A.F. that appeals to me but I'm not old enough to do either.

Mary keeps getting her letters from Eric and she shares bits with us from time to time and what seems to be long ago, he's finished basic training and has taken loads and loads of tests that to me just sounds like being at school. He's doing well and going for aircrew, then he had to go and tangle up with some barbed wire on a cross country run, his leg turned septic and was in a military hospital for a month. So this put him back to the next intake course to start again. All the ground training behind him for the second time, he was posted to Desford for flying training in Tiger Moths.

Then the last letter and Mary seems pleased and relieved both at the same time, as Eric has flown solo at a place called Braunstone with the airfield covered in snow. In all probability he will be going to the U.S.A. or Rhodesia to do his advanced flying training after two weeks embarkation leave.

On the few times that I go into Town it's surprising how often the buses are at a standstill while long transporters go through carrying fuselages of planes in a convoy with other vehicles accompanied by either R.A.F. or Army Police on motor cycles.

Dad says the transporters are going to and from the factory at

Broughton and are called 'Queen Mary's' because of the size. I have seen them going through town with sections of submarines on so they won't have been from Broughton.

A lot that passes through Town ends up on the big Roodee and its really filling up with all types of vehicles, some trucks and huge wooden crates, some covered with tarpaulins. Convoys of tanks and bren gun carriers go through in numbers. I stand and watch on the kerb as they pass by swivelling on their tracks as they go round sharp corners. You don't see the driver, only the one with his head and shoulders above the top of the gun turret. He usually waves. Goodness knows what damage the tracks do to the road.

There are a lot of soldiers, airmen and sailors in and around Chester now, mainly soldiers, and more and more Americans by the day. Now they are all soldiers.

Arthur and I are always looking for something new to do and he's come up with the idea of joining the Boy Scouts. A friend of his from school is a Scout in the 8th Chester's, and if we would like to join he would have a word with the Scoutmaster. Arthur's Mum and Dad approve of the Scouts and so do mine.

They meet at the scout hut one night a week and as it's on the other side of Town and dark nights, we will be going on the bus, "even so we will have a fair walk to Parkgate Road" says Arthur. It's a church troop which I didn't know when I told Mum and Dad, so we'll just have to see how it goes. Did we have a job finding it in the dark! Luckily someone else was going in as it happened, just as we got there, a boy much older than Arthur and me. We knew he was going to the same place as us as he was wearing a wide brimmed scout hat. We went down the side of the church towards a dim light and then carefully and slowly going down a lot of stone steps to a partly open door. Through the door and shouts of 'Close it quick, don't want to let the light out and the cold in.' Of all places, we were in a big cellar under the church. I always thought of scouts being in huts and how I wished we were.

Now we're in the light, even though it's gloomy, the older boy we met outside looks more like a young man. His name is Eric and shows us where to hang our coats. Then we meet the 'Skipper' as he's known to all though his name is Mr. Williams. I thought it most strange seeing both men in scout uniform. I suppose it's the short trousers. There was a lot of running around and very noisy, just like a school playground but it sounds noisier being inside; then Mr. Williams blows his whistle to restore some order. It wasn't very exciting or interesting.

We didn't seem to do much the first night. Just trying to fit in, getting to know them all. But, we have done some serious things. We have been sworn in, that is taken the scouts oath as we are now 'tenderfoots' as Skipper says, "the first rung on the scout's ladder, and to always remember the scout's motto, 'Be Prepared.'"

Away from the place, I begin to wonder what we've got ourselves into and I'm not so sure about where we meet, being in a cellar isn't ideal. I know the first visit was on a cold dark night and it was preferable being so but it's going to be just as bad in the summer. The two ceiling lights don't really light the place. I wasn't aware of any heating and I don't remember seeing any other rooms, say like a lavatory. Maybe I will be more aware of things as I get used to being one of them. Thinking through it all, the scout motto comes to mind and how appropriate if only Eric had spoken of it as he took us down those steps. Anyway next time we should be getting some badges and a list of things we need to have which don't have to be bought at once. So Mum will be pleased. I suppose the first thing to buy will be the shirt to sew the badges on.

Mary says, "I've something for you," and hands me a couple of pink tickets for the Majestic Cinema. I don't know of the Majestic and ask where it is. "Well you know the way to the Gaumont in Frodsham Street, over the canal bridge then it's just a short walk past the Gaumont on the other side of the road. You can't miss it." How often do people say that when you ask for directions. "Now the tickets are complimentary staff tickets, so that means you and Arthur will be allowed in without paying. Now isn't that good?" "Yes Mary it's good, but anyone will know Arthur and me aren't staff without having to ask." "Now the lady that gave me the tickets for you, Mrs. Walsh, Eric's Mum, told me not to worry about that as in all probability she would be on the door when you go and looking forward to seeing you. And when you do go don't expect the Majestic to look like the Gaumont as it's nowhere near the size or as plush. And don't forget to thank her." Not being plush doesn't bother me when it's free; it's if we don't see Eric's Mum before anyone else sees us.

Arthur has to tell them all at home about our free tickets and his Dad seemed very amused by it with a grin on his face saying, "it was always thought that you came out of the Majestic with more than you went in with, we called it 'the laugh and scratch'. But that was a long time ago." We have got a lot of cinemas to choose from in Town and this is the only one where we don't have to pay.

Dad always insists on calling cinemas 'picture houses', which I think sounds old fashioned and I don't think he's all that bothered about going to see films anyway. Having a lot means you can pick the film you want to see and if one cinema is full you can set off and try another one. Sometimes if a very good film's showing they allow you to stand up behind the rear stalls, then hopefully you find a seat at the interval.

166

There's the Odeon, Music Hall, Tatler, Regal, Gaumont, Majestic and The Park in Saltney. Up to now if I had to choose my favourite cinema it would be The Tatler even though as yet I haven't been to the Majestic or The Park. The Tatler is very small, plush and I don't think it has an upstairs. It's the newest of all the cinemas and they say it was built to be blast proof from air raids.

They show news and lots of short films, funny films. It's the warmth, the comfort of the place that I like, mainly the seats. Not like any of the other cinemas the backs of the seats are at a much lower angle, is the word rakish? - but just as thickly padded as the seats. The arm rests aren't bare wood they're also padded. If the films weren't so good I've seen some people nodding off, (asleep) - then when the lights went on hastily having to pull themselves together when leaving their seats to stand for the King.

Now this is where the blast proof thing comes up and I'm not sure about it, so if the siren had sounded when we were in The Tatler watching a good film, maybe The Three Stooges or Edgar Kennedy or the News, would we have had to leave this lovely warm and comfortable place to go looking for an air raid shelter? Hopefully the blast proofing would have let us be - enjoying our films. Come to think of it I can't remember ever having an air raid when I've been in the pictures or if you were when the siren went, would you get a refund? I suppose not, as you'd be a heck of a lot longer queuing to get out than you were queuing to get in. Was it sixpence or nine pence we paid to go in The Tatler?

Some of us are getting interested in football. I don't think Arthur is. It's not that we haven't been interested before but it's always been with an old tennis ball in the road or on the way to somewhere, on The Green with the trees for goal posts. The small ball isn't very good on grass; we need a big ball - a proper football.

My pals are around The Green, Park Road West and that's it really. Say eight of us, not enough for a game of football even if we did have a ball and all of the eight aren't bothered about football. Alan's one that does, a good dribbler with a tennis ball. He goes to the College School on the other side of town. One of his teachers plays for Chester.

Three of us thought it a good idea to go and see how Chester played as we hadn't seen a professional match before.

We meet up on the Saturday afternoon and only as far as the end of our road. I'd never seen it so busy; there must have been hundreds of men and boys coming up from Saltney; the whole length of Earlsway, all talking away about the match as they went along. They seemed a friendly lot and we were soon amongst them. By the time we got across the Dee Bridge and on the Gas Works path we got talking with some lads from Mount Pleasant and managed to kick a tennis ball about on the grass down as far as Paradise Street. They had been before so we stayed with them all the way and after the Roodee and into Sealand Road it was impossible to even think of having a kick of a ball. We met up with more men than before and all walking in the middle of the road. Then, what a surprise, a lovely sweet smell of flowers as though we were in a greenhouse full of them, it was so strong. A man walking next to me may have heard the sniffing and said we were passing the scent works. I never thought of a scent works being by the gas works or even making scent in Chester. I suppose that's why it smelt so nice having had earlier passed the gas works.

The football stadium looked a big place just off the road and we got in through the turnstile for less than an adult. The whole place looked really good. We were in the ground half way down by the side by the halfway line opposite what they call the Stand where they all sit down, under cover. We were under cover but it didn't go all the way down.

There were a lot of men in front of us, some leaning on bits of fence which I think would be less tiring than just standing all the time, and I'm beginning to think we're going to be well tired by the game's over. Then a few men shouted "make way for these lads down by the wall so as they can see the game." We just kept saying 'thank you' so many times as we made our way down. Then the loud speaker came on, 'Hello Spine Cop, Hello Albert.' I didn't know what that meant and as it went on and on about things the teams came out from under the stands and having a kick about before the game started. Chester were playing in white shirts and black shorts. The noise - everyone shouting and cheering, I couldn't hear a thing, not even Alan standing next to me. He had spotted his teacher.

A man standing next to me was doing a lot of shouting and seemed to be used to the place, so I asked about Mr. McNeil and what position he was playing. "Who?" he asked. I said again, "Mr. McNeil." He seemed to think it funny before saying "Left back, one of the best with a kick like a mule." We hadn't a programme so didn't know anything of the team or who they were playing.

When the whistle went for half time and it was quiet enough to talk with the man behind me who I think realised I didn't now much about football and I thought it best to say that it was the first time we had been to a football match, a proper one. Second half - the same man got into an argument with another, shouting across to him that "Chester were a hell of a lot better than the dock rats." I later found out that the other team were Tranmere Rovers but where they came from I didn't know. Chester supporters left having won. I think

Tranmere Rovers supporters were complaining having scored a goal or goals that hadn't been allowed.

We enjoyed the game but being new to it all I didn't know what was going on, a bit like the first night at the scouts. When I got home Dad wanted to know what I'd been up to so I asked him about the scent works in Sealand Road, the Spine Cop and Albert at the football stadium. Dad look puzzled. I suppose he expected me to be full of football match, and I wasn't. My reasoning was that I didn't know what was going on, how they played or the rules. I just didn't understand then to my surprise; "doesn't surprise me, Peter - never understood the game or the men that played it. You'd never find me kicking a round ball about the park. I don't know about the scent works and its Spion Kop - came up in the Boer War. What the connection is with Chester football club I don't know, nor Albert."

That was the only time I had ever talked football with Dad but I soon found out that it was the wrong football. Dad had played rugby football and talked of playing for Runcorn or Widnes when he was a young man before going into the army. I just don't fancy Dad's game and will stick with finding more about what he calls 'the softy's' game played with the round ball. I only know as much of one as I do than the other but he's partly right.

I think of rugby as being more of a rough game than football, just being allowed to handle the ball makes for more physical contact. I'd prefer to keep the ball at my feet no matter what Dad says. I just don't like being thought of as a softy. What surprises me, I don't think Dad's ever been what you would call a big man. He's very much on the light side, but then amongst it all he did mention 'fly half' whatever that might be.

As well as a lot of troops being transported through the Town there's still the convoys of tanks and field guns and just recently I've spotted quite a few of our aircraft with black and white stripes painted under the wings. They're not in my aircraft spotters guide so it's something new. The markings have been mostly on fighter planes - Hurricanes and Spitfires. They could be on our bombers as well but as they fly from airfields on the east side of England, I wouldn't see them.

Wilf, a pal of mine and Arthur's, lives at Number 15. He's a few years older than us. We haven't seen him for a while - then we find out from his Mum that he's left home to be a soldier in the Irish Guards. When Dad comes home he doesn't seem surprised about the news of Wilf joining up and can understand why the army want him in the Guards. "They want tall lads for the Guards, but why the Irish I don't know, and no matter how tall he just seems no more than a lad." When a friend leaves home you think of the times we had together as boys. We always played together I suppose at being soldiers which he and we always wanted to be but there were other times we had a spell when Wilf's Dad, Mr. Ball, showed us his expertise in making sailing boats. He made Wilf one and then Arthur and me. They weren't like yachts that have a keel; he shaped a lead weight the full length of the hull so they never went completely over when the sails caught the full wind. We had a lot of fun with them.

All three of us with Mr. Ball went down to the Cop and sailed them out across the river from the stone steps on the quayside, just a bit up river from Crightons. They would go bobbing across the Dee depending on how much string we had to let out.

Wilf came home on a few days leave. Arthur and I couldn't wait to see him - he was so proud of his uniform; showing off really. Somehow he seemed different to the Wilf we remembered from just a few weeks ago. He seemed much older and was just full of being a soldier. Wilf went back to his unit - I don't remember any goodbye's neither do I remember ever seeing him again. But I do have memories of those simple happy days we had together going to the illuminations in The Groves and across The Meadows. We missed the illuminations in the Town having spent too much time in The Groves, playing in the road with an old tennis ball and Arthur's older sister Phylis's hand-me-down tennis racquet and hockey stick, and launching those sailing boats.

Eric's stationed at a place called Heaton Park not far away in Manchester, waiting on a posting for advanced flying training and is now at home enjoying his embarkation leave which has been extended, much to his surprise. On return to Heaton Park they were told by the AOC that air crew training for pilots, navigators and bomb aimers would cease, but some could re-muster for air gunner or ground crew. They weren't surprised by this as the Americans were taking over most of our airfields and there must have been at least a year's supply of aircrew already in training. Eric said they created uproar and wouldn't leave the building and only changed their minds with the offer of a travel warrant and further week's leave. On return, he was posted to RAF Eastchurch on the Isle of Sheppy awaiting re-muster.

Due to reserved occupations status Eric was discharged from the RAF as surplus to requirements. He wasn't given any clothes other than his RAF shirt and trousers and came home to Chester, going back to work for the GPO. I can tell Dad's quietly angry and after a while he has something to say. "They were handy enough giving him something to wear when they wanted him, when he volunteered. What a way to be treated." We were all silent and I got the feeling that Mum and Mary though disappointed for Eric are pleased he's home without saying so.

The last time I went up to Overleigh Road to trim Granddad's privet hedge we talked about me getting about a bit on my bike and my interest in engine spotting, spending some of my pocket money on a penny platform ticket at the General Station. "Next time you go, see if you can spot the name 'Joyce' on the platform clocks - it might have Whitchurch where they were made, or was it Northwich? You will have to let me know."

I asked Granddad why he was so interested in the name 'Joyce' on the platform clocks. "Well it goes back to early in the war when we were getting bombed and this man (as we all got to know as Lord Haw Haw) would come on the wireless all the way from Berlin, spreading his propaganda. Now this may have been before your Dad bought your wireless, but in any case yours, being a utility set can only get the home services, whereas I can go to all sorts of foreign places at the push of a button and some careful tuning. Berlin, Paris, Moscow, Rome, Amsterdam, Brussels and Battenburg." Granddad looked at me with a smile on his face and winked. He thought he'd caught me out. I couldn't see the connection between the clocks at Chester Station and this Lord Haw Haw but from the expression on Granddad's face I took it that he was trying to put some reasoning together so I remained silent. Then; "Well Peter?" Whenever that 'Well Peter' comes it's nearly always to tell me something that requires my full attention. "This Lord Haw Haw was the son of an Irish born American, William Joyce and a former British fascist. This of course was before the war when trouble was brewing between us and the Germans. There was another fascist, Oswald Moseley, can't think what happened to him. We called them 'blackshirts.' Anyway, I think that's the family connection with the clocks." We talked about it for long enough before I go out to cut his privet hedge.

The propaganda (as it was called) that followed the 'Germany calling, Germany calling' was just like Granddad's 'Well Peter' - to get our attention, to listen. Lord Haw Haw's message was all about being bombed, of losing the war, the hopeless situation we were in and all our young men being killed when all we had to do was surrender and all Germany wanted was to be friends of the British people.

I could see what Granddad was about with his fascist thing, I just find it difficult to believe that he might have lived not far away from Chester, and how he ever came to be a fascist, I just don't know. I can see why he thought it best for him to leave before we got into this war with Germany, and where else could he go. Granddad's words 'a turncoat and an absolute traitor through and through.'

With a sandwich and a bottle of water I was on the bus with the lads all the way to the General Station to spend the day train spotting. We passed what was once Dad's shop and I thought of all the happy times I enjoyed there, not just playing about over the shop in the stockroom, but the view from the window across the busy street to the Grosvenor Park beyond. Dad and I would sometimes take our cups of tea up there when he wasn't too busy and Dad would say "Just watch the world go by."

Across the cobbled back yard was the big warehouse, a barn-like place where I would occasionally find some hens eggs, chop wood to bundle up into kindling to sell in the shop, and helping out serving when I had the opportunity. Memories occupied my mind until the conductor sounded his bell, calling 'General Station.' I hadn't been aware of going up City Road after Dad's shop but how I wish he still had his shop to go to each day.

With a penny surrendered to the machine in the entrance hall we have platform tickets that I think are intended for travellers just wanting to meet people arriving or seeing them off. The man on the gate snipping our tickets gave us a look, knowing full well what we were up to. We were there for the day. Not bad for a penny - cheaper than the pictures. An unbelievably big place, busy with people, so many trains coming and going all the time - it never seems to stop. It's good fun running from platform to platform across bridges to collect numbers, sometimes not quick enough to catch the trains before they're off again. I got lots of numbers and names that I hadn't seen before and one beyond my wildest dreams, the Royal Scot an LMS Shielder class. It had a bell on the front and a commemorative plaque in recognition of its tour of Canada. Just think of it - this engine having gone all that way to Canada.

When you're near to it, the size and the power of this engine, the constant hissing and clouds of steam; I looked up in wonderment and envy at the driver. He caught my eye and above the noise I heard him shout, "Would you like to come up onto the footplate?" I have a 'Yes please,' back before he'd finished asking and my hands on the rail and up the steps. On the footplate I shook hands with the driver and his fireman, two very friendly men that told us all about the engine and that when in Canada it had a cow-catcher on the front as well as a bell. I could have listened to them all day but they had to be away.

Carriage doors were being slammed and all secure, then came the sound of the guard's whistle and a wave of his green flag. With a smile and a wink from the engine driver at me, the engine eased forward and became noisier than it was before, steam and smoke everywhere. With the power of the engine the wheels were spinning on the lines for some time before the noise of the engine was taken over by the gentle trundling of passing carriages with windows open and people waving. Then at the last, the goods van with the guard, and a wave, they were all gone, leaving the platform empty and quiet. It wouldn't be all that long before they were passing Mr. Brown's signal box and full speed for Holyhead.

We had spotted loads of engines from other sheds that we hadn't seen before and would never have seen passing our usual spot on the tip. As it happens we would have seen the Royal Scot, the tip being on the way to Holyhead. We met other spotters from Crewe who told us that a lot of trains from London change engines at Birmingham or Crewe, never finding their way to Chester, so we wonder now that we have big bikes, that we might get as far as Crewe Station where the sheds are much bigger, to do some train spotting, seeing engines that rarely ever pass Mr. Brown's signal box.

We were well pleased with our day and decided it was time that we made for home. The West View bus was waiting outside the Station. Through Town and going down Lower Bridge Street, we were via Handbridge and it was as we passed 74 Overleigh Road I thought of Granddad's station clocks. We did see the big clocks on platforms, checking on time and trains coming and going, but in the excitement of the day, clean forgot to notice any of the maker's names. What will Granddad say? I thought it through so many times over so many days.

On seeing Granddad I had no option but to admit that I had forgotten. Thankfully he didn't seem to be all that bothered. "Well Peter I have given it some thought and if my memory serves me right the names on those platform clocks may well be Gent - but I'm sure Joyce was from a Cheshire family of clockmakers, maybe not station clocks. Where this leaves Lord Haw Haw I don't know but it doesn't get him off the hook when all this is over he's still a traitor.

It seems unreal that what seemed ages ago the Italians surrendered to the Allies (that's us), and then declared war on the Germans - and now Dad talks of our lads fighting it out still in Italy at a place called Monte Casino, and of landing at Anzio. I thought that the Germans would have tailed it out of Italy long ago when Mussolini became unpopular with the partisans, but no, they are well dug in at the great Abbey of Casino. When Dad talks about the war he doesn't mention the Yanks anymore or the Allies, its now 'our lads' which sounds better to me - and to Dad I suppose they are lads, as were the soldiers when they lived with us after Dunkirk.

After a few battles and a bombing there wasn't anything left of the Abbey and I wondered whatever became of all those monks. I wasn't bothered about the Germans. In no time at all we were hearing news on the wireless of Allied troops entering Rome and being greeted by crowds of cheering Italians. Dad didn't have much to say about the news. I don't think he's ever forgiven them for being on the side of the Germans. He's got a thing about how the Italians behave when times change and its best left alone.

Summer's with us and the long light evenings. Double British Summertime, a government thing to help the farmers with more time to spend in the fields when it's most needed at harvest time. It's not just the farmers that benefit from more daylight time; I can get out to see my pals or spend some time to work in the garden after tea as Dad doesn't get much time to do the garden as most nights he works late. It's usually a round half past eight when he comes through the back door. I've noticed that in the summer time it takes him longer to get home and Mum also notices the difference as she's taken to saying, "Your Dad's late again." That's later than his usual late, and it's all to do with the double summer time.

Now Dad's a great one for his newspaper and when he gets off the bus in Saltney the newspaper's opened and he reads it all the way home until we eventually see him turning the corner out of the entry at the bottom of Greensway. Paper opened to the world he continues to read it making several stops before he opens the garden gate. A meal Mum has cooked and being kept warm in the oven hasn't been given a thought. It seems to be an age before the latch goes on the back door and he's home. We get a "Hello" (from the back kitchen) and, "get that wireless switched on Peter so as we can get the news." It comes on, it's the wrong channel and Dad fiddles with the knobs from station to station and just can't find any news while repeatedly uttering the word "strewth, we must be in between programmes. I just can't understand Annie why you haven't had the wireless on all day. They've been interrupting programmes all day on the factory wireless with special war news bulletins, D-Day, its D-Day!"

He looks beside himself as we pass around looks of complete puzzlement. "We've invaded France. The Allies, us the Yanks and anyone they could lay their hands on, a hundred and fifty thousand men in all. Would you believe it, five thousand ships crossing the English Channel, the biggest armada ever known to Man. "Those lads are having one hell of a time over there and you haven't had the wireless on! It'll all be in the papers in the morning and I can't wait to get the Picture Post. I just hope to God that they establish the landing then move on into France and that it doesn't end up in another Dunkirk. I'm not convinced about Eisenhower being the right man for the job. My man would have been Monty."

Mum thought the name Eisenhower sounded German. This triggered off a long discussion about the mish-mash of nationalities from all over the world but mainly Europeans that go to make up the United States of America. Dad talks of the great depression and mass immigration after the last war (1914-18). Perhaps Mum wasn't far out with her thinking on Eisenhower. This went on for long enough and then tells us that it was around that time his brothers emigrated to Australia which was news to me as I only know of his sisters, my Aunties Effie and Martha. With all this going on Mum's reminded of the soldiers we had billeted with us and can't help but worry about them. We went to bed very late that night without hearing any more news other than what Dad had told us earlier on.

Just a few days after D-Day and we were full of what was going on over there. Our troops were holding their own and in some places making slow progress. Dad says, "The priority is keeping a constant landing of supplies and reinforcements, a good solid back up. The RAF lads keeping the skies clean while the lads on the ground go for the big breakthrough. It's going to be tough but there's going to be no stopping them as so many will have memories of Dunkirk."

With D-Day our war seemed far away from England and to be fought on foreign lands far away. Then comes the news that London was being bombed again, prompting mass evacuation of school children to the countryside. They weren't like the air raids we had experienced in the early war years - the ones that came in the middle of the night, well not many came in the daytime, but these come day or night, it doesn't matter. They were mechanically guided, pilot-less aircraft, more of a flying bomb launched by a catapult and powered by jet propulsion. It was the German V-1. It soon becomes known to us as the 'doodlebug' or 'buzz bomber' by the noise it made as it fell to earth when the buzzing stopped and it ran out of fuel. I don't know how much a bomb load it carried but it was much more than a conventional bomber.

Thankfully for the rest of us the V-1's could only carry enough fuel to reach as far as London. I wonder if we will be getting some evacuees? I kept asking Dad time, time and again what the V-1 stood for because my thinking was in Roman numerals. 'V' being five followed by a '1' which made six was confusing. I think Dad got a bit fed up with this; then he comes home one night and says, "Peter, your constantly troubled questioning's resolved. One of the men at work, incidentally of all things an ARP Warden when he gets home, has come up with the answer. The 'V' before the '1' is for a 'Vorgel-tungswaffe.'

This name went around the house and up and down the road whenever I had the opportunity and almost everyone thought it sounded funny and brought a smile to faces until they were told it was the German for what we had named their doodlebug. Even that sounds a bit light hearted for a very nasty bomb and only goes to show what tricks a different language can play.

Mum was only saying the other day that she hadn't heard anything from Lill, that's my Great Auntie Lill at the farm; I'm always wanting to go to and never seem to make it.

Things I hear from Mum of Auntie Lill, she seems to be a nice lady and, for some reason, I don't feel shy about having to meet her on my own. It's as though I know her already. I suppose it would make it easier if I went to see her with Mum as she is Mum's friend from a long time ago from school days. But I can't see that happening. If I want to spend a day on the farm, and I'm sure there's loads to do for a whole day, I will just have to make my mind up and set off good and early as I don't know how long its going to take me on the bike, and have some time to spare in case I get lost. But I do know the way as far as Balderton crossing. It's strange how things happen. Just by coincidence, Mary's favourite saying whenever this happens is, 'funny peculiar' or sometimes just 'spooky.'

Mum has had a letter from Lill. Dad, sat in his armchair in a world of his own, pauses from reading as he slowly lowers his newspaper and looking straight at Mum says, "the Reds have re-taken Minsk, taking would you believe it, one hundred thousand German POW's. I just don't know what they will do with them" as though asking a question. Then Mum comes up with, "Lill says they have two at the farm." Mary and I couldn't stop laughing and it soon caught up with Dad. Mary said, "Now that Peter was funny hah hah."

I don't think Mum was quite sure of the funny side and when it quietened down, came out with, "They seem such nice lads and Alf says, hard workers with whatever the job was, always done and looking to do more." Dad's nodding his head without a word spoken as he goes back behind his newspaper, so we gather he agrees with Uncle Alf's views of the Germans, which surprises me. But as it's my turn to make the toast, if I throw a question up it will only delay the toast.

It's going to be either I go to the farm on my own or try and persuade Arthur. I'm sure he would like a day on the farm. I had a word with Arthur about going to the farm for a whole day starting off early and decide a Saturday would be best for Arthur with being in St. Mark's Choir. We managed the early start and getting to Balderton didn't seem as far as we thought. I suppose having been before and as Mum said, we took the road to the left after the crossing. We didn't meet anyone to ask if we were going the right way so we just kept on going and what didn't seem to be too long a time, we came to a house or two and a school. We were in Dodleston.

We got off our bikes by the pub for a rest and to gather our thoughts before looking for the farm. I don't know why or how it happened but looking at each other without saying a word, we knew we had set off from home with nothing to eat or drink and we hadn't any money. A man soon came by on his way to the pub and as he was the only person we'd seen in Dodleston I thought it best to ask the way to the farm. All I could think to tell him was that it was my Uncle Alf's farm. "I think that would be the Johnson's yonder on the left, the farmhouse just before the church." I realised I should have asked Mum their address or just the name of the farm as well as the sandwiches and a drink. After the man had gone Pear Tree Cottage came to mind and I suppose the farm may have just been 'the farm.' Whatever, we found it. We got off our bikes and pushed them across the gravelled yard to the back door and it was while there that I wished Mum had been with us as I knocked on the door.

It was soon opened by a rather thin elderly lady with white hair in a bun. She was wearing a brightly coloured flowered overall and busily wiping her hands on a tea towel while saying, "Yes?" She had a nice friendly smile and a gentle voice. I somehow knew that she wasn't my Auntie Lill so I told her my name was Peter and that I had come to visit my Auntie Lill that I hadn't seen before and that this is my friend Arthur. The lady said, "I'm pleased to meet you Peter - my name is Pat and I will go and get the mistress for you, your Auntie Lill." This was spoken as she held her hand out for me to shake and I couldn't help but notice that her fingers were very bent and she didn't walk too well as she took us into what was a very big kitchen where Arthur and I sat down at a very big table to wait for Auntie Lill. I counted the chairs - there were ten and two had arms which I thought maybe for Auntie Lill and Uncle Alf.

Time seemed longer than it had taken us to get from Balderton; then Auntie Lill came in all of a rush. Pat had found her busy with the hens across home field and of course she had no idea that we were coming to see them. "What a lovely surprise this is and this is the first time I've seen you from being a baby." I didn't know what to say and

Arthur had nothing to say either.

Whilst it was still quiet I just looked at Auntie Lill and she was everything that I had expected a farmer's wife to be. She was a cheerful, round soul with a fresh rosy face and a lot of curly white hair. I'm going to like my Auntie Lill. Though surprised, she seems pleased that we came and we talked and talked while Pat busied about in the kitchen. All this time Arthur had kept quiet and made it quite obvious fidgeting on his chair that he was getting fed up listening.

Still not parted from her tea towel Pat is with us again busy wiping while saying, "These poo'er lads must be well clemmed (starved). What about some treacle sandwiches and buttermilk." We couldn't say anything other than "Yes please!", even though we weren't sure about the buttermilk. It's relieved the problem of having left home without either food or drinks. Thank goodness. We eventually left the farmhouse with Auntie Lill carrying a rather nice woven straw bag that I hoped contained our goodies for the day as by this time I was feeling quite hungry.

Down the narrow garden path through a rickety gate we were on the lane and could see the farm buildings across what Auntie Lill calls the home field. "I don't quite know where we'll meet up with your Uncle Alf, probably in the dairy or the shippons as he likes to see everything clean and ready long before milking.

We met Uncle Alf coming out of the dairy. He looked a real country farmer, mind you when I've seen pictures of farmers they've always been red faced and fat and he was neither. It was the clothes he was wearing - brown boots, leather lace-up knee length gaiters, fawn corduroy breeches and a nice yellowy waistcoat. He stood with us whilst he busily put his arms through the sleeves of what, when on, was a long light brown twill coat. "Almost ready for the ladies now."

Auntie Lill says, "He always calls the cows his ladies."

He had a friendly country way of talking and seemed pleased to see us - he would keep calling me Annie's lad. With coat buttoned up he was rooting through his pockets and produced a packet of Churchman's No. 1 cigarettes. I'd only ever seen Dad's packets of ten before and they were never Churchman's. He hadn't got a lot to say and I felt that he wanted to get on with his work and we were in his way.

"Come on then, follow me, and I'll show you round the farm and maybe meet some of the others idling away the time somewhere out of sight " and off we went, passing buildings that we didn't go in, the pond with ducks on, a few noisy geese and a bull, thankfully behind a locked half door who seemed to be in competition with the geese. Beyond the bull's stable was the shippon and across the yard was the old barn with massive high wooden doors, painted red.

It was only then that I became aware of Uncle Alf having a walking stick as he propped it against the wall before he heaved the door open with both his hands. Maybe farmers have a walking stick, something useful to have with animals around.

It was dark inside the barn and we'd certainly disturbed a few hens - they were clucking and flying all over the place. In the middle was what appeared to be a stack of straw bales covered with a big grubby white sheet. "Would you like to see Ruby, she's been sheeted up for the duration?" Before we could say yes the sheet was off. Ruby was a little two-tone crimson and black Austin Seven, no longer on four wheels but resting on four bales of straw and no petrol. Having had a good look, we helped to cover her up again for the rest of the war.

Uncle Alf points with his stick; "And up them ladders is where we keep the hay and you can go up there and eat your sandwiches. But mind now, no smoking. And afterwards feel free to wander about until milking time." Auntie Lill handed over the bag that I'd taken a liking to and no sooner had they left we were up the ladder.

We sat up in the barn amongst the hay in a nice spot where through an opening in the wall we looked down on the pond with lots of ducks, the orchard and open fields for as far as we could see. Hens strutted about never stopping pecking and all the time listening to pigs grunting away. What a nice place it was to have your sandwiches. We were so hungry and they were lovely. I do like treacle. This was the first time Arthur had had treacle. We ate the lot, but one taste of the buttermilk was more than enough! Neither of us liked it. It was horrible and we had a big pop bottle full. I'm sure Auntie Lill will want me to take the bottle back empty as she seems to make out that buttermilk's a treat so I have to pour it away somewhere without anyone noticing.

We walk round the farm with our bag and the bottle of buttermilk having an explore and I reckon the trough at the pig sty is the place as the pigs, from what Uncle Alf says, are always hungry for anything, so when we're sure there's no one watching, the bottle comes out of the bag, screw cap off and the buttermilk gone down the trough, and by the squealing and grunting of the pigs they have a liking of buttermilk.

We got a bit bored after a while and found some trees to climb, not the fruit trees, trees naturally mixed up in the hawthorn hedge and unfortunately some barbed wire that had been nailed to this tree. Arthur had to slip on the way down and ended up with a nasty cut on his bottom, so we had to go back to the house. Pat patched him up and we had a cup of tea and a scone with jam, both of which Pat had made, and the butter. Uncle Alf's in for his tea and scones as well. I met my two cousins Albert and Peter, and Dell, she's so like her Mum.

Then Uncle Alf's ready for the off; "How's the wounded Arthur? -

fit enough to get the cows in from the top field?" We seemed to walk quite a way along the lanes before we found the padlocked gate to the top field and the cows were all there by the gate waiting for us. Uncle Alf said "they know when it's milking time and know the way back to the farm" - it's just that he had to keep an eye on them to see they don't get into mischief. He seems to use his stick quite a bit just to guide them away from things on the way back. They seem very nosy things when they're on the move; they kept stopping at gates and looking into fields whenever the opportunity, all the way down the lanes on the way back to the farm - just being nosy - they knew perfectly well they weren't home. There was no stopping them once they were at the farm gate.

Uncle Alf had to put some speed on finding his way through the cows to open the shippon doors. Each cow knew exactly where to go and Uncle Alf says "they're creatures of habit." Pat, Albert and Peter were waiting, ready for milking. The Germans, who I hadn't met, had been in the fields all day and had left for the night. It was quite a performance getting the cows in as they had definite thinking on which stalls they should be in. I suppose this was determined by the order they came through the door. Some thought they were going the wrong way and decided to turn round and go against the flow. It was quite chaotic but they eventually got into their usual stalls and settled down to what Uncle Alf calls, "some bran."

Whilst they were chained up ready for milking, I was ready to have a go myself and was shown how to do it by Pat who likes to be known as a 'milk maid' but from what I see of her, she does almost everything and I've only been here a day. I'm sat on my milking stool busy pulling away with both hands at the cow's udder whilst resting the side of my head on the cow's side so as I can reach the cow's udder, which isn't easy, when I become aware of being wet with milk.

It's Albert and Peter a few stalls away who are managing to aim the cow's udders at me with some accuracy to drench me in milk. I find it hard enough to get it in the milking pail that you have to hold between your legs whilst sitting on a three-legged stool in a most uncomfortable situation with a live cow that doesn't seem to like me! All of this they find very amusing, and Uncle Alf does to a point, then it's no longer funny and they get into trouble.

I feel better for having tried; I don't think Arthur wanted to have a go at milking. We didn't see the milking finished and wended our way back to the farmhouse where Auntie Lill met us and thought it was time we made for home as Mum would be getting worried about us. I've no idea what the time was but it seems we should be on our way.

Auntie Lill handed back the bag that I'd become familiar with throughout the day, saying, "Be careful, there's a few eggs in there, some freshly churned butter and a bottle of buttermilk, and next time you come we'll see what we can do about a chicken." I thanked her for the things which seem heavy to have on my handlebars. I couldn't help but think most of the weight's in that bottle of buttermilk and should I ditch it shortly after leaving the farm? I got a hug from Auntie Lill before we left the farm and I can't help but think that Arthur had been left out of today and might not want to come again.

It always seems less time going back home than going away from home. We were tired when we got there and Mum was in the mood for talking of news from her old friend Lill, and for once I was ready for my bed.

Mum was looking very knowingly as I handed the bag over and obviously very surprised by the weight that I'm pleased to get rid of. Her head almost in the bag and then, "It's buttermilk. I can't remember when I last had buttermilk, it must have been at Gran's farm well before the war." Bottle in hand she was off into the back kitchen. I could see the disappointment on Dad's face as Mum came back with only one tumbler full. I was well pleased and I don't think Mary was bothered about having any as I think she caught a whiff from Mum's tumbler full. It took no time at all for Mum to down it. She obviously loves the stuff. To think my thoughts were to ditch it somewhere or other shortly after leaving the farm. I would have been found out in the end, that's for sure. Just as well I struggled home with it, thank goodness.

Dad appears with a tumbler full having been to help himself to the bottle and catching Mary's eye points to his tumbler of buttermilk; then looks at me. We take it the gesture means 'would you like one?' Mary puts both her hands up with a grimace on her face as though she'd already tasted something nasty and I instantly did the same.

None of us had said a word but Dad got the message. I thought I might have got into trouble but I didn't, maybe because I was encouraged by Mary.

Surprisingly, the butter and eggs though gratefully accepted as we have so little, didn't reach the same level of excitement as the buttermilk, and of course the promise of that chicken. Mum looks across seeking my attention, "Now Peter your Auntie Lill is sure to want this nice big bag back next time you go, so don't forget to take it. I was questioned for what seemed hours. Mum wanted to know about Lill, Uncle Alf, the boys and Dell. With Dad it was just the German POW's that I hadn't seen, but with going to bed late I found out all sorts of things about Auntie Lill that I never knew before!

Mum remembers what they did together long ago when they were at school. Most of it seemed to be playing tricks on lads, but I never found out what the tricks were. She just kept on getting into fits of laughter when remembering a boy's name, then saying, "Oh, the things we got up to," then didn't share it with us. They obviously had a lot of fun together.

However, I did pick up in all this going on that poor Auntie Lill could only see from one eye and had something odd about her feet, which were sort of joined up between her toes. I asked if she had been a good swimmer at school. It seemed to go unnoticed and I didn't ask again. I knew Dad was disappointed that I hadn't seen the German POW's to have a talk with. How he thought we would have a talk I can't imagine.

Mum remembers that in the early years of them being at the farm they had financial worries and Lill talked of this with Mum. They both thought a fortune teller could give Lill some idea of what the future may bring. I don't know where they would find one in Chester but find one they did. I can only think that they struck lucky with Pat Collins's annual fair being on the Little Roodee. Mum spoke of the fortune teller as 'the gipsy.' She had quietly listened to Lill's problems whilst holding and looking into her hand. Then she spoke of good times ahead as she was going to be lucky and could see some money coming her way. Then, without having to think about it Lill decided to have a gamble on the Football Pools, and won! Mum didn't know how much, but they continued to live at the farm.

Mum went on to say that some years later the situation repeated itself and she won for the second time - the only times she had filled in a football coupon. Now that really impressed me and I asked Dad about us doing the Pools, which I had heard of before. With no time to think from Dad, there was an instant, "Never!" I went to bed very tired having decided that I wanted to go to the farm again and to do some work.

A couple of nights later I had a word with Dad about going to the, well not so much going but coming back home with what might be in that bag because I was convinced it would grow. Well next time there was going to be a chicken and I'm sure as long as Auntie Lill churned for butter, there was going to be lots more buttermilk. Never mind just the coming home, it wouldn't surprise me if that bag was full of empty pop bottles when I left home for the farm. What the weight would be like on the way back I couldn't possibly manage on the handle bars. "Is it possible Dad that you could think of maybe a saddlebag; then I could fit considerably more in, or you could have a word with Mum about some control on the buttermilk thing?" I didn't get an answer but I think he understands that I have a problem and says he's going to give it some thought. I never quite know what that means. Mary says I could borrow the basket from her bike which I have thought about, but a basket with a cross bar doesn't seem to go. A saddlebag somehow seems right.

Being in the scouts is going well and I'm enjoying it, but there's something not quite right and I don't know what it is. When I first joined I really did feel the odd one out and I think the reason for that was going dressed as a school boy and not as a boy scout, whereas now the only thing I'm short of is the scout hat. The most important thing and the first to get was of course the shirt to sew all your badges on that came about by having done various tasks which Skipper has to approve of. Some badges or things just come by being a scout. On the things side, I've got a couple of tags that hang from my garters that hold my socks up. Only scouts wear them and I don't know why. Two longer tags hanging from my shoulder, one green, one white, the colours of the Eagle Patrol, and then my favourite badge, design-wise, a blue shield with a gold sheaf of corn - the badge of Cheshire.

Other badges you have to earn; my official scout badge, so I'm on the first rung of the ladder. The Skipper's very fond of mentioning the ladder which comes up time, time and again at meetings. It could be that by day he's a painter and decorator. I've a neckerchief in the colours of the 8th Chester Troop held through a very nice platted leather toggle that mostly Mary made - whilst I watched. Being platted I can fiddle my scout lapel badge into it to look that little bit special. Scout-wise I'm well kitted out.

Now I've two very special badges; proficiency badges - and from what I can see you can get dozens of these more than you can fit on the sleeve of your shirt. It's these proficiency badges that I'm not sure about as the two I have, cook and artist, that I'm very proud to have, didn't seem all that difficult to come by.

Going for cook's badge was one Saturday at the Skipper's house, spent in his back garden. There were a few there and I think Arthur must have got his badge that morning. The first thing of course was to lay a camp fire from wood found lying about in hedgerows. We had been told of this at the last scout meeting so I arrived at the Skipper's house with more than enough well dried out wood collected in the Dingle along with a couple of newspapers and a box of matches. When I had been getting all my gear ready for the day I remember Dad just looked, then says, "You, a scout, taking newspaper and matches. Now that's a turn up for the book. It'll be firelighters next or a bottle of paraffin." I didn't know whether he was joking but he did look seriously surprised.

We had some guidance on how to make a camp fire, read some leaflets with diagrams and had laid a fire, but doing this as a practice on the cellar floor isn't the same as in the Skipper's back garden, and putting a match to it. However, all went quite well; some of us had problems mainly with damp wood, filling his back garden with smoke and unfortunately not progressing the cooking, having failed to get a fire going. Mine was going well along with a couple of others and we've placed a few house bricks around our fires to support an iron griddle. Then we wait, keeping the fires going whilst Skipper's back in the house. We're all still in the dark about what we're expected to cook, only Skipper knows and insisted all along on providing the food for us to cook, which Mum thought was very good of him with rationing and all that, and using his pans. I got to thinking of frying - sausages and bacon - I could manage that, but I don't know about an egg. I've never fried an egg - far too precious. I'm good at doing eggs with powdered egg with maybe, if we're lucky, a tin of beans.

The Skipper appears carrying some saucepans. Mine seems to be on the large size compared with the others so my dream of a nice fry up isn't going to be. I ask you - saucepans! "Now lads, I know it's got a bit late in the day having had a few problems.

Nevertheless you're going to cook a breakfast - the scout's favourite breakfast at camp." Then producing from behind his back what looked like a container of oats. Surely it's not going to be porridge. I instantly went off the idea of summer camp.

It's Dad's favourite breakfast but most certainly not mine; I hate the stuff though Dad says it's much nicer with a trickle of golden syrup. From what I see of Dad with his porridge he enjoys more than a trickle whenever he has the opportunity - it has become quite a rare thing on shop shelves.

I've just no idea what to do, can't make porridge, never watched Dad making his. All I can manage at breakfast is toast and this fire for certain will not make toast, not that I think I would get a cook's badge for toast. I thought for certain that my chance of a badge had gone, or maybe I'd get a fire fighter's badge if there was one. I'll just have to have a word with Skipper. He assures me that things have gone well so far and that a little guidance, if accepted, doesn't come amiss.

Well here goes, pan on the griddle, in goes a good mug full of cold water and in no time at all steam's rising and starting to boil. Skipper's busy going between us with his container of oats and it seems that I was too enthusiastic when helping myself and took too much, as my mixture became a bit cloddish to stir.

Guidance from Skipper was, "to get a happy consistency between thick and thin, too thick, then add a drop of water; too thin then add a few more oats until you get it right," - sounds simple enough. I seemed to add water then oats so many times before I got a nod from Skipper after a tasting. Just as well - I'd been given the biggest pan as I ended up having enough porridge to feed the troop, much to the amusement of the lads and Skipper.

Skipper quietened us down, "Now the good news - you are all capable of making porridge at camp, especially Peter, but before I can award your proficiency badges for cook I want to see the pans emptied before we pack up for the day," as he hands out pudding spoons. How I hate porridge - never expected having to eat it! In fairness to them all I was helped and Skipper had a fair whack of it. Looking back on the day I'm sure I was set up by Skipper and a few others from the start and that badges come along with having a good laugh providing sometimes you don't mind being the clown. I'd got my badge but I wasn't at all well leaving the Skipper's house.

The other one I have came easier as I wasn't even trying to get it - it just came about without me thinking. From the first night in the cellar where we met I decided to keep a diary. I would keep it in a book the same as I had at school for nature study. It was the only book

I liked as it wasn't all lined paper, every other page being unlined rough cartridge paper which provided me with the opportunity to draw and colour as well as to write. So I just kept an illustrated diary of scout nights in the cellar, other activities and some weekends in the countryside. This came to the Skipper's notice from our patrol leader and I came by my artist's badge.

Dad's home from work and 'cock-a-hoop,' an expression of Mary's when things are going well, and from how Dad's going on it's more than going well. He's excited.

"You just won't believe it Annie, the military hierarchy! One of his own Generals has had a go at him; I knew it would happen sooner or later, but never by blowing him up." Dad eventually calms down and we all listen carefully to what he thought to be the better option, which was poisoning.

All the excitement seemed long gone, then we get the rest of the story, and as we thought Hitler was the one they'd had a go at but it had all gone wrong - he hadn't been killed by being blown up at all. It would appear that he had summoned all his Generals and Senior Staff Officers up for a meeting and a few of them who were a bit fed up with the war, as they were now loosing, had plotted against him, with one officer having taken in a bomb concealed in his document case with the intention of killing Hitler and I suppose a few others at the same time. However, it hadn't gone to plan as Hitler had already left the meeting when the timing device exploded the bomb. Whether others had been killed Dad doesn't know but thinks Hitler must be well scared and it's just a matter of time before someone else has a go at him.

Maybe Dad's thinking the better option of poisoning would have worked but then Mary and I think a man like Hitler would have a taster to try out all his food before he eats it and Dad thinks we could be right. One thing for sure we won't be seeing any photographs of this in Picture Post - just words in a newspaper which isn't quite the same.

Skipper's mentioned church parade more than a few times at scout meetings. He obviously wants a good turnout so in the end I agreed to go Sunday morning. I'm sure I mentioned to Mum and Dad about scouts being a church troop but I never mentioned anything of church parades. I can't say that I'm looking forward to it and don't know when the next one is. Let's hope maybe two or three months. I'm sort of wishing Arthur had found a troop without church connections. Come to think of it Arthur's been my best pal for as long as I can remember and I've never thought of him being in any way religious, but then he's a choir boy at St. Mark's Church in Saltney, but from all accounts he's thinking of packing it up. I sometimes go with him for company and sit on the back row out of the way.

I usually take something to do and the thing I do at present is different coloured electrical wiring that some of us make up into ladies bracelets. The problem is managing to find an Electrician willing to part with leftovers from jobs, so when I do, it finds its way into St. Mark's and other such places. When I've a few made up I usually persuade Mary to take them into the Exchange to sell to her friends and it never fails - they seem to love them.

I just don't know whether church parades, church or chapel or what, but I'm sure it's going to get complicated and probably ending up in trouble with Dad; best to put it on one side and concentrate on what badge to go for next. I just don't know; knots seem to be the thing with scouts and I just can't reason why, as I never come across a piece of rope or string that's needed joining together but this we do most meetings.

Other than doing up my shoe laces and wrapping parcels when Dad had the shop, which I always managed to do, so why all these other complicated knots with names I can't remember and will never have a need for? Whatever the reason it's something to do to pass the time and so we all have a length of cord to stuff into our trouser pockets so as we can practice on the way home or whenever we're at a loose end with nothing to do. One of the first things Skipper greets us with at meetings is, "How's your knots?"

Dad noticed this one night when taking a break from reading his newspaper. I was trying to fathom out my way round a knot. He really surprised me by taking my length of cord and doing all sorts of knots, quite different to anything we do at scouts, and splicing - that we never do; I was really impressed. Skipper hadn't ever mentioned splicing this is going to be another badge for sure.

This was one of the few times that Dad and I talked for what seems hours - of when Dad was in the Field Artillery in charge of horses on the gun carriages in the last War (1914-18) and before he went into the Army, he knew nothing about horses, of leather harnesses or ropes. "Rope was always there to replace the leather harnessing for when things went wrong and couldn't be repaired in the field, and you could always do something with a rope. Many a time I've got us out of a mess by splicing a length of rope together."

Some evenings we would spend time together with my well used piece of rope, now getting a bit grubby and I'm told 'not up to army standards.' I think, other than a few words in passing, this has been the only time when Dad has talked with me about the last war, his war, and his army pals.

There were obviously interesting and happy times for Dad; then he would dwell too long on the bad, the sad times, go quiet and shed a tear or two before a sniff and a good loud blow of his nose with the white handkerchief which he always kept neatly tucked up the left sleeve of his jacket. I always thought it best not to ask Dad anything about the last war; somehow I knew it would upset him. As far as I can remember the only time he has talked of it was with the soldiers when they were billeted with us. Exchanging experiences which I think they enjoyed. Enjoyed somehow sounds out of place when this war has altered our way of life from day one, if not before.

Every day something different to cope with, having to make changes especially for Mum and Dad, and has been for such a long time, so much of it that you wouldn't think room for anything but doom and gloom, but it's not all bad and sad. We have enjoyable times a bit of a laugh and get on best we can, making the best of it. All things considered I'm quite enjoying the war; all talking away and thinking on the light side of life, what they call 'morale boosting' on the wireless. Dad comes out with, "It's not quite all swings and roundabouts you know - we've still got a long way to go."

The morning of the church parade and as always wherever we go we get there much too early, all because we're scared of being late, and more so on church parade. Time seems to go slow on purpose when you're waiting. Then, thank heaven, the odd one or two file in; then at long last the rest arrive and we've all gathered around the back of the church in a bit of a rabble. Skipper shows his presence and soon gets us into shape, formed up in a line, two abreast, "made to measure," he calls it, to fit down the aisle, flag bearers to the front.

I was a bit worried as we hadn't had a rehearsal. Don't know about Arthur, but the others seemed to know what to do - I think they'd done it all before; this was my first. All in all, together as a troop, I think we looked pretty good going into church and felt proud of being a scout. It went down well escorting the flag to the altar. I had already decided not to take my 'bracelet makings' into church, which was just as well as we were nowhere near the back row.

Time passed fairly quickly and it wasn't long before we were out of church, the flag once again stowed away in the cellar until the next parade and we were on the way home after a 'thank you' from the Skipper. It was good really and we decided not to get the bus. I had worried for long enough about what Dad's reaction would be after all things, a church parade. I still don't know what religion our troop belongs and Dad doesn't seem to be at all bothered, which I just can't understand.

I suppose his views on things have changed over the years since he's been at the aircraft factory. The big change, although I was too young to realise it at the time, was giving up his Sunday lay preaching; this he would do most Sundays travelling to outlying country places by Crosville bus from Delamere Street. He was usually away for the day.

Over the years of lay preaching he had found a few like-kind people in the congregation, and they would invite him into their homes. He never went without his Sunday dinner and might well have gone into an afternoon tea. Because of this war all that is long passed. It's now into store management and a Union official. He's well thought of, dedicated to the Union and the workers as he was to his religion and congregation. I never thought his way of life would change this way but then I suppose neither did he.

When Dad's listening to the wireless or reading his paper, he'd come out with the odd word or two, like 'Monty' or 'General Somebody or other' usually American, sometimes Russian and we're not really listening, then one slips by that I'd not heard of before, so I interrupt his listening as he leans across from his chair to turn the news off. Looking at me I get a 'now then Peter.' It's nearly always serious when I get a 'now then' and what he really means is for me to listen and to pay attention, or I've done something wrong.

"This man's name is de Gaulle, General de Gaulle and he's just led a triumphant victory parade through the streets of Paris. He came over here with what was left of his defeated French army and our lads at the time of Dunkirk; maybe on one of Bithell's pleasure boats for all I know. We then gave him the grand title of 'Leader of the Free French' and has had a nice cushy time of it all through the war. I don't think for one minute that he went over with our lads on D-Day or even took part in the liberation of Paris. No room for the man and from what I hear of Churchill and his Generals, neither have they." I just knew it when I got the 'now then', but give Dad his due he always gives me a pause to get my thoughts together which is something that Mum never does but then I never get a 'now then' from Mum.

When I came in from school Mum was having her usual pot of tea, what number cup she was on I don't know. I'm home well before Mary so she talks with me of a lady by the name of Ciss, who she tells me is my Auntie Ciss. Now this is where I get confused with some of my so called aunties, as I then find out most times from Dad or Granddad that they're not aunties at all but old school friends of Mum's like Auntie Abley, and I suppose in a way like Auntie Lill, but then she put it right by marrying my Uncle Alf; so I'm in doubt about this lady Ciss.

I now know that she lives in Rosset which is a ride on the Crosville bus. She had a boy, Fred, maybe Cousin Fred, and I think his age must be about the same as mine. I suspect soon we will be on the Wrexham bus on our way to Rosset. I wasn't wrong, and we were on our way; just Mum and me. Mary and Dad thought better of it and I didn't really want to go either. I think their names are Roberts, so they will be on Granddad's side of the family, but I can't remember Granddad ever saying anything about having a relative living in Rosset. Come to think of it Granddad never talks of family, it's always Gran and I know all of them.

We left the bus and with the help of some passers-by and it wasn't long before Mum was knocking on the Roberts's front door. I got a nudge from Mum, "Peter, this lady is your Auntie Ciss;" she did look a bit like Mum. We sat down in the front room whilst Auntie Ciss made a pot of tea. Everywhere we go, whatever the time of day, there's always a cup of tea; you don't have to be thirsty, it just comes about. Nothing much happened; Mum and Auntie Ciss just talked.

I got on quite well with Fred and his Dad who went on and on about his motor bike - then suggesting that we go down to his shed. Inside there was a white dust sheet in the shape of a motor bike, just like Uncle Alf's 'Ruby' at the farm, resting for the duration of the war all for the want of some petrol. When I go out with the lads for the day on our bikes we don't see many cars - if any at all. I just can't imagine what it'll be like when its dust sheets away, and petrol to buy.

The wireless news is the Allies are well into Belgium and have liberated Brussels. I remember all of these places on Granddad's posh wireless - Paris, Rome now Brussels and the final one I suppose will be Berlin. The Army must use one heck of a lot of petrol getting to all these places and the combined services use - I just can't imagine.

How it gets to them or where it comes from I don't know. Dad says, "It's all to do with pipes and transport to the front line - is what wars are all about and the longer the war goes on the tighter it gets for Jerry. Now the end can't be far off". It's only recently that Dad's been calling Germans 'Jerry's.' I was used to 'Nazis' and I'd heard of

'Krauts' but 'Jerry's' I didn't know who he was talking about.

Since our visit to see Auntie Ciss which I told Granddad all about, he seems to know quite a bit about Fred's Dad and tells me, "He was an army dispatch rider in the last war and was badly wounded. The outcome was that he now has a metal plate in his head and doesn't mind having it tapped on; sort of amuses him. I remember he was awarded a medal for bravery - could have been the VC".

Some weeks later I went with Mum to see her friend Ciss again. Fred's Dad was at home and when I thought the time was right, when we were in his shed, I mentioned my conversation with Granddad. He gave me a smile while tapping his head with his knuckles to the sound of a tin can. I didn't know really what to do and we quietly left the shed.

I didn't say a word about it to Mum but when I got home I couldn't help but tell Dad, who thought for a while, then asked if at the time we were in his shed. "Yes," I replied. Then I can see from Dad's expression that he's going to be very positive about it all. "Without you seeing, Peter, he probably tapped the empty petrol tank on his motor bike with his free hand." Dad sort of ruined this for me, but I still like to think that Fred's Dad had won the VC. I'm still not sure of their name being Roberts or if they are related to Granddad.

Well surprise at school! We are all off to the Odeon to see a film - Henry V - it's in Technicolor and what's more it's free! All the schools in Chester are going to see it and for us it's an afternoon showing. I would have liked to go at night when it's dark but I suppose we have to go in the afternoon school time. We haven't done anything about Henry V at school so it will be new even if it's a long time ago, if you know what I mean.

We were all on the bus at first afternoon lesson time and that wasn't free. Soon off at Bridge Street and on our way to the Odeon. The Market Square was full of school kids from all over Chester, all wearing what was left of their school uniforms which have become quite depleted through the war and we've grown out of them. We just seem to have cloth school badges now that can be sewn on whatever you wear.

Most of us have our gas masks that have gone a bit lax over the last few years. Some of us have our school satchels which have lasted well as they are made of leather and I suppose all in all we look a rather tacky lot of kids - that reminds me of the evacuees from Liverpool in the early forties; thankfully it's not quite the same; the difference being we are a happy lot of kids compared with the evacuees. Some of the kids had goodies to eat in the Odeon which I hadn't thought of taking, not that I had any goodies to take and Mum hadn't thought about it. We eventually got in, and boy was it noisy. The Manager kept coming on stage trying to establish some order all to no avail; just like Saturday mornings - so he decided to show the film, I suppose in the hope that we would quieten down, not that I'd done anything to let the side down, I just wanted to see a free film and a change from cowboys and Indians and Flash Gordon.

Teachers were with all the schools and seemed to be in a completely helpless situation to control a full house at the Odeon. I'd heard of William Shakespeare having done a bit at school but knew nothing of Laurence Olivier who's taking the part of Henry V. I sit next to Betty Ashton who filled me in about Laurence Olivier being a very famous stage actor on any of Shakespeare's plays. We were having a good chat about him and how they had managed to make the film while the war was on what with conscription and everything. We thought they may have had special leave from the Army or maybe Laurence Olivier could be a conscientious objector. Tongue in cheek and having a bit of a giggle really when Mrs. Hill one of the teachers with us overheard and looking straight at me, with a finger to her lips, I got a "Shush." She didn't look pleased.

I didn't really understand the film and lost interest as most of the others had; quiet mutterings were on the increase throughout the cinema. But I did enjoy the battle scenes and some of the characters, especially the Welsh knight with a funny eye. I didn't rate Henry V. Mrs. Hill told me that the film was made to present to the nation to lift our morale in the time of war. I just couldn't see the connection - it was hundreds of years ago we were fighting the French with bows and arrows - our secret weapon that the French just couldn't cope with.

The Odeon was soon left empty as was the Market Square as we found our way to various bus stops and on our way back to school. I had time to think about the film we had seen. I would have preferred to see a selection of up-to-date simple black and white newsreels. We are now on the winning side in this war from what we hear on the wireless, our morale has already been boosted; seeing a progression of newsreels would have confirmed this. The wireless is great but it can't compare with pictures - these we see in Picture Post - but then they're stills and don't compare with what the Americans call 'movies'; 'movies' - a name that Dad can't abide.

We shared our views on the film in the upstairs of the West View bus, much to the amusement of the other passengers, and decided that whilst battling with the French the countryside had looked pretty good - then I suppose it was intended to look like France, not that I have any idea what the countryside looks like in France. They most definitely couldn't have filmed it in France with D-Day and all going on. Wales maybe or here in England, but then there's too many give-

203

aways here of a war going on. It got a bit noisy and it wasn't long before we heard the voice of Mrs. Hill from the back of the bus. "Peter! I know this is going to get me into further explanations, but, in answer to your questioning, it was filmed in Ireland. Now let it rest until next we have history." Why is it always me to be picked out? It was off the bus and straight home.

Mary's concerned about Eric as he's gone on a crash course down to London for a pre-Royal Signals Mechanic and he's getting buzz-bombed very day with the first of the area around St. Paul's Cathedral. They just drop wherever they may be when the fuel runs out, so selective bombing is a thing of the past - not that the Germans kept to the agreement when they flattened Coventry Cathedral.

Dad says that now that aircraft bombing raids as far as Jerry's concerned, would appear to be over, that the government in their wisdom are going to replace blackout with 'dim-out,' and no one knows what the difference will be, so we shall just have to wait and see what the difference is when it happens. We don't do anything and we stay with the blackout. Dad's fond of coming out with things like this; then before we can talk about it he hides behind his newspaper again.

If we'd done anything wrong in the weeks that followed the Warden would have been blowing his whistle and shouting about the place. I think we still have the ARP, the sirens and everything else to do with air raids. We shall just have to see.

We still don't hear any news of Mussolini but did I get a lovely surprise the other night when Dad came home. No sooner had he got settled in than he said to me, "Peter, I have something you have waited for, for so long." I couldn't believe it - it was a saddlebag for my bike, an absolutely super saddlebag; green canvas with brown leather edging and straps. It has side pouches and straps on top to take a rolled-up oilskin cape, not that I have an oilskin cape, but I may have one day. It's so big I could get everything in it for a whole day out. I just can't thank Dad enough. It's just fantastic. "It's no thanks to me Peter. I just happened to mention it to one of the men at work that you really enjoyed your bike and would have liked a saddlebag, and as it happened he took it unto himself to make you one. I travel to work with him every day. He lives down Mount Pleasant close by one of your pals, John Thompson."

I think Dad thinks that I should know him but I don't. I can't understand how this friend of Dad's can design, pattern and sew up such a super saddlebag when every day he's building Wellington aircraft bombers. Dad then comes out with, "Ah well - you see before the war, as you know Peter, we all did very different things and we have had to change and one day, hopefully soon, it may well return, who knows. So now, like me, he is working on aircraft. Before the war he was employed as a master craftsman at Shuttleworth's in Bridge Street making all sorts of leather goods, ladies handbags, purses, wallets, briefcases, suitcases and travel goods for the aristocracy, and I'm told for the Duke of Westminster!" Wow! And this man has made me a saddlebag!

Dad points a wriggling finger at me whilst saying, "Now you have a saddlebag - next time you take it to go to Dodleston to see your Auntie Lill, let's have no complaining about bringing back buttermilk for your Mother." I didn't know the man's name, so I wrote the man a 'thank you' letter addressed to Mr. Shuttleworth and gave it to Dad.

I seldom catch on to songs and can't stand Gracie Fields; Vera Lynn's alright, but the other day I did hear a song on the wireless I really liked and I've asked Mary if she knows all the words. I manage a few lines then I'm lost. I don't think Mary's going to be able to help with this one as she's a through- and- through Glen Miller fan. Mum and Mary get fed up with it and don't mind saying so; then Dad joins in, "This is so monotonous Peter." I don't know about monotonous but from his tone of voice and the look he gave me, I gave up on "Don't Fence Me In".

Days go by and some girls come up to The Green from Saltney. We just talk and generally just fool about, you know, like you do. One of them, Ann Rimmer, lives near Nash's corner shop just down the road from the Park Cinema. Ann knows all about what she calls 'hit songs.' I didn't know there was such a thing but she tells me, "The singer is Bing Crosby backed by the Andrews Sisters." I'd not heard of them before but I will remember the Andrews sisters; the same as on the tins of liver salts in our bathroom cabinet.

I don't know about Bing Crosby but Ann's offered to write all the words down for me, then I will know all the words and won't annoy Mum, Dad and Mary. I wonder if Bing Crosby is a cowboy. I think Ann's friend was Beryl O'Hara - she seems a nice girl.

Mum's had news from the farm and puts it to me that Auntie Lill wonders if we (that's me and Arthur) would like to go down for the day to help with the harvest. I know I would, but I'm not so sure about Arthur so I'm off to ask when Mum stops me. "Now think on Peter before you go chasing off to see Arthur, it's going to be an early start for a long day in the fields and for the first time for both of you, some hard work. It didn't take long for Arthur to make his mind up so I'm going on my own; something to look forward to.

Come the weekend, it's going to be a nice sunny day according to Dad, a good day for getting the corn in. I get there very early, much to the surprise of Auntie Lill who seems to be on her own in the kitchen.

She glances up at the clock as though she can't believe the time. "You are early - your cousin hasn't left yet on his milk round. Well I suppose you'd be best making your way down to the yard. They'll all be around the dairy somewhere with your Uncle Alf. He likes to see them off then he can get on with his day."

I remembered the way from the last time I came and I could soon see the milk van alongside the dairy, both doors open and well stacked with crates of milk. I found Albert and Pat in the dairy. We talked for a while and I could hear Uncle Alf - he's not far away. "Mornin Annie's lad (looking around); come on your own then, no Arthur? It's about time you were off with the milk." I don't think Auntie Lill noticed that Arthur wasn't with me as she was so surprised on seeing me so early. I don't think much surprises Uncle Alf. From the first time I met him he seemed in control of everything; he knew what had to be done and got on with it and expected others to do the same - always having to chase people to see how they were getting on.

It seems Uncle Alf's in a talkative mood today. "You can help me this morning; we might just get the last cut out of the clover field while Albert gets back from Chester, then we can put our mind to the afternoon. Likes talking with the ladies does Albert; that's what delays him. In the meantime a nice little job for you - have a good look in the hay loft, the Dutch barn - and you might find a few eggs to take back to Pat. Most likely you'll find her in the dairy. This'll keep you busy while I get along and harness the Bossey up for mowing. Now think on, careful where you put your feet." And without a goodbye, Uncle Alf was off.

Whilst looking around the Dutch barn amongst the bales of straw I found a few eggs and some more in the hay loft that I managed to knot up in my handkerchief to take back to Pat. She seemed pleased about the eggs and tells me they have so much to do on the farm from morn till night and there's just not enough hours in the day to be looking around for a few eggs. I liked being with Pat and we talked of the farm and things. I know that I'd stayed too long talking with Pat when I heard Uncle Alf shouting for me. I just know there can't be two Annie's lads!

I was met by Uncle Alf holding a rather restless big brown horse all harnessed up. I assumed it to be 'the Bossey.' He's enough to have to cope with so without saying anything I just follow into one of the barns and there's the mowing machine just next to Ruby still under her dustsheet. The Bossey shafted up and we're on our way to the clover field. I was surprised to find the clover field so close to the farm just on the other side of the Dutch barn where I'd found most of the eggs.

Uncle Alf sits himself down on a bale of straw whilst he fingers through pockets and producing a box of matches and a packet of cigarettes; Churchman's No.1. I remember from the last time. He enjoys a smoke but I thought not the thing to be doing when sat in a barn full of dry straw, but best not to say anything. Looks like we're not in a hurry to get on and I felt I had to say something, so I talk about fields on the farm, how many and what you do with them. "Well then let's see; there's the pastures, standing grass for hay, some we bale; fields for grain and our clover field. Not what you'd call a big farm. Enough to keep us busy along with the orchard and a few hens that your Auntie Lill looks after." "Yes Uncle Alf I think I know what goes on with these fields but not the clover field. I've never ever heard of a clover field. I've seen a few bits of clover in fields amongst the grass and Dad complains about it in the lawn as though it's a weed. But you grow a whole field full." I can see he's amused. "You don't know of one Peter because this one might be the only one. It's very special is clover and I'll show you for why when we get it up in the silo. Now we've got to shape up with the mowing and raking." It looks like I'm on the rake and it's a big wooden one.

I don't think Uncle Alf realised when he was saying it. It seems I'm not Annie's lad any more and I prefer it. The mowing was finished. I'd been raking all the time and there was still quite a bit to do. Uncle Alf was aware of the time as he's got a gold pocket watch and chain. He thinks it's about time we made our way back to the house for a bite to eat.

I think the house is called 'Pear Tree Cottage' and it would sound much nicer than saying, 'the house,' but a bit of a mouthful, so I can understand Uncle Alf saying 'the house' and 'the farm.' It was then that I noticed I had blisters on my hands as that bit of finishing off in the clover field was about as much grass as they get off The Green at home.

Pat and Auntie Lill were busying about in the kitchen; the big table laid, lots of bread, butter and cheese, a basket of apples; then Pat comes round with a steaming bowl of soup with a, "there young man; tuck in, all made on the farm apart from the apples and them's grown." She seems a happy lady.

Albert comes in late and gets teased about his ladies at the Barracks. He takes it all in good part; I suppose he's heard it all so many times before. I can't help thinking there's a lot of food for us. Then Pat, looking at me, reads my thoughts. "They don't all come in at the same time - its dribs and drabs whenever they think on." Uncle Alf had an enormous mug of tea and a second fill up whilst he has a smoke. He does seem to smoke a lot. He then reminds Pat that we'll be in the clover field till milking and we will have to be fixing this lad up with a few things before he leaves.

We have a tour of the farm - I suppose Uncle Alf keeping his eye on things - and it gives me a break from raking. We eventually get to the clover field to find Albert already there with a horse and cart and a helper at the far end of the field who seems to have taken over the raking where I left off. Uncle Alf doesn't seem to be bothered about that, then, "One of our German POW's" - the war's over for them - they know they're in safe hands and enjoy being on the farm. Hard workers not like the Italians we had a time ago. One of them wants to stay when it's all over as he thinks there won't be much left in Germany to go back to."

Uncle Alf took me across the field and he talked with the German telling him who I was, that my name was Peter. He was a quiet tall man, very brown with fair hair and wore brown trousers with round patches, some of different colours. His shirt didn't match - it was much the same as Uncle Alf's. There didn't seem anyone with him other than Albert. No armed guard. Why I don't know but I didn't feel at risk. He looks down at me and smiling holds out his hand, "Hello Peter." We shake hands. He seems pleased to meet me and a pleasant enough man. I never thought that one day I would shake hands with a German soldier. It had left me confused. I'd heard and seen so much to hate Germans for such a long time. I just can't believe what I've done and what will they say when I get home!

They soon had the last of the clover carted away and I can't help but think that they made more of an impression in that clover field than we had in the morning. We made our way following the cart to what Uncle Alf calls the silo, a tall round building made of concrete slabs. Sort of straight bits made in the round. Is it called a hexigan?

While Albert and the German sort things out; I honestly don't know his name and never asked because I don't know if he would understand my asking. He knows mine and I think it's fantastic that he manages to talk with us.

I was quite happy just watching whilst Albert climbed his way up the ladder that he's placed on the silo, then disappeared inside. Uncle Alf mumbled something about Hans throwing up on the end of a pikel. I wonder if his name is Hans as Dad and Granddad now seem to think that all Germans have the name of Fritz. I was aware that Uncle Alf thought I wasn't paying attention by the way he started speaking to me. Dad does the same. "Well now Peter, this is where you get the answer to the question of the clover field. The clover is special but it's also to do with what we do with it. Like most jobs the work gets easier as it goes on and this job's almost finished; a couple of cart loads will see it full.

This is how it goes - we put in a layer of about four foot of clover spread out and well trodden, then a good dosing down with 'watta' and cow treacle and so on - that's Albert's job inside and it can get a bit warm and sticky, best done in the evening. Then it's capped off to keep out the weather whilst it all sweats and part ferments into a very desirable sweet fodder that 'the ladies' love; keeps them well over the winter, and from what Pat tells us it's not only the ladies - you and Arthur can put a few treacle sandwiches down along with the buttermilk." If only he knew! This made me think again.

First the shaking hands thing, then Pat making us sandwiches of treacle intended only for cows - crude molasses or cow treacle. I thought it was the Tate and Lyle treacle we used to have at home. That's maybe why Arthur didn't want to come - was it perhaps he wasn't too well after the treacle.

Uncle Alf thinks that if I stay for milking it's going to be too long a day and its best that I make my way back to the house. I take it that's a must. On the way back to the house I find Auntie Lill in the orchard surrounded by a few boxes and baskets of fruit, apples and plums as far as I can see, and she's looking at bit hot and bothered. It has been a hot day so I help her with the picking for an hour or so before taking what we could carry back to the house. It meant leaving some boxes to be picked up later and taken to the dairy for washing. Auntie Lill says, "They'll all come together by morning ready for Albert to take out on his round.

Auntie Lill and Pat got about busying together in the kitchen and I could see a few things on the sideboard that they call 'a dresser,' that I think might be for me to take home and if so it's going to more than fill my new saddlebag. I can hear Pat talking with Auntie Lill, "What about something to drink?" My thinking was it's going to be buttermilk and maybe a treacle sandwich.

They'd both come in from working and were nowhere near ready for tea. Pat had already said that Peter would be back very late with a couple of the men as they'd had trouble with the tractor in the morning from what Uncle Alf said. I think they were getting the corn in, in what field I can't remember, and something about next time they could be threshing and baling. I'm beginning to think that running a farm is much more difficult than managing a shop and in the shop situation you are inside, shutting out all the bad weather. But then Dad hasn't a shop anymore, but I can't see me working on a farm.

I was given a warm buttered scone that Pat had baked and a mug of tea which I wouldn't get in a shop!

I ended up with a full saddlebag; so full that the straps were on the last hole and more bags on the handlebars than before. This was ridiculous! Mind you I have got more than expected and some hand-me-downs of Cousin Peter's that could come in useful but I'm not so sure. A shirt that I could wear for football, dark blue and green with a white collar, so I think it's a rugby shirt, and a pair of white canvas cricket boots. The way we play cricket on the tip, none of us have anything to wear to do with cricket, so I would look a bit silly. Buttermilk I have, but as far as I can see, missing out on a chicken, but then it isn't Christmas and from what Uncle Alf has hinted, he expects me up again whilst there's still work to be done on the harvest. I might one day get to help Albert on his milk round. He might even pick me up at home then I would miss out on the farm as he'd drop me off at home before going back to Dodleston. Thinking about it, it gets a bit complicated - maybe not a good idea.

Uncle Alf has explained about the threshing, baling and the giant steam engine that belt-drives it all. It's not machinery they have at the farm. I've seen the odd lorry or two driven by steam and of course railway engines. Dad says, "They don't look unlike steam rollers we see when they're repairing the roads. Steam engines just have different wheels with solid rubber tyres so as they can get out onto the road and travel from farm to farm doing contract work. It wouldn't be viable for your Uncle Alf to own that sort of machinery. Always well painted and decorative, the drivers take a pride in their steam engines. It's the same with the bargees on the canal and the gypsies. You'll have to get yourself off. It'll be a busy time and you'll just have to see how it goes. I can't see you throwing bales of straw about but seeing all that machinery on the go will be quite something and I'm sure your Uncle Alf will find you a job or two to keep you occupied."

I am going to go. I do really like being on the farm; it's the going and the coming back on my own that I don't like. Dad understands and has a name for it - a lonesome road - and it is, I never see anyone until I get to Dodleston. The same on the way back. Then Dad goes on again, "I don't know why I'm telling you all about steam engines give or take the odd thing or two when they're identical steam engines that you've seen at Patsy Collins' Annual Fair on the Little Roodee. Dozens of them - they tow everything to do with the Fair all over the country and when parked up work all the rides and generate electricity; hundreds of lights everywhere. That's another difference you won't see fairy lights in your Uncle Alf's baling yard. The Fair will be back with the races when it's all over.

And I suppose it will. So many things you miss when there's a War. I don't remember there being races - for me it was just the Fair, the organ playing that never stopped, the laughing and screams of the girls all having fun. It was a very noisy place and you just had to shout to be heard. Oh! The candy floss and brandy snaps; and I suppose toffee apples were OK but didn't compare with the rides. The Waltzer was best but pennies soon went - as did the ride. Sadly one of my Uncle Roy's pals fell from the top of the big wheel and died in hospital. I think they were trying to get some excitement out of it as it stopped when they were at the top. It was Gran that told me.

So many things I miss. I suppose it's more or less everything, but surprisingly everyone gets used to it. We hadn't an alternative. I think what I really missed the most was light and after that it's when Dad had the shop. I loved being at the shop and Dad always brought home sweets on a Friday night from Noblett's sweet shop. Sugared almonds for Mum; if he couldn't get them it was chocolate covered Brazil nuts and Callard & Bowsers butterscotch for Mary and me. Each double piece was individually wrapped in silver paper - I always sucked mine and Mary crunched! We always shared with Dad - he had a sweet tooth.

My favourite at the Fair, after I'd had my candy floss was the 'wall of death' where a couple of men on motorbikes raced up the inside of a wooden vertical tower which creaked like mad while we all stood round the top as they rode up; it was scary! Then it was the small circus and the strongman who wore a leopard skin and sandals and apart from lifting an elephant, he hammered big nails through a thick wooden plank with his bare hands wrapped in a bit of cloth. When the war came I don't know what happened to the Fair, the circus or the strongman. I can only guess that he volunteered for the commandos.

Everything went well with all that was in my saddlebag. Mary and I enjoyed the fruit, especially the plums, leaving the bottled stuff to Mum and Dad. There was no mention of a chicken but Mum said something about remembering a walnut tree. I'd never ever thought of a walnut tree growing in England. It was then that I thought of shaking hands with a German POW and spoke of it with Dad. Mum and Mary didn't say a word, then Dad broke the silence and I thought, 'this is where I could be in trouble.' To my surprise I wasn't. Dad says, "Your German soldier knows that for him the war is over and shaking the hand of the enemy is a relief. I did it so many times with Germans in the last war. It's a good sign - the end hasn't happened yet for us but it's not far away and when it does you will remember it for the rest of your life." I hope I see him when I next go up for the baling.

When we, the lads from Northway and Park Road West, get together with the lads from Mount Pleasant and not forgetting Glan Aber Park, there's about eight of us, enough to have a good kick around on what the lads from Mount Pleasant call the back field. It's always the tip to me, but it's flat, no trees to get in the way and a place where we can put our coats down for goal posts. A proper inflatable full size football has appeared, from where I don't know but it does seem big after a tennis ball! It takes some shifting when you kick it.

I've been given a pair of black shorts, what I think is a rugby shirt and a pair of old cricket boots. Having them on will save my shoes but I'm short of shin pads, so I decided to make my own. I know what shin pads look like as I've seen them in Hacks' sports shop in the Arcade. Something hard and vertically ribbed on the front to take the kicks, backed with something soft against your shin. Simple really, bearing in mind that they couldn't be too big or bulky as they had to be stuffed down your socks, and I hadn't got any football socks – then maybe a Christmas present.

I find some old garden canes in the coal house which never made it as an air raid shelter. These I cut up into short lengths and find an old pair of corduroy trousers to cut up. I sew a couple of pieces together with a backing of brown felt carpet underlay. This provides pockets for me to shove in the canes. When it was all fastened together they didn't quite look the same as the ones I'd seen in Hack's but no one else would see them stuffed down my socks. They served the purpose, took the knocks, but after a while the rough felt carpet underlay made my legs feel very, very itchy. Some of the lads used to stuff a folded comic or 'Boy's Own' down their socks. My own homemade ones did work, I just hadn't got the right materials and Mum wouldn't let me use her Singer sewing machine. What a mess we must have looked on the back field but what enjoyment we had.

Cousin Peter's old canvas cricket boots - I did manage to find in the shoe box some brown leather dye that didn't work too well as they turned out on the patchy side and rather bright. I didn't get into trouble going home with shoes covered in mud but can't help thinking how great it must be when you play for a team and have all the proper kit and a pitch all marked out with goal posts and nets; and Brown's field in Curzon Park has a pavilion, or is it now the field belonging to the Rustproof Metal Window Company?

The war goes on and there's good news and thankfully it's all going our way. Summer seems to be fading and has a feeling of 'back-end' not really autumnal. The next thing to look forward to would have been Bonfire Night and that will come and go without really knowing when it was or should I say when it should have been. No bonfire, no fireworks. Not allowed - not even an Adolf Hitler for a Guy and I don't know why, because we don't have blackout any more - it's dim-out.

This is all looking forward and it's still summer, well late summer, and Mum asks me if I would like to go and spend a few days with the Peacock's in Weaste. I don't have a problem in finding the answer. No! I think Dad and Mary have been asked and I can't see either of them being too keen to go. Why is it always left with me? I really don't want to go. Then Mum mentions that Uncle Eddie has said something about a scout shop in Manchester just a short bus ride from where they live. I'd sooner stay at home with Dad and Mary and do without the hat, but it's looking like a few days with the Peacock's.

Getting there was fairly dreary; bus and train, a change, a wait and a bus again before at last finding where they lived - in the rain. I am not interested enough to know the name of the road or numbers. Why we're going I don't know. We arrive when they were all at work and have disturbed Auntie Nellie having had to attend to our ringing the doorbell. She's still a very large lady and I was to find out on our visit that she spent most of her day sat in her armchair.

When they all came in from work the house is filled with constant bickering; this seems to come about by the lack of a meal being prepared due to Auntie Nellie's inactivity. This happened every night and I would be sent down to the corner shop with money and a list

217

for meat and potato pies, mushy peas and pop. The same list every night for a week that seemed like a fortnight, and I was only asked for a few days. I've no memory of breakfasts or dinner times or even pots of tea. Auntie Nellie has a liking for pop and there's always a big bottle on the table. I don't mind, but it doesn't go down well with Mum. She likes her tea and I think this alone could make this our one and only visit.

We went out on two occasions, one to Manchester to buy me a scout hat and the other in Uncle Eddie's car to visit some relatives in Sale by the name of Legge. I enjoyed being with them; they were very nice people but I had a feeling that they didn't get on too well with the Peacock's. I'm still not sure how we are all related and I find it so difficult to say Uncle and Auntie. This was the longest time I ever spent away from home. One thing I can't reason out is that going from home whether it is a short or a long journey always seems to take longer than going back. Maybe one day when I have a watch I might find each way's just the same.

I ran all the way from the bus stop at Selkirk Road and was so pleased to be back home. What a lovely place where we live. Mary put her arms around me, gave me a hug and asked if I'd had a good time. I didn't say a word and she didn't ask me again. Dad was still at work where he wanted to be along with his pals and when he's finished for the day he enjoys being at home. I'm beginning to think the same way.

School days and weekends come and go and I thought by going to Weaste I would have missed the opportunity of spending a weekend at the farm, but I haven't. I'm going to help if I can with the threshing and baling. Dad was right the work was too heavy for me. A bale of straw is impossible for me to handle but to watch the men working together is an experience to remember. The steam engine is fantastic, the power, the noise and the speed that the grain is separated from the chaff and then the straw made up into bales; it's just beyond belief.

Straw was being forked up into the top of the baler whilst what I think Uncle Alf calls a 'nodding donkey' goes up and down. This compresses the loose straw into bales and somehow they keep coming out at the other end neatly tied up with wire. It seems never to stop and the rate they come out keep the men on their toes to-and-from the Dutch barn, stacking. Everyone is covered in dust and chaff; it's almost like being in a snow storm - it's all over the place.

I was quite useful constantly going back to the house for jugs of tea and bread and cheese, and I notice there's never a treacle sandwich. On my travels back to the house I did see a couple of hens meet their doom that I prefer not to have seen. The brick sty where the pigs are kept is roofed with a small yard to the front and on all three sides a low wall - the side wall is gated and this is only opened to muck out and freshen up the straw.

Now for convenience sake when not having to go into the sty there's an aperture in the wall which is the start of the feeding trough, where feed and any swill can be thrown in. From what Uncle Alf tells me pigs can be quite nasty. One of them, a whopper, is named 'Tarzan' and as I get near to him the grunting and squealing going on, it's obvious that they'd just been fed. They are enjoying the feed. Then I notice some hens scratching around in the grass. One jumps up into the trough to sample the pig feed and then with much frantic flapping of wings and clucking the hen disappeared down the trough and within seconds and before I could get into the sty the clucking had stopped. I look over the wall to peer inside; there were two enormous pigs and no trace whatsoever of the hen. I didn't tell anyone. Auntie Lill knows all her hens by name and will think it's been a fox.

No sooner had this happened Uncle Alf must have thought that the men were doing quite well without him, I spotted him by, of all things the walnut tree. He manages to lay his hands on a hen with a lot of disturbance of feathers and clucking going on.

The next thing I saw was a hen running around the field without a head. It seems to run around for quite a long time and this might well be the time that I thought farming wasn't for me, but I do like the getting in of the cows, the milking and most of all the thought of going out on the milk round. Maybe it's the mystery of the ladies at the Barracks! It's the hens, ducks and animals I get attached to and then they're gone. It's not the same with corn, grass and clover.

I went home with some eggs that night and a chicken and the buttermilk goes without asking. I know because today I churned the butter and it is hard work!

Time goes by, the nights get colder, frosts making nice patterns on the inside of my bedroom window. Guy Fawkes night whenever it was has long since gone and one of my must haves was a collection of Army Regimental cap badges, collected since the beginning of the war that I have fastened onto an old leather belt, and I've sold it to one of the lads. I should have asked Dad's permission but I didn't. The thing is I've got some extra money to spend; is it going to be football socks or some proper shin pads?

Most of what we hear on a daily basis is air raids on places sounding German. So many thousand tons of bombs dropped and how many of our aircraft are missing. Then Tokyo's mentioned; bombed last night by American B29's - now they can carry a huge amount of bombs. I think this must have been our first air raid on Japan. Dad says, "The Yanks have never forgotten Pearl Harbour and now they've found the way to Tokyo there'll be no stopping them. Mark my words in a few months time there won't be much left of Japan."

Thinking of what to do on winter nights other than going to scouts isn't easy but talking of finding your way somewhere, pocket money permitting, we've taken to walking down to the West View 'chippy' for a bag of chips and a scoop of scraps - the scraps are free and there always seems to be plenty of them, providing you ask for chips first. The walk there and back talking as you go passes the night away.

One night on the way to the 'chippy', just after going under the railway bridge in Saltney, we notice light coming through a doorway. Going down a short path on an explore we were in a big dimly lit wooden hut just about empty except for a few chairs, a billiard table and a dart board, and a bored looking elderly man, slouched on a bench by a coke stove. He could have been asleep and we disturbed him as he did seem surprised on seeing us. We joined him round the stove and talked. We had discovered the Saltney Railwaymen's Social Club and not a railwayman in sight other than the man looking after the stove, who I think was retired from the railway. He knew of our friend Mr. Brown from the signal box.

This place was to become our haunt for the winter nights, that's if we wanted to play snooker, billiards or darts. Snooker and billiards I tried and dropped and darts just seemed a novel way of doing arithmetic. I've enough of that at school so I spend my time with the man by the stove, whilst the others play their games, just talking about anything. I'm quite sure he enjoys passing the night away with me. We make a pot of tea which the others don't object to before making our way home. I never knew his name and found him a very knowing man about most things, especially football and remember him giving me a tip to prevent my throat getting dry when playing football - it was to suck a piece of coal. This I never questioned and never tried, nor ever felt my throat feeling dry.

Apart from the news that Dad always likes to listen to, the wireless is left on for most of the day, turned down low. It's sort of there but isn't. I don't really notice it. It's Mum and Mary who want it on and every now and again the volume is turned up when one of their favourites comes on. Dad says it's much the same at work but the other way round - they can't turn their wireless down. It must be awful having it on loud all day and I'm sure it must be on very loud with all the noise going on making planes. No wonder he likes a bit of peace and quiet when he gets home.

Mum and Mary know all the singers. They're not my favourites and when I come in the volume is up and they're sat listening; it's obvious something's happened. Dad's not saying anything. Then Dad looks at me, "It's Glen Miller's plane Peter. Reported missing somewhere between here and France. He's in the American army, plays in a band and they've got some of his music on by way of respect." It sounds to me as though Dad's a bit fed up with it but we all listen, saying nothing, and it goes on and on and I can't say I like it. I don't know if it came to an end or not but Mum got up and turned it off.

Mary says, "The music's called 'swing' - played all the time in the dance halls, Quaintways, Clemence's, all over the place. 'In the Mood' with Glen Miller's American Air Force Band; Oh! and 'Moonlight Serenade' - that Mum likes. It's the sound of the saxophones that make it so special. He was awarded the first Golden Disc for his 'Chattanooga Choo Choo.'" Dad keeps having a look around to see how things are going and every now and again looks up at the ceiling as though everything is passing over his head. I think it was the

'Chattanooga Choo Choo' that did it.

A few days pass and we don't hear anything more of Glen Miller. Dad and I talk about it and it wasn't what I thought, it was his playing of, 'In the Mood.' It reminds Dad of the wail of an air raid siren; something I shouldn't share with Mum and Mary.

Luckily we don't hear the siren any more, only of V2's dropping down south most times on London, if the Germans have got their aim right. The civilians cop it every time, night and day. The last one sounded particularly bad as it dropped on a Woolworth's store crowded with Saturday morning shoppers, killing a hundred and sixty people, mostly women and children. This really got through to Mum. From what I understand from Dad and the news, the closer the Allies get to Germany reduces the risk of V2's as the Germans keep having to relocate the launch sites, so very soon London will be beyond the range of a V2 rocket - buzz bomb. So it's all good news ahead and a good feeling of being on the winning side.

It's getting close to Christmas and I can't believe that my going to the farm has provided us with so many chickens which we've never had before, other than at Christmas. Thinking on it, there's one thing I can't understand. On the farm Uncle Alf talks of chicks when they hatch out from eggs, then later they become hens and he tells me, "Go and feed the hens, or collect hens eggs - muck out the hens." Then when they're dead they become a chicken again. "What about a nice chicken to take home for your Mum?" Gran says the same. Anyway I shouldn't bother about it as long as we've got one and I can't see I'll be going to the farm till well into the New Year. So I'm hoping Gran will come up trumps, along with a few hens eggs.

Mum and Dad have brought up the birthday and Christmas thing again and it looks like I have to try on something for size before they buy it, so it won't be a surprise. Not that I mind but I hope it's something to do with football. I wasn't far wrong and Mum took me to Bradley's corner shop. She knows the man in the boot-and-shoe department from when Dad had the shop, Mr. Dowthwaite. He fits me up with a super pair of Hotspur football boots and even gets me a pair of football socks from another department just to try on with the boots, not to keep. Mum bought me the boots. I've got them in a box complete with long laces and Mr. Dowthwaite has put in a tin of Wren's dubbin that we haven't had to pay for. When we left him at the shop he said, "Remember me to Harold," which was nice. I've got enough here for birthday and Christmas. I just couldn't believe I was going home on the bus with a brand new pair of Hotspur football boots.

Dad's old shop looked much the same except there was nothing in the windows to attract people to come into the shop. Dad always thought that was important. I used to love helping him dress the windows as it was called, and there were two big ones. I don't think they sell anything and it does have the look of an office, was the name now Pickfords? I wasn't sure and neither of us talked about it.

Dad was pleased about Mr. Dowthwaite remembering him and says, "Yes, Bob Dowthwaite took a big interest in local football with Blacon United. A nice man, his son must be about your age Peter."

Mum and I go most Sundays to see Gran and Granddad with the same old things, the shortbread and ginger biscuits that Granddad has come to expect - he'd be disappointed if Mum couldn't make them. Gran also gets the same things every Sunday - scraps, stale bread and egg shells. That's for the hens - the stale bread and eggshells. She breaks them up with a cobbler's flat hammer and mixes in some corn. We spend a couple of hours with them. Gran always manages to make us a nice cold meat sandwich and a cup of tea. Before we set off for the walk home she tells us that some of the hens have gone off laying so we won't go short of a chicken and hopefully some eggs. There we go, hen one day and a chicken the next. What would we do without Gran and Granddad!

Most nights we, the lads, go down to the Railwaymen's Club, knocking on doors to pick up a few more in Mount Pleasant. Mum says she always knows where I've been as she smells it in my clothes. I know what she means because the place smells musty a bit like a church with the added smell of coke stove and the caretaker's smoking. I was home a bit late. Dad was in the bathroom getting washed and shaved ready for an early morning start. It must be well after nine o'clock, probably a bit late for me to be making toast.

Our path isn't the easiest to come up after dark and I know Dad's in the bathroom as I can hear him singing. There's a chink of light finding its way through the blackout but it won't get us into trouble as I don't think we have a Warden anymore since we went on dim out. Mum's sat at the table with a pot of tea. There's nothing said of me being home late, then - "Oh, your Dad's brought home a roll of papers from the factory. I think he must have left them in the hall, but I wouldn't touch them as I think he wants to give them to you."

I can't think what, and know he takes ages in the bathroom having a shave. What it is, Mum doesn't approve of Dad smoking. She thinks it's just a waste of money so Dad really makes a shave last much longer than it should so he can have a smoke in peace. That accounts for me seeing the chink of light in the blackout as Dad opens the window slightly to let the smoke out so as Mum thinks he's not smoking, and this disturbs the blackout. Even so when he eventually comes down he smells of smoke! So there are two of us tonight being a bit on the smelly side.

He hands me a long roll of papers held together with an elastic band. "Go on, open it up." I do, and was it difficult trying to unroll them and get them to lie flat on the floor in front of the fire - I don't think Mum was over pleased. But they are super posters, mostly to do with safety at work, 'careless talk costs lives' and for blood donors. Dad says, "They've been up around the factory long enough and were being thrown out. I thought they were nicely done and might be of interest to you knowing your interest in drawing and painting." The posters had names of the artist just like on paintings - 'Tom Eckersley', 'Abram Games' and 'Fougasse', his were cartoon- style drawings. Dad says, "They call themselves 'commercial artists.'"

I never gave it much thought before seeing all these posters, then Dad goes on to tell me of a commercial artist in Watergate Street that used to do show cards and price tickets for him when he had the shop. The posters have provided a problem as I wanted to stick them on my bedroom wall instead of the one in a frame over my bed. It's been there longer than I can remember, far longer than the posters have at the factory. Time for a change I thought, but got a most definite 'No!' So 'The Light of the World' has to stay there, Jesus looking down over me with his lamp and my posters all rolled up lie in the bottom of my wardrobe.

There aren't many days without me having a look at my posters on the bed. I'm sure Jesus wouldn't have minded sharing the bedroom with a few posters, but then I hadn't asked for a sharing and I'm sure the 'No' was because both Mum and Dad thought the bedroom wall was not the place for sticking posters. I can't see the sitting room or the hall being an option, so in the wardrobe they remained.

I've still got the money from selling my regimental cap badges. It hasn't burnt a hole in my pocket and I've saved a bit more so I'm going to buy Mum, Dad and Mary each a small present to open on Christmas morning. If I'm careful what I buy I should manage it. I know Mum would love to have a nice warm scarf. Didn't think about clothing coupons so she'll know I'm up to something, but a scarf will still be a surprise and I've seen the one I want to get in Marks and Spencer's.

As I'm not sure about Mary, I've asked Mum's advice and she thinks either face powder or cream, so it helps having a choice of two, though sometimes the choice isn't in the shops. Dad's easy; I know he would really like a box of Manikin cigars; five in a box and I remember seeing them in Gerrard's shop next door to Dad's old shop. Again, like Mary's I don't need coupons and Mr. Gerrard knows me and he'll sell them to me because he knows they're for Dad. So that's it all sorted.

I got my shopping done as planned, all on my own in secret. No one knows except for the coupon thing. I decided on the powder for Mary just because I liked the box and I think I have enough money left to get some football socks for me. I'm not having time to do that before Christmas. I just wish I was good enough to play for a team each week so as I could get the right coloured socks to go with the shirt.

Everything seems to be going well and it looks like being in all probability the best Christmas we have had in the war but to think of it, I haven't heard a word from Mum about a cake or a pudding. Well, what if we don't have a pudding or a cake, they will all have a surprise in the morning around the time when Dad lights the fire in the sitting room - that's always good for a laugh - although it's not intended to be. Then, with only a few days to go it all starts to go wrong.

Mary tells us that Eric has had his call-up papers for the army and he won't be home for Christmas. He has to report to Maryhill Barracks, Glasgow on the twenty third. Mary's obviously very upset - all three of us are - and after saying all the sorry things with arms around each other, what else can you say. We tried to talk of other things to take her mind off it, which didn't seem to help.

Dad had to know when he came in from work. He usually puts the wireless on but not tonight and he listens to Mary's news from Eric. It went much the same as it had for Mum and me earlier on, and gone silent again. Dad, like us, wasn't prepared for it and neither was Mary. The war's been like this all the way through.

I think how uncanny it is of all places to go, Eric's leaving Mary to go to Maryhill. Dad had a word with me later on when we were on our own. "Like you Peter and your Mother I honestly feel sorry for Mary having this news, but there's not a lot we can do other than help her along as best as we can. But what about Eric in all this - he's not only leaving Mary, it's everything else precious to him - his family, his way of life, everything and most of all his independence. It was his name on the envelope - 'On His Majesty's Service.' Before opening it he knew what it was - call-up papers, a travel warrant and the King's shilling."

I can't remember Dad sounding so upset and we were left silent for long enough before I could ask Dad about the King's shilling that I had never heard of before.

Dad's reply was "It's a long standing tradition, how long I don't know, that you accept the King's shilling and by doing so, to serve your King and country. I don't think that for one minute it's come out of the King's pocket or that you can send it back. There are alternatives but that's for another day and it's about time young man that you were in bed."

I know what Dad was on about as one of Mary's friends who lives in Earlsway and was also a friend of Joe Brown's decided to be a conscientious objector, everyone called them 'Conshies' and he worked as a farm labourer all through the war and so many people gave him so much abuse. I thought it a very brave thing to do and never ignored him. His name was Peter Mulvey and I always said 'hello' to him. If ever I got sent the King's shilling I'd have to go, like Eric. I felt very pleased that Dad thinks of me as 'a young man' but I still can't stay up late.

Woke up early Christmas morning to see patterns of frost on the inside of my bedroom window and I'm the lucky one having the hot water cylinder in the corner cupboard. Mum and Dad's bedroom and Mary's have fireplaces, only small ones as I'm told hot bedrooms aren't healthy, not that they ever have a fire in them. You have to be ill to have a fire.

I remember when I was ill with scarlet fever the fever hospital was full so I had to stay at home and moved into Mum and Dad's bedroom and a fire was lit for me. I remember a bucket of smelly disinfectant with a bed sheet soaking in it as it hung over the door. The doctor came every day and he would talk with Mum in the bedroom as to how I was. I think I was beyond being bothered most of the time, the rest I was half asleep.

Then I caught something about 'if he sees this night through then he will be on the road to recovery.' Apart from me being a worry, ill in bed, Mum was also in fear of a spark from the open fire setting alight to the bedding and it was probably her only bedding. The fever van as we called it was painted dark green, so as not to be confused with the white ambulance. We became very used to seeing it. I don't remember when this was and it may well be before the war, perhaps before I went to school. It was a long time ago.

Christmas 1944

This morning it's Christmas. There's a decided smell of paraffin oil as I come down stairs and head for the sitting room. Dad has been busy long ago - the fire is lit and sprigs of holly all over the place. On the fluffy hearth rug, a full size leather football, a 'T' ball, the best. Holding this football, time stood still. Oh! I haven't got their presents - they're still hidden under the bed, so I dash back upstairs hopefully unnoticed. I can't help thinking that my presents to them don't seem fair compared with a football, but I suppose I can make up for them when I'm working.

Back downstairs and I think everyone was really surprised by having presents. Mary says it's her favourite powder. Mum likes her scarf and Dad's already going around the house with more shovels-full of coal openly puffing away on his cigars without having to go into the bathroom - they smell lovely, I really like it. I may smoke cigars when I'm grown up.

I'm not sure if it's safe having my new football so close to a roaring fire, as it might explode. Dad agrees and it goes behind the settee. I can't thank them enough for the football, but what do I do when it needs blowing up? I don't know. Then I find a little thing hidden in the rug, it looks to be brass.

Mum says, Oh you've found the adapter that screws on to your bicycle pump and if you have a problem pumping the football up you can take it into Mr. Hack's shop - the sports shop in St. Michael's Arcade. If its in by the Wednesday he'll have it done by Friday ready for the weekend as he thinks you might have a problem lacing it up." Well I haven't got a lace for a start! Not that I've been in his shop but I think that this Mr. Hack plays cricket for Boughton Hall and Cheshire County.

Mum's got pans on the stove with lids rattling away, the kitchen windows well steamed up as is most of the house. My job's going round the window sills with a cloth mopping up and getting in the way. Gran's chicken sounds to be roasting well in the oven, making quite a bang, and spluttering every now and again. On my round the smell of cooking is everywhere. Mum's got some scent on or is it Mary's powder and I can tell where Dad's been by the whiff of his cigar that tends to linger. Mary is keeping cheerful and helping Mum whenever things get a bit hectic in the back kitchen. We are all in and out when everything is cooked, and settle down at the table. Mum as always, and I don't know how, has managed to do us a lovely Christmas dinner. I do love sprouts and roast parsnips and we have a plum pudding with custard. Dad leans back on the back legs of his chair whilst patting his stomach with both hands and said, "More than an ample sufficiency." We then, as Dad puts it, retire to the sitting room where the fire looks decidedly low, in need of coal.

Dad likes being in charge of the fire and is soon back from the coal house with a good shovel full. He always carefully places the coal by hand piece by piece. With not an ember in sight, it looks like it's gone out. Mum, looking sadly at the fire, said, "In trying to be careful with the coal you let it get too low and now you've suffocated it." Dad doesn't seem at all bothered by this.

The coal shovel is propped up in front of the fire and a full sheet of the Daily Express against the coal shovel; in no time at all it is back to a roaring fire before the Daily Express went into flames and is sucked up the chimney. I could see Dad is in a panic as he thinks the chimney might catch fire. We seldom use this room so a build up of soot in the chimney is unlikely; nowhere near enough to cause a fire. Then from Dad, "The lad's right Annie." I don't think Mum was all that bothered anyway.

Enough coal on the fire and banked up with damp slack we were set up for the afternoon. Mum settles down to making a pot of tea to go with the mince pies and Dad gets out the draughts set so Mary and me play draughts while Mum and Dad talk. I half listen between moves and now and again Mary's concentration went as though somewhere else and I have to remind her of her move. I can understand and so can Mum and Dad as they keep butting in with our game; all trying to help and probably not helping at all. Then Mum comes up with something that finishes off our game of draughts and we settle down whilst she talks. I've an idea from the way Mary looks that she's heard it all before and this is really intended for me.

I've thought for a while now, well since I first went to Uncle Alf's farm, that Uncle Norman was the go-between as his milk round isn't just Curzon Park, it goes into Handbridge, Queens Park and then into the town. This is where he meets up with Albert's milk round and they pass the time of day. This is going on when Uncle Alf thinks he's talking with the soldiers wives at the Barracks in Nicholas Street. But that's beside the point.

So this is where my visits are planned and Mum says that Auntie Lill isn't expecting me at the farm until the spring. Not a definite time but I know for sure that winter visits are out and that's what matters.

It's nearly always Uncle Norman that comes with our milk and always more than a good morning, but Mum never offers a cup of tea like Charlie used to get. I think Mum had a soft spot for Charlie. We never hear of him and all we get from Tom is a passing shout 'Hello' as he goes with next door's milk. That's the Dyes, not the other neighbours, the Irlam's; they have the Co-op and have to put milk tallies out with the empties by the gate post. They don't have a bill as they pay for the tallies at the Co-op shop in Saltney. The Irlam's accused me of stealing the tallies when their milkman didn't leave them any milk for almost a whole week. Dad said to take no notice. I was worried to death but the police never came round so it all blew over.

Uncle Norman and Tom always sound happy as they busy around the houses, whistling. Then Mum says, "Your Uncle Norman is also uncle to Tom." Now I've never thought of Tom other than being employed, working the dairy, so I have another cousin. Mum must have seen I was looking a bit nonplussed and goes on to say, "The eldest of the three boys at the farm." As if she thought I hadn't understood. So Uncle Alf's his Dad. I didn't like to ask about him not living at the farm.

After that news of my new cousin Tom and having a winter break from the farm I ask about Pat at the farm and of Charlie who used to come with the milk before the war. Could they be like Tom, relatives I never knew about? Mum soon put that one to rest by saying she had an idea that Pat went to the farm, that's Great Granddad's farm, Five Ashes Farm in Wrexham Road, from an orphanage and then on to Uncle Alf's farm at Dodleston. Charlie could also have come from the same orphanage that she thinks was in Wrexham Road, but then who knows, and we never hear anything of Charlie. I couldn't think of anyone else but I think I could ask Gran when I think on.

We talk and talk so much that afternoon it was dark and tea time long since past. So what time it was I don't know when Mum cut into the Christmas cake. Neither do I know what Mum had got for tea as we never had it. Dad had forgotten the blackout but we didn't have the light on, just the light from the fire and somehow it was very comforting. It has sometimes been sad when we had our cake and a cup of tea. We have tried 'Camp' coffee but it never caught on. All in all what a lovely Christmas and as the fire needed more coal we went to bed.

A strange day, Boxing Day, a real 'after the day' feel about it. We all felt much the same, like not doing anything. Not much happens after Christmas - then New Year and that's never been anything special to celebrate in this house. Dad says it's more of a Scottish thing as they celebrate Hogmanay being the night before New Year and don't go much on Christmas. I wonder if it's that they're not Christians? I don't ask, I just wonder. Hogmanay to me sounds pagan. I might ask about it at school.

I've never like January. It's always so dull and cold. Spring seems far away and its dark coming home from school when all you want is to be in by the fire and be warm. I always feel sorry for Dad as I know he feels the cold. Not that he ever complains. I get chilblains on my ears; they itch like mad and the cream Mum gets doesn't help any. It's nice just watching the fire.

Mary tells us that Eric's finding the weather severe and cold. He's at the HLI's Depot in the Gorbals. Dad doesn't know of any army barracks in the Gorbals but knows it as being a very rough area of Glasgow; not that I think he's ever been there. Dad might not know the HLI but I do. The Highland Light Infantry, a crack Scottish Regiment - I had their cap badge in my collection. There's a song about someone McKay - Johnny McKay of the HLI. We used to sing it around the piano at Miss Baker's music class. Dad's response was, "It sounds like the lad's in a rough place with an even rougher outfit. Sounds typical of the army and thankfully only to do his basic training and it will keep him out of the war for a few weeks before he moves on."

The end of the war in Europe can't be far off with the Russians well into Poland and having taken Warsaw. They'll be into Germany soon and then it's a chase between us, the Yanks and the Russians as to who gets to Berlin first. I'm not a betting man but for me it's got to be the Russians, for them it's payback time with a vengeance. They'll be absolutely ruthless and we and the Yanks just don't compare.

Dad was right about the rough place as Mary talks of them being forty to a room in condemned barracks from Napoleonic times and run by a bunch of sadists. So different from the RAF - and I thought Maryhill sounded such a nice place.

There is a feeling around of the war coming to an end and preparing for it, of how we will celebrate; when it comes. It'll be so unreal, so it might well be that we won't know what to do for a few days before we believe it. As a family, I don't think we're much good at celebrations. Christmas seems the only one, and that's always good but birthdays aren't what you call celebrated. You know when it is, then you're a year older - now that's important to me, as this year I can leave school.

End of the war - I can only think of fireworks and bonfires; of burning Adolf Hitler, maybe some pop and I think that's about it. Where fireworks will come from I don't know. There are still a few soldiers about who might be persuaded to part with some Thunder flashes as they won't need them anymore.

I've spoken with Dad about celebrations and I don't think I picked the right time as he didn't seem at all interested. "Nearer the time Peter and in any case it's up to the Town Hall to sort something out when it ends." So there we are.

Almost every night now when Dad comes in it's about the Russians advancing through Poland and it's not about the fighting and how many men killed - it's about what they're finding. Huge concentration camps not filled with prisoners of war but civilians from all over Europe - mostly Poles and Jews. Labour camps - and when they can't work any more with being starved or sick they go into the gas chambers and then the cremation ovens. We listen, well we have no choice; we just have to talk about it. Dad must get it all day at work. We don't hear these things on the wireless at home.

The Germans seem to have a thing about not liking the Poles and Jews. I remember Dad saying, "Auschwitz, - a name that I will never forget and probably never forgive them for, where they killed and cremated twenty four thousand Jews a day; men, women and children, just making up numbers." I've never heard Dad so full of hatred and eventually he stopped. We were so shocked, so had nothing to say. Then Dad says, "Just what do you do with these people when the day of reckoning comes?" When Dad told us about it, it was of shock and horror but seeing the photographs in the 'Picture Post' was unbelievably horrible. How people can stay alive looking so ill, just skin and bone and dead people just stacked up in heaps waiting for the ovens.

Then a few days later we find out from Mary that she's seen it all on newsreels. She'd been to 'The Tatler' with some friends from work and it had got so bad that she had to shield her eyes from it and lots of people just had to leave the cinema before it had finished. Was this intended to lift our morale like the Henry V film or was it to confirm our hatred of the Germans. I can't see either way, it being necessary. You wouldn't think this is possible of human beings.

We think the worst of the winter's behind us. Eric's finished his basic training and is away from the Gorbals and seems to be in a more acceptable part of the country. He doesn't mention sadists any more. From what Mary says he seems to be enjoying it. He's at Catterick Camp on signals training and been recommended for officer training. Something to look forward to for a change and Mary seems happier about it all.

As a bunch of lads we go to see Chester play most home games and they've got a pretty good team together; mainly local players and a few good players from the army stationed in Chester - Burden, Hamilton, Marsh, Foulks and Short. A few of the others might be servicemen for all I know. And of course the favourite of us all is Tommy Astbury, a war time Welsh International. They do well in the league but from what I see the two teams that keep them from the top are Rotherham and Doncaster. Dad insists that's because the majority of their players are coal miners, a job of national importance, so they're exempt from call up and consistency always being the basis of a good team.

Dad sometimes has Saturday off from work and I don't like leaving him in the house, so I like to think I take him to watch Chester and we go in the stands. I know it costs a lot of money but he likes to sit down. There's just something missing - it's not quite the same in the stands. When you're in the ground you seem more involved in the game, sort of taking part, and it's much cheaper. No one talks to you in the stands, but someone did with Dad - a man discharged wounded from the army and he'd played football in the desert in unbelievable heat with an ex-Chester player, centre half Trevor Walters. "What a player," he says, "dedicated, just wait till he gets home then we'll get promotion." I got Dad to go a few times and it was a change for him. We saw Chester lose and win but he was never really with them and at the end of the day for him, I know they played with the wrong shaped ball. So I went back to watching it with the lads in the ground.

Mum's had a word from Norman about the other Johnson's - that's Uncle Alf at Dodleston, for what I've been looking forward to for long enough - going with Cousin Albert on his milk round. It means getting up and going early but I don't mind. It's quite nice going from home on my bike when everywhere else is still asleep. Dad's very good, he's always up very early every day and he wakes me. He has an alarm clock. When you work, you're able to buy things like watches and alarm clocks.

I find the farm really quiet apart from Albert and Pat going backwards and forwards from the walk-in fridge to the van with tankards of milk from last night's milking. They have a knack of rolling them on the base rim without having to lift them, a skill that I might find with practice. It's not long before we wave to Pat and are on our way to Chester. No sooner left than we are at the Overleigh roundabout; it beats the bicycle. When in Chester I discover streets I never knew of - I only knew of around Dad's shop and scouts. How, in a big place like Chester, one can be so confined seems quite strange to me. But I am enjoying being with Albert delivering milk. Measuring it out from the tankards into jugs and I can't help but notice that some milk is already in glass bottles; Albert says a pint measure, and Pat's made up more than a few sandwiches for us.

After all the streets we end up at the Barracks; the married soldiers' quarters in St. Nicholas Street backing on to Nuns Field. Through the archway entrance it was castle-like and I would have expected a portcullis or even a drawbridge had there been a moat. Not even a soldier on sentry so all probably in lands far away. We were in a big courtyard square empty apart from a few children playing around. Then within minutes of Albert parking his milk van ladies appeared from all over the place as if by magic, carrying jugs, and what had been peace and quiet became a place of chatter and lots of fun.

It was all that I had ever expected of a milk round. I wasn't disappointed I just knew it would be like this. As true as Uncle Alf said they were Albert's ladies. Albert seemed to get rid of more milk than we got rid of in the streets and without knocking on doors. I was to ladle out milk into jugs like nobody's business whilst he chatted away with the ladies who seemed very pleased to see him. By the time we left the Barracks we only had a short measure left in a tankard and a few bottles. From what I can see this must be the last call on Albert's round and we haven't met Uncle Norman, which doesn't bother me. So I expect to head off for Lache Lane and the farm. But no, we made our way back into town where Albert left the milk van by the Falcon Tea Rooms and I followed him across Lower Bridge Street to Griffiths' cake shop. It's my favourite place and he asked for two Chester cakes, so it looks like I'm having one. They know him by name - Albert. We ate them in the van - they were big and took some shifting. I'd never had a cake like it but then Griffiths' are good bakers even though Mum only buys their bread or buns.

On the way back down Lache Lane Albert winds down his window and out went Pat's sandwiches, which was probably the best thing as I was full and more than likely cow treacle; then the window went up with not a word spoken.

Back at the farm there was some milk to churn; nothing worth speaking of, not enough to take any butter home but I will have a bottle or two of buttermilk for Mum and Dad. What else I don't know.

I don't think I've enjoyed a day as much as this for a long time and I don't know why but somehow I knew I would. I can see why Albert enjoys what he does at the farm but after a while can get a little bit repetitive, sort of boring. I think it's going to be joinery when I finish with school.

I helped with the washing of bottles and tankards and the inside of the van. Always a cold job and I left before the end of the day with fewer things than before - a few eggs, some butter that I hadn't churned and some buttermilk; plums, apples, pears and the soft fruits all gone with the summer. Mum and Dad were well pleased with the buttermilk. But I have a feeling that I won't be going to the farm anymore.

News about Eric from Mary is confusing as he seems to be being messed about yet again. First it was the RAF and now by the army. He's doing all sorts of tests through a long day with breaks when they are well fed and waited on with wine in the Officer's Mess; makes a change from roughing it in the Gorbals. He's obviously not sure how he would fit into this way of life and we hear that some of the would-be officers with him appear to be real idiots, even having had a public school education. With his elementary, he felt a misfit. Tests finished and the selection board decided that the army requirements were for Infantry Officers for Burma as the war in Europe was drawing to an end. There were no vacancies for Signals Officers.

I can understand Eric being disappointed as signals was his training, what he was good at. As was being a pilot - it just didn't work out. As Dad said, "At the end of the day, being messed about by the system has kept him out of trouble and God willing to the end of the war."

I've played 'footie' that many times on the Mount Pleasant tip that the studs on my boots are becoming a problem with the nails showing proud of the leather stud. The football is showing a few scrapes as the pitch isn't ideal, it's either the long grass or lumps on the wings or the gritty middle where we keep finding bits of glass. On the plus side we're never troubled with cows just the odd dog every now and again - usually a greyhound. I wondered if I could file the nails down or even knock them in so I put this suggestion to Dad about the file and he said that if I was careful how I went, I might find in the coal house on the top shelf, a last that belonged to his Dad.

As nothing was said about my idea of filing the nails down, he didn't think it worth doing or maybe he hasn't a file, but a last? I didn't know what on earth he was talking about but on looking in the coal house way up on the top shelf I could feel a strange shaped thing, cold and made of iron. Dad was right in saying to be careful as it was seriously heavy. Why he put it way up on the top shelf I can't imagine - had it come down on someone's head - doesn't bear thinking about.

It was dirty up there with coal dust and cobwebs and when groping around in the dark I found what I think is a pair of pincers and a screw driver. Not at all pleasant, but when wiped clean they were covered in rust and I couldn't open the pincers so I took it that the big heavy thing was Dad's Dad's last. I carried it in to show Dad and got into trouble from Mum for taking it into the house and for getting dirty. I thought what a good job it was that we hadn't used the coal house as a shelter in the air raids as the Town Hall suggested.

Dad says, "Yes, that's the shoe last I'd forgotten all about it till you mentioned your football boots - a cobbler would be lost without it that's for sure." This is what I can't understand about Dad. He is so meticulous about his garden tools and keeps his eye on me whenever I do the garden. The tools have to be scraped free of soil, dried and wiped with an oily rag that he keeps in a screw topped jar on the lower shelf. Hedge and grass shears always well cleaned and oiled and his lawn mower, a Qualcast Panther, is a showpiece. It's been instilled in me that a good workman looks after his tools.

I haven't really got Dad's attention and I need to know more about this last if it's going to be any use to me with my football boots, so I put it to Dad if he has ever used this last or seen his Dad using it, or anyone for that matter. The newspaper lowered onto his lap and then it's a 'No.' I know I've interrupted his reading and then comes a long explanation from Dad. "What you will have to understand in life is that there are trades and skilled trades and I was neither. I was a retail trader. Your Granddad and Uncles have skilled trades apart from your Uncle Roy and Sid who have professions."

Now I already know what they both do - Uncle Roy's the architect and Uncle Sid's the accountant and this isn't helping me with my football boots. I can tell Mary's fed up - her knitting has gone back in the bag and she's away upstairs to her bedroom. It's going to be a Fair Isle pullover for me.

Dad's going on again. "Now Mr. Irlam next door, to him the cobbler's last is his life blood; without it he's unable to perform his skill." So with that I gather Mr. Irlam to be a skilled retail trader. I know for sure that I'm not going next door to see Mr. Irlam for some advice and so does Dad. Dad obviously knows nothing about the shoe or cobbler's last whatever it's called. He's not a handyman, he's a believer in every man to his trade, leaving jobs to tradesmen who know what they're doing and not tinkering around with things that he doesn't know anything about but I'm blowed if the only alternative is Mr. Irlam.

I go hunting around under the kitchen sink in Mum's grate cleaning box and manage to find a piece of emery cloth. With this and a lot of rubbing, I get the last free of rust; then wonder if I should black lead it with some of Mum's 'Zebo.' Maybe not, it looks pretty good as it is.

Strange looking thing this last. Three things sticking out, one with a heel shape on the end and two with what could be sole shapes, one smaller than the other. I think this could be pretty straight forward if only I had an old pair of shoes ready to throw out that I could practice on before having a go at my football boots. I can't see me getting a file so with all the kit cleaned up and a boot on the last the larger of the sole sizes I manage to pull out three nails and off comes the first stud; one gone, eleven to go. A bit slow but then it's a skilled job and if I make a mess of it I'll never hear the last of it. Why do they call this cobbler's thing a last? After a few nights work I manage to get all the studs off and I'm well and truly fed up as well as not being able to play football on Saturday without studs in my boots.

On Saturday morning my first call in town before doing Mum's shopping in the market will be Mr. Hack's shop in the arcade. I always leave my bike by the policeman at the Cross as he looks after it for me whilst I do the shopping. I do lock it to the railings by the church. He gives me a nod when I get there and when I leave so I know he's looking after it. Well Saturday afternoon - no playing football and Chester away to Doncaster and going to lose, so I might as well have a go at putting my studs in.

I got them at Mr. Hack's shop in a packet of twelve, just enough, and I know it's going to take me all afternoon. Well it didn't and I got all twelve in and I can see why you have to have a last, as the nails in the studs that I found out cobblers call pins, are longer than the thickness of the sole, so when hammered in the pins hit the iron last and turn over, so as they don't stick in your feet and make a mess of your socks. But I need an inner sole, so I've cut a piece of corrugated cardboard to the right shape. I just hope I can find a team to play for that has a decent pitch to play on so as I don't have to keep replacing studs, as I'm going to end up having boots full of holes where the pins came from.

I find I've a chance of playing with a team at Blacon from Mr. Dowthwaite at Bradley's shop, and one from Upton, how I don't know. After having a trial game with both I decide to go for Upton as it seems more of a lad's team and I'm not ready for men's football so I'm going to be playing for Upton at home this Saturday. They have a good pitch near the Zoo and I'm looking forward to playing on it.

Come Saturday, the bus got me there in plenty of time, only to find the game cancelled because of an animal having escaped from the Zoo. What sort of animal no one seems to know, but it was something I hadn't considered when turning down the offer to play at Blacon. I was quite relieved to get back on the bus for Chester. Two lots of bus fares for nothing so next time it's going to be the bike. Dad thought it strange when I got home earlier than expected - found my reasoning very amusing. When he stopped laughing he said, "Probably one of those giant lop-eared rabbits," and he was off again.

Even though I haven't had the opportunity to try out my new studs, Dad has suggested that I might like to have a go at repairing his shoes and mine and that we should pencil an outline on some paper round our soles and heels to take to Woolworth's and see what they have to offer, to get kitted out to do a proper job. This doesn't sound like Dad at all. He didn't say at the time but he must have been really impressed with the way I did the boots.

It wasn't long before we got into Town for our shoe repairing kit but first to my surprise we were off the bus in Bridge Street, walking out of town down Grosvenor Street to Mr. Bounds' shop, just by Mr. Irlam's Co-op cobblers shop. Dad gave me a passing look and said, "I don't think so," and we were in to see Mr. Bounds to get my black and yellow football socks. What a lovely surprise and what a lovely loud bell there is when you open the door. We have a good long talk and to my surprise Dad tells him that I'm good with my hands and what a good cobbler I am. "So you won't be calling next door then?" says Mr. Bounds.

Mr. Bounds lives four doors up the road from us. His Dad was left with only one leg after the war as was their next door neighbour, Mr. Speed, a strange name for a man with one leg. He works nights at the Telephone Exchange. Mary sees him at work now and again. Mr. Bounds talks about him repairing the family shoes and I can't help but think how upsetting it must be, having to mend one shoe. I often talk with Mr. Speed and Mr. Bounds' Dad as they're passing our house. I get some new football boot laces before we leave his shop and Mr. Bounds tells me, "Now don't forget next time you need new studs for those boots of yours I sell them singly and I'm expecting to have some rubber studs in by then that should last that little bit longer."

We were soon up Bridge Street and I looked across the road to the Bon Bon Café at the Cross to see if my police friend was on duty. He wasn't and I tell Dad about him keeping an eye on my bike. Then I thought that I never come into Town with Dad, it's nearly always on my own, and now, only now and again with Mum when we always manage to bump into someone she knows and today with Dad - no one. Maybe this is the wrong end of Town for Dad to see people he knows and we've had no reason to go down as far as Foregate Street and City Road.

Woolworth's is always busy and I've got to know the lady on the biscuit counter when I come in most Saturday mornings to see if she has any broken biscuits. They're much cheaper than the whole biscuits but today it's another lady and no broken biscuits, so I'm not doing any better than Dad. But when at last, after wandering around Woolworth's for ages, we find what Dad calls 'Cobblers Corner,' a counter stacked and stacked with every possible thing you could mend a shoe with. Soles, heels, leather and rubber either to pin or stick on; metal studs, tips for heel and toe or are they called 'segs' to make things last that bit longer. These are all sold on cards so you get a lot. Dad says, "What a good job we made those templates," producing them from his pocket that I'd forgotten all about, as he goes looking for the right size in rubber soles.

Then Dad shows me a thick round piece of black rubber with a small centre piece in leather. I just can't believe so much stuff. "Now, Peter that's what I call a good idea - two or more heels for the price of one. Don't you see - you fasten it to the heel of the shoe and when it wears down you slacken the fastening off and rotate it to a good bit."

Dad's buying that much stuff and it's OK for him as I'm the one that's going to be the cobbler. Dad's even spotted a cobbler's hammer that I can see a use for as it's got a much broader head than our hammer at home. I eventually manage to get Dad out of Woolworth's and he thinks it would be nice to walk home. He decides we go back down Watergate Street and along the racecourse. We go across the footbridge passing the sentry box and not a soldier in sight. It's been one of those days of not seeing familiar faces.

Dad's still excited about everything we've bought, well what he's bought, as he proudly lays it all out on the dining room table, so carried away that the clean, freshly ironed table cloth just wasn't noticed. Mum has a long look and says nothing about the cloth or of anything. Just nothing! I feel sorry for Dad as he'd had a lovely day and now everything has gone flat, which makes me think that she doesn't go along with home cobbling. Probably thinks it's all been a waste of money. Or is it just that she hasn't got the same faith in my cobbling ability as Dad?

Somehow I don 't think I'll be mending Mum's shoes being high heeled court shoes and that's probably what did it all along - she's just been focused on my football boots. I wasn't bothered any way, just having Dad's and mine to do will be enough. Now Mary's - I don't

247

know as I'm almost sure that her shoes have what they call crepe sole and heel - all in one piece. I think they're all the rage in America and that's the one thing we didn't see in Woolworth's.

Right out of the blue the other day, Mum said to me that it looks like a new suit for me, as I can't very well be seen at Mary's wedding in a school blazer that's not looking its best. My word, they've kept this quiet or is it me that just hasn't noticed what's been going on. I gather it's not far off and I'm away to get rigged out for the day at the Etonian for a grey suit, and I don't take a liking to new clothes but I have no say in it. It's going to be on a Saturday so it's no football and when I seriously think of it, I get to feel quite sad as I know I am going to lose my sister Mary who I dearly love and she's going to leave home and I don't want to be left on my own.

I suppose it's being selfish but I can't help feeling this way and I do like Eric and I know she will be happy. We will just have to see how it all goes. And it's going to be at St. Mark's Church in Saltney - not Methodist or Catholic, sort of neutral - what a turn up for the book. Whatever the faith I get a new suit.

The day comes and I enjoy it at the church. Thankfully I wasn't asked to be a page boy as I didn't enjoy being one at Uncle Sid and Audrey's wedding, dressed up in yellow trousers and a girl's frilly blouse, so thank you Mary!

The wedding went well and I enjoyed seeing Margaret - she came in her Red Cross uniform. The reception was at The Stafford Hotel where I met Eric's younger brother, Michael. I think he plays for Clare Rovers in the same league as Upton, so I'll look forward to meeting him again.

When we sit down for food I am opposite one of Eric's Uncles who I hadn't spoken to before. Amongst various pieces of cold meat on my plate I have some particularly hard pickled onions, one of which I fire across the table and it unfortunately hit Eric's Uncle in the chest. Well I hadn't intended to fire the pickled onion at him, it just came about. Thankfully he saw the funny side of it and lobbed the pickled onion back at me with a smile. I thought everyone was watching and felt very uncomfortable.

When we left the table he managed to find me and we talked about the pickled onion. It had brought back a memory of a friend's wedding and a situation much the same as my embarrassment over the pickled onion, only this time it was over a three-tier wedding cake and an absolute masterpiece in icing decoration achieved mainly in what must have been hundreds of shiny silver balls, the size of small ball bearings, the sort you get on your bicycle and every bit as hard.

I know what he was talking about, just like on my bike. Well he had his piece of cake, maybe a second as he loved cake and the icing and marzipan from other guests' plates who only really wanted the cake. So by this time he'd gathered together quite a mouthful of these steel-like things and looking around the table decided to avoid the embarrassment of being seen spitting them out on his plate in front of all these people, he swallowed the lot.

I knew just how he felt and was very concerned so I asked "Well how was your friend, was he ill?" Eric's Uncle thought about it for a while; then said, "No! I don't think he was, he was fine when he got back home, made a cup of tea and it all went wrong when he bent down to light the fire in the front room and unfortunately shot the cat asleep on the couch, and riddled it in cake decorations." Then, a broad grin came over his face and we had a laugh. I didn't think it was a friend at all, it was a made up joke, but he told it well and I still think it's funny. I told it to Dad but he didn't think it was funny. Arthur did and so did his Dad. I thought about it and for Eric's Uncle to share a man's joke with me made me feel I was growing up.

The Peacock's weren't at the wedding nor Auntie Abley, Ciss or Dad's sisters and I suppose the Johnson's would have been too busy on the farm. Close family were there and Mary's best friend Margaret which was all that mattered. We all had a lovely day. Mary and Eric looked well and they both went away happy to Blackpool. The house doesn't seem the same without Mary being about - not seeing her coming home from work each day and in her own quiet way, looking after me. Dad's home and quietly talking with Mum. It is quiet without Mary - it's not that she's noisy it's just that we all talk at the same time when she's in the house.

I'm just listening and I gather someone has died. I don't know of anyone being ill so I suppose it could be a friend at Dad's work. I keep quiet and then Dad mentions the name, "Roosevelt, President Roosevelt, a good man. What a time to go and not to see all this through to the bitter end. Always got on well with Churchill and he'll be missed." Whenever I've seen photographs of Roosevelt in the 'Picture Post' when he goes to conferences with Churchill and Stalin, he's always been sitting down or in a wheelchair with a coat around his shoulders and although he's never looked well he had the look of being a nice man, a friendly man.

Mary's back home and Eric's gone back to his regiment awaiting posting, so it's all back to normal until the postman came and I picked up the letters in the hall and thought for a minute they weren't for us. No Mrs. E.M. Walsh lives here at number five. Then it dawns on me it is my Mary, not Mary Rowland any more, and it's going to take some getting used to.

Mary reckons she's going to be finishing my Fair Isle pullover soon.

The front that is, so I couldn't see how she thinks it's going to be finished soon when the front's taken so long. Then within days I'm trying it on all sewn up, finished. It's got a plain back and it looks super from the front. Then Mary tells me that all Fair Isle pullovers have plain backs so no one's going to laugh at me thinking she ran out of wool. I'm going to love wearing it but it won't be allowed for school so it's going to be for best.

I had a couple of games with Upton, one lost, one drawn and they seem quite pleased about things so I look like becoming one of the regulars. It's really good having all the kit playing for a team.

The girls still come up from Saltney every now and again. More frequently now the weather is getting better and we just talk and they tell us of plans for having a big street party to celebrate the end of the war. It sounds to be well organised and one of the Dad's is on the party committee so some of us might well get invited. Then we're back on the usual things we talk about, singers, film stars and pictures and before I realised I was making up a foursome to go to the cinema. I'm going with a girl by the name of Beryl who I haven't even spoken to yet and I think Arthur's got June.

I'd got so much to talk about when I got in, of the people in Saltney planning a big street party and them being properly organised with a committee. Dad really understands them wanting to get together for a street party as they live in, what he calls a very close community. He says to me, looking over the top of his glasses, "You know well enough what street life is like, Peter, when we went to visit your Auntie Effie and Jim in Runcorn. They live in each others pockets every day of the week. It's a different world than the one we live in round The Green. Then there's the food - where does it come from with rationing? Your mother does well for us every day of the week as I have no doubt all the other ladies do but they can't perform miracles." And this is when I think I know who could and it's Uncle Eddie with his dealings in the black market, but we don't see the Peacock's anymore.

"Then there's the timing, the end could be days away, weeks or even months. Whenever it comes will be a surprise, no matter how you plan. And about being organised there's a saying that a camel was a horse designed by a committee." That I thought was so funny. Dad's what you call a realist and he's right it's not the same as a street living round The Green, it's the gardens and the open space make it more private but I still know all the people to say 'hello' to and have a talk. I can't see a party happening and I never said anything about going to the pictures with Beryl.

Mussolini executed : Hitler commits suicide
The end can't be far off

Then word of Mussolini who we hadn't heard of in ages has been on the news and for once we've heard it before Dad tells us; he's been found shot by partisans. Well the actual words were 'brutally killed', him and his mistress and it's thought when trying to escape on a German aircraft, I suppose hoping to get safely to his friend Hitler; then it all went wrong. He's obviously been in hiding somewhere in Italy until the partisans managed to flush him out and both of them have been left hanging upside down by their ankles by some petrol pumps at a garage in Milan. It all sounded very nasty to us and Mum says that, "We'll most likely see it all on photographs when your Dad picks up his 'Picture Post' from Moulton's shop along with his Park Drive. He just can't resist." Mum does go on about Dad's smoking and I'm sure he thinks that she doesn't know.

Then only within a day or two I get in from school and Mum meets me with "Hitler's dead," and I didn't believe her, I thought she was having me on. "No Peter he is dead." When 'Peter's' mentioned I know it's for real. She goes on to say, "No, he is dead. They found him dead in something they call a bunker in Berlin." I ask if that was it, and Mum says "Yes." It was as though she wasn't listening to the news, it was a brief interruption of her usual programme and that Dad would probably have more details when he came in from work. And he probably would as they have the wireless on all day and I notice Dad's now saying radio. It's all gone mad just like Dad said about the party thing - you can only predict what might happen and it looks like now it has!

More news of Hitler came home with Dad, not a great deal more than Mum had to say maybe that will come tomorrow. News comes in small pieces now what they call 'news flashes.' Dad is really surprised that it's all happening so quickly and he confirms Mum was right. Gone; committed suicide; poisoned himself in his bomb-proof bunker along with some of his cronies. I think Dad means some of his officers and staff though I did catch a mention of a mistress.

When they talk about our Allies, they're high ranking military and government men, there's never a mention of mistresses, so I put this to Dad and all I get from him is, "It could apply to the French." And without a pause we're back on Hitler again and discussing his fear of being found by the Russians and that by this time he must have heard of Mussolini's fate in the hands of partisans.

So I took it that Dad thought any other way to go, and this got me thinking by which time Dad's got settled in his chair with his newspaper and I notice he has the Daily Herald - a change of newspaper, so it's 'goodbye' to Rupert bear, not that I read it any more. Dad shares bits of it with us.

I've seen the photograph of Mussolini and his mistress; the two of them look a mess, covered in blood, just hanging there on show. I just got a glimpse of it before being taken back by Dad and he tells us that, "This reporter's saying, unceremoniously executed by partisans and being strung up by piano wire." With Mussolini dead and now Hitler it must be the end of the war, but Dad says, "No, it's not as simple as that, papers to sign."

As I didn't get a straight answer about mistresses I didn't see any sense in asking about papers. I've talked with Mary so many times about Dad when he talks like this; Mum does the same and Mary says, "It's called a red herring and its given when you don't know the answer or don't want to give " Mary said what Dad should have said was, 'signed an unconditional surrender.' I'm getting so mixed up with what's going on that I could have forgotten my date with Beryl.

Well I meet Beryl to go to the pictures as planned. She was waiting in front of Kennerley's Chemists. I was surprised as I didn't think she'd show up. I'd managed to come by a bar of chocolate, you could say 'on the secret' and I paid for the tickets. We went to the Music Hall and of all people I caught the eye of Mr. Mulvey, the Manager, who gave me a nod; he's a friend of Dad's and always wears a big 'dickie' bow tie. I think he knows me, but then maybe he just nods at everyone.

The Music Hall isn't one of my favourite cinemas, a place I only go when all the others are full but as it happened they were showing a film of her choice. It was all a bit boring and I can't see me doing it again. It seemed to last such a long time. Beryl was my first girl friend other than Betty Ashton, but then not the same really as she's a school girl friend so she's different. I can't even remember what the film was called, but I don't think it would have been Betty Ashton's choice.

It's hard to believe what's happening and so fast. Dad's beside himself but won't admit it. It must be just a matter of days and he hasn't done anything, so we haven't even got a flag to put out. I think we should but can't see it's going to happen. I've an idea to make one and pester Mum for an old sheet or a table cloth - it wouldn't surprise me if she had neither as she's been making them with aircraft fabric for years. I'm going around The Green from door to door asking for blue and red paint. I know the structure of a Union Jack from my book on scouting and it's really complicated but I'm going to have a go at painting up whatever Mum manages to find and hopefully end up with a couple of Union Jacks.

Mum comes up with a single bed sheet which must have been one of mine. Avoiding the torn and threadbare bits with careful cutting I end up with two good pieces flag-wise, enough for a flag to put out from Mum and Dad's bedroom and one from Mary's. That leaves me out but I can't see any sense in me hanging a flag out anyway from my back bedroom as the only people to see it would be the Adams family. Well, it is a bit of a disappointment - no one had any dark blue paint but loads and loads of red. I'm going to have so much left over I just don't know what I'm going to do with it. So it's not going to be Union Jacks its going to be St. George for England - just like in the film Henry V. So the morale booster had worked after all.

I've had a word with a couple of soldiers in the bungalow across The Green when I was on my rounds looking for paint that I'd kept friendly with over the years, playing football and cricket from time to time but they would always come out for sure when the girls were around playing Rounders. They say they're going to join in when it's all over with a Thunder flash or two, but they seem reluctant in handing them over to me and Arthur. Some of the engineers down at Crighton's ship yard might turn up if we had a bonfire.

Dad tells me that I'm getting far too excited about it all and to just calm down and wait - but why so long? Then it happens. A high ranking German officer by the name of Jodl Donitz has signed an unconditional surrender. Now that surprised me as I'd only heard Dad speak of an Admiral Donitz having taken over after Hitler. Dad often talks of them now they're both in the news and I know it's serious but when Dad says 'Donitz and Jodl' to me they sound a comic pair, like Laurel and Hardy. Funnies apart I'm sure Jodl must be at least a General. Then when I think of him without Donitz and on his own, General Jodl sounds even funnier! Dad wouldn't think it at all funny so it's something to tell Mary on the quiet. When Dad comes out with some statistic or other that isn't anything to do with what we're talking about, which he often does, Mary has a word for it. It's a 'pearler' and I think it must mean a gem.

One night after scouts I am talking with Mum about summer camp, then without an 'excuse me' from Dad - "Do you know Annie that to date by the end of this war we will have on this island of ours five hundred and fifty thousand German prisoners of war to get back to Germany?" I suppose Dad collects these 'pearlers' at work though this one is very much of the time, and he has to share them with Mum, Mary and me as we are always good listeners. I was dying to say there would be one less as there was the nice German prisoner of war I'd met at Uncle Alf's who wanted to stay on the farm. With my best interest in mind I decided to keep it to myself.

Germany surrenders and we celebrate
Victory in Europe.

V.E. Day, May 8th, 1945

In no time at all Churchill and Truman, who Dad now calls Harry Truman, the new President of the United States of America, have said that the Eighth of May should be celebrated in Europe as V.E. Day and I'm sure we will.

On the day, brass curtain rods came down without asking Mum, so no curtains in the bedrooms apart from mine, which didn't go down too well. Went out early morning, saw a few Union Jacks around The Green and we were the only house flying the St. George flag. With being painted in household paint they didn't seem to blow about like the bought flags but who cares. We had a couple of flags. And tonight, who cares about curtains - we're going to have every light on in the house!

Church bells keep ringing all over the place. Most of the shops had flags out and the windows decorated. The pubs were full not that I knew they were full, it was just so noisy and so many people about in funny hats going around hugging and kissing anyone and everyone, not usually seen when I'm out shopping. The Council workmen have been busy building a bonfire on the Meadows and boy has it grown over the last few days. I've an idea they're being helped along by people dumping things so we might even end up with a Hitler or two, so we're not going to miss out on a bonfire.

This is one of those sort of days when you're that busy that you lose track of time and this is a one-off day, a very special day. No more war! It's going to be different and it's past dinner time by the Market clock. It was on the way home that I thought of the soldiers at the bungalow not having seen us, something we must do later. I went round with Arthur in the afternoon. They always seem pleased to see us and I think it's because they're bored. We told them all about what's going on in Town - that didn't cheer them up any. I think they felt like being left out of things; stuck on duty with not much going on round The Green. Well nothing really, so they look even more bored than when we came in.

The funny thing is I've met up with these soldiers so many times over the months, if not years and I don't know their names - they're just soldiers. Then leaning back on his chair one of them, who I think is the senior man, says, "Well what are we going to do with these 'bangers?' We can't put them back in stores." I thought he was looking for an answer from his mate, the other soldier, and he didn't say a word nor did Arthur. On the spur of the moment, and why I don't know, I said, "The swill bin could be a good place." The other said, "We can't risk leaving them live in a swill bin." Now I had never thought of them being dumped so I said, "Why can't you set them off in the swill bin? It'll be a lot of fun and they won't be needed after today - bins or the Thunder flashes."

We all looked at each other for a bit and one of the soldiers, the senior man looking at his watch says, "Why not." The metal cabinet was unlocked and he's not going to part with the Thunder flashes, which is just as well as we've only messed about with spent ones down by the river when they've been having manoeuvres. You know, tapping out what's left in the hope of making a firework. It worked sometimes but setting it off was a bit tricky. I can't help but think how much bigger these Thunder flashes look compared with the spent ones we used to pick up.

The lid was lifted and I could see from the expression on his face that he thought it a bit pongy and said, "Half full and could dampen down the impact." This is when it's good to have some experts with us - feels like being looked after. Then comes "Stand back lads," and in a couple of seconds went in a Thunder flash, then instantly, "Run for it lads." Running for it we were overtaken by both the soldiers. Then there was a tremendous explosion. I stopped running and looked over my shoulder to see the bin lid hurtling through the air out of a haze of smoke, before coming down in one of the front gardens - it could have been the Jefferson's. When it all settled there was swill everywhere. The bin wasn't in too bad a state sort of crumpled and it had been through a long war, so being knocked about could be an excuse.

When we rescued the lid that luckily had landed on grass it was just a bit out of shape. By this time a few people had come out to see what was going on, a bit shocked I suppose by the bang. It was a good one! They just looked around the place and knowing they hadn't been bombed, went back inside.

Anything we could pick up went back into the bin and I honestly can't say we were worried. It was fun, but the soldiers weren't for having a go with the other one in the bin outside our house.

The soldiers asked us in for 'a brew' - I hadn't heard this before. It's a cup of tea and another 'not had before' was an enamel tin mug and they had sugar that I hadn't had in ages. I decided I didn't like sugar. One of the soldiers said 'he was starving,' and when putting the Thunder flash back in his cabinet, produced a big tin of chocolate biscuits. He said, "From me mother's - brought them back last week, might as well finish them off." I can't remember seeing a tin of chocolate biscuits before and they were assorted. It wasn't a full tin but not far off. His mate looked surprised as if he hadn't seen them before. We had another 'brew' and weren't those biscuits lovely! We didn't eat all of them, there were a few left!

Mum, Dad, all of us - and we collected a few others at the end of the road - were off to The Meadows. We joined up with a lot more people up by Hunter's field, I expect going to the same place as us, and of all days, quite a few men working in their allotments. Dad just couldn't resist calling across, "No digging for victory any more!" There was a casual glance from one as he straightened his back. I think it was that they hadn't heard him, or maybe they'd heard it so many times that it just wasn't funny anymore. I can't remember us having had our tea, but there might be places selling something to eat when we get there. We're going to have a good time and anyway I'm full of chocolate biscuits so I won't go hungry.

There was a continuous stream of people all the way to The Groves - it's just like going up Earlsway on a Saturday afternoon when Chester's playing at home. And it's got more and more people going from the suspension bridge along the river path. Those on bikes have given up and are pushing them. There's something about being with a lot of people all doing the same thing that makes you feel good. As we walked along, all of us being aware of keeping close together, I can see quite a few people in their boats, most of them with lights on and flags, music, all having parties. Even with rationing everyone is trying to put on a show. On the way we've seen a few cars with flags on and horns honking - everyone has just got to be noisy. It's all part of celebrating being happy.

There must have been hundreds of people all around the bonfire. It looked enormous and we weren't even near it - so many people you could hardly move, all waiting to see it go up in flames. Trying not to lose each other, the nearer we got the bigger it looked. There are a few bangs - fireworks going off, nothing compared with a Thunder flash, but had one gone off here people would have panicked, thinking the war had started again.

I've seen men selling flags and hats with 'kiss me quick' and there

263

seems a lot of that going on; plenty of flags, and a man selling baked potatoes; nothing that you'd really fancy. I haven't seen any ice cream. Then the singing of 'why are we waiting' so they must be late in lighting the bonfire, probably as damp as the swill bin. I've no chance of seeing what's going on being behind so many tall people as well as being a long way away; just like being at the pictures.

Then a great cheer goes up and the steady crackle of burning wood, and then we soon see flames leaping up to the sky. I wonder who lit it, I don't know - it could have been the Mayor. We were soon being showered with sparks and then followed the heat - and we thought we were too far back from the bonfire, not thinking of the heat. Well I can tell you we were glad to get away from it and we weren't the only ones pleased to view it from afar. We found lots of friendly people to talk with and pass a few hours away as the bonfire died down. I suppose in a way it became a bit sad. Maybe we were thinking of the past, memories.

After a while Mum and Dad suggested it was time to go home. We'd seen the best of it and I think we all felt tired but didn't admit it. Even as we left, more people were coming and I couldn't but think they'd be a bit disappointed. All over, and it didn't seem the same going back then amongst all the people. A man passing with a gang of 'full of fun' girls grabbed me by the shoulder and shouted "How yuh doin?" He'd gone when I realised they were the two soldiers from across The Green; out of uniform they looked so different. They'd gone by unnoticed but then it's only Arthur and me they know.

The trees in The Groves were full of fairy lights and there were floodlights. It was just like fairyland. How they'd managed to do all this in just days of the war ending I don't know. On the way home we saw cars with lights on, full of happy people hanging out of windows, all shouting and singing. Not just lights on cars, headlights full on, not masked. Then over The Dingle footbridge into Curzon Park were we in a mess - no lights, pitch black and we hadn't brought a torch; left at home like tea. We've never ever been out at night without a torch. And was it fun! We just couldn't stop laughing all the way down Curzon Park as we stumbled our way in and out of potholes - the more potholes the more we laughed.

Now if this had been in the war Mum and Dad would have moaned like mad. As Mary's older than me she would have thought it best not to laugh; I would have laughed and got into trouble from Dad. But today has been different and if the truth be known, Mary and me are laughing at Mum and Dad. They are so funny and we're not getting into trouble; and the worst is yet to come. The worst bit, the darkest bit, is out of Curzon Park and down by Hunter's field and the allotments. But way, way away we have the Chief Constable's house in sight with the lights on. With the 'digging for victory' men long gone home in the dark, we or should I say Dad, insisted on forming a human chain - he leads and holding hands, I became the last. My only memory was from Dad and I distinctly heard through the darkness, "Damnation, that b....y manhole again!" Obviously one he used to dodge when borrowing my bike. All remained quiet, it was probably shock. No one dared to risk a laugh. Funnies were over.

In Park Road West we were as good as home. Mrs. Jarman, the Thorington's and Miss Bean on the corner had all left their lights on with a few extras and we were as good as home, safe and sound. Northway and Greensway were, I can only say, a blaze of lights - must have been every house and bungalow fully lit with all blackout gone except for one bungalow across The Green, and they were in all probability still in The Meadows; who knows. Dad was quite annoyed as we'd left the bedroom windows open all because of my flags.

Even so we put on all the lights we could and Mum put the kettle on for a cup of tea; that's always good in a crisis and for once I wasn't down to make the toast. Mum made it under the grill and plastered toast with strawberry jam that she must have been saving for a special event. All this was because we'd been out of the house so long after tea time that the fire had gone out. Dead as a doe-doe! - No one in to damp it down with a shovel full of wet slack.

We were tired but just didn't want to go to bed. I think we wandered around the place and the front garden with our tea and toast. Then I was aware that unknowingly Mary had drifted off to bed and Mum was looking sleepy so I said 'goodnight' to Dad and it was then that I thought that I'd never kissed Dad. I left him to lock up which he'd always done alone. But what a day and what will tomorrow bring?

~ ❦ ~

My memories of the war ended with the defeat of the Germans who I had built a fear and hatred of since 1939. Now it's all over with Victory in Europe, VE Day. I know the Japs are still around and I think we are leaving that to the Yanks to finish off as it's their payback time for Pearl Harbour. Sort of like our Dunkirk.

Now just a couple of weekends or so after VE Day is all I ask to complete my memories and its always nice to finish things in a light hearted mood and this was the best laugh; the only belly laugh that we had had probably since it once started way back in 1939. I'm sure it was a Sunday. Dad was still working though the pressure of war effort was off, he still needed his wages. Weekend work and overtime on weekdays had become as normal. As for me, school days pre-war or war were much the same except for time spent in the cellar when the siren went.

It was Sunday – we had nothing to do and out of absolute boredom we could only come up with a walk in The Groves. That's Arthur and me, so we called on a few of our pals from Park Road West, down through Mount Pleasant and then meeting up with the main road in Saltney. It was bumper to bumper with cars; a road that we'd hardly ever seen a car on for at least five years, a long time in a lad's life.

Every now and then they would edge forward, no more than a couple of feet or so. We supposed it was people coming in from Wales as they don't have pubs opening on a Sunday, but then they usually come in by Crosville bus or train, so where's all this petrol coming from all of a sudden. We all agreed to follow them up Hough Green passing the Rookery and we soon realised that they were following us.

It didn't get any better in fact it got worse as we progressed to the Overleigh roundabout where we decided to take a seat for a while before heading off down Overleigh Road for The Groves. In fact we never made The Groves that day. We just sat there and watched the world go by, this new world of motorists. However slow it was enjoyable, something we hadn't ever seen before and accompanied by the constant playing of horns from impatient motorists. Or was it just a reaction of war over and they just wanted to make a noise?

As we sat there it soon got way beyond pleasure for us and was to become the biggest laugh we had had in years. We watched motorists abandon their cars for what appeared no reason at all as soon as they came in sight of the Overleigh roundabout, sometimes being followed by their fellow passengers, leaving the cars in absolute abandonment, doors open and running across to the gun emplacements on the roundabout in a desperate state, frantically trying and beating on doors to no avail – all lettered Ladies and Gentlemen to fool the Germans when they were expected after Dunkirk.

Then without thinking, one by one, we stood up while waving hands in the air and at the same time directing them down into the Dingle. They soon caught on and sped past us. In no time at all we had two-way traffic, the way back being much slower having been relieved. We did casually mention to the odd one or two, of the lavatories on the Little Roodee but the interest had gone.

The laugh was long, the day too short, the show went on and we had to leave it as it was time we went home, this time down Curzon Park away from the traffic, however amusing it was, we were now tired and set for home. How long the show lasted into the night we shall never know.

~ ❦ ~

The seeds of this book were sown by Jenny Joinson and supported by Kathy Astbury. I think they only expected a few pages, a brief of my growing up through the war to V.E. Day. Then I have to confess I got hooked on it and it just grew and grew and I loved every day of it as the war went on and on along with my memories.

I find it difficult to draw a line under my memories and say that's it, so after having a few words with my brother-in-law Eric, he suggested "Why not continue as readers may like to know What happened to the Lad?"

What happened to the lad?

V.J. Day came and we didn't celebrate it really but Dad did recall memories of that little old lady that used to come into his shop in the early war years when waiting for her bus, the Jehovah's Witness and she had predicted that this war was going to be the end of the world – 'Armageddon.' Dad said, "She wasn't far off – those atomic bombs are the nearest to absolute destruction you can get, and the Japs will never forgive us for it!" It didn't seem a time to celebrate; just relieved it was over.

I can't say that I really disliked school but I liked the thought of leaving and working. Unfortunately leaving at fourteen didn't happen. The leaving age extended to fifteen. This was a long year and Skipper's not pleased when I give up scouting for night school with the prospect of being a joiner in mind.

Leaving school wasn't the event I thought it might have been. I just left at the usual time at half past four. And that was that!

I enjoyed the evening class drawing the construction of windows and doors, all the different joints in wood. On his rounds of the class, the teacher, Mr. Pearson, asked if I had thought about going to art school. We talked about it and then he moved on. I never gave it a second thought.

A letter from the art school found its way to Mum and Dad and they agreed that I could go providing there were no fees to pay. I spent a day at the Art School in Grosvenor Street sitting my exam and several days later a letter came to say that I had won a free scholarship. I was to become an art student no longer a school boy.

On the first day this lad arrived in short trousers and my old school blazer minus the school crest embroidered on the top pocket which Mum had carefully unpicked. I stuck out like a sore thumb but it wasn't long before a trip to the Etonian with Mum, leaving with a pair of grey flannel longs with white and green pin stripes and a dark green shirt. The only tie I had was a school tie, crimson with black horizontal stripes which didn't go. I left the Etonian with a bright yellow one with white spots. I now feel the part and would get on, and I did.

It wasn't long before I discovered that my free scholarship entitled me to return for night classes. This I did five nights a week. At last doing something I enjoyed. I had no time for doing anything else other than pals at the weekend for a game of football and a night at the pictures.

Even with a free scholarship it was difficult for Mum and Dad and I managed to find occasional work in summer working at Groomes' farm picking fruit. I swatted up my history on Chester with a view to escorting American tourists around the city. I put it to the Manager at the Blossoms Hotel. He was willing to go along with the idea and I was to be well tipped. My Christmas job was with the Royal Mail at their sorting office opposite the General Station. Every morning there would be a mountain of parcels that a couple of us would climb, shouting addresses as we threw parcels down to be sorted. That done we were out on the road in a hired furniture removal van.

Tips weren't up to American standard. Over many Christmases I was only offered one by a little old lady which I couldn't accept. Her delivery was a turkey from Ireland with no packaging whatsoever, plucked of feathers and naked to the world, apart from the address label tied round its neck. The first time I'd seen a turkey.

There weren't any commercial artists in Chester, so jobs would come into the Art School and there always seemed cake decorations to do for Bolland's in Eastgate Row. They would send parcels of assorted pieces of hard icing for me to paint designs on, usually heraldic shields and coats of arms which I was never paid for, not even a free cake.

I drew up some advertising for Williams & Williams, the metal window company. This came via a printer in Watergate Street Row and by way of thanks he printed off some Christmas cards from my pen drawings of Chester which saved the family a bob or two.

One of my jobs didn't work out too well and it was with my barber, Ernie Coe's on Grosvenor Street. In chatting as you do when having your hair cut, he discovered that I was at the Art School across the road studying to be a commercial artist and saw an opportunity for some free advertising. We agreed on a trade of four haircuts to include Brylcream, not the usual rubbish he usually sprays on that sets like a starched shirt collar.

I drew him up a full colour show card to stand up in his window that he was over the moon with. I thought it was rather fun and enjoyed doing it; a good caricature drawing of a bearded tramp with knapsack on a shoulder stick. The caption in a balloon from his mouth, 'I'd walk for miles for a haircut and shave at Ernie Coe's.' I managed haircuts one and two, then at three Ernie had a word that he wasn't his usual busy self so the show card came out of his window and I missed out on two haircuts with Brylcream. So I made a move to Newnes on the Eastgate steps. In chatting I never shared my being an Art Student. They always thought I worked in a bank.

My sister Mary gave birth to a baby boy, John Patrick. I can't believe it – me an Uncle. Eric was demobbed from the Army and moved in with us at 5 Northway. A full house again just like in the early war years when we had the soldiers. We haven't got a shed and it's getting difficult having two bikes in the back kitchen of a night time.

After the war, it wasn't having to save for a house, it was all what Dad called, 'red tape'- permits and a licence to build from the Ministry of Works. Eventually it all came together with Walker and Dawson, who were going to build in Curzon Park North. Eric found Mr. Walker was one of the few builders that worked without a backhander, but progress was slow due to the scarcity of building materials; the land where the ATS had their huts in the war.

Mary and Eric's house was to be number six Curzon Close – it backed on to the railway and had been the smallholding of one of our neighbours, Mr. Jones, a retired railway worker who lived at 'Gwynfar' number fifteen Greensway. He was related to the Blakes in Watergate Row; what a small world. I thought he was rather posh as he had a pony and trap as well as a two wheeled trailer that he towed around on his bicycle; a nice friendly man whom Arthur and I always had a chat with.

Arthur's sister Phyllis who worked at the Co-operative Building Society managed to get a mortgage for them so Eric and Mary moved into their new house. What a house! A very basic house by today's expectations - screeded concrete throughout the ground floor with taps and sink in the back kitchen. Just bare walls and floors, fitted kitchens just didn't exist. Furniture was difficult to buy and when available I think it was all about collecting points. Furniture was rationed just like food and clothes and the war's gone but why is all this with us? Furniture was branded 'Utility Furniture' though I did rather like it. It was painted, simple and it served the purpose.

Eric was to become one of the first 'do-it-yourself-ers' and he worked very hard. But he did find time to play football and we would go together for a kick around on the Civil Service pitch on the Wrexham Road opposite Great Grandma's Farm.

At Art School I had entered a design for a road safety poster at the Welsh National Eisteddfod at Dolgellau. I was helped along by a fellow student, a Mary Rowlands. Her father spoke fluent Welsh and he would translate for me. I only remember the English version – 'Look twice before crossing the road.' He also suggested that I add an 's' on the Rowland name on the entry form as it then became Welsh. I was already ahead of him. It was always an issue with Dad.

I won first prize; a cheque for five pounds was way beyond the national weekly wage. I spent most of it on a lovely decorated jug for Mum which I knew she would like from Browns of Chester. It's amongst a few of the memories I have in an IKEA display cabinet at home.

This was followed by another five pounds when I won the Randolph Caldecott Memorial Prize for Illustration. I have since found a plaque on a house in Bridge Street Row where he lived.

Whilst on the lighter side of life I put on a football shirt for the Art School as well as for Upton Athletic. At Christmas I was given the opportunity to play for the pub landlords eleven in a charity game. This came about by Arthur and I going into the Pied Bull on a Sunday night whilst walking his dog 'Blackie.' We would settle down at a table with a glass – we only knew lager - whilst Blackie did a tour of the pub; regulars knew him to be a nice friendly little dog.

It was obvious that the landlord didn't want to play football, neither had it appealed to the regulars so he asked if we fancied a game. Arthur wasn't in the least interested as his interests had gone over to rugby, so it was down to me and I was to play for the landlord's eleven. How on earth was I going to tell Dad that I'm going to play on behalf of the Pied Bull or even been in the Pied Bull! This was going to be some game and I was going to play with the greatest centre forward of all time, 'Dixie' Dean, landlord of the Dublin Packet in the Market Square. He scored a fantastic goal from a power drive off a centre that I would never have put my head to, but he did. I can't remember the final score or even who won – it was just good fun.

Sunday night at the Pied Bull became the regular thing for us to do with the company of Blackie, up Earlsway, down onto the Roodee and up Paradise Street into Town. This was the usual way we walked into Town. The chaps behind the bar didn't seem to mind Blackie being in the pub. Let off his lead he would happily snoop around the place being made a fuss of and he'd appear from behind the bar when it was time to go.

A couple of glasses of lager, a packet of crisps and we would be off back home, but for some reason Blackie never seemed to have the same sense of direction on the way home and would have wandered off if it wasn't for his lead.

Then one Sunday when I went round for Arthur Mrs. Carsley opened the back door. She said that Arthur wasn't in. We talked for a while and then she put it to me that she couldn't understand why, after we'd taken Blackie for his walk on a Sunday night, that more often than not he was decidedly off colour for a couple of days. The silence seemed endless and all I could think to say was – "I'm afraid I can't help you there Mrs. Carsley." Arthur had found a girl friend and things were never to be quite the same again.

On leaving Art School I'd collected three Union of Lancashire and Cheshire Institute certificates at distinction level, two annual awards for best student, the Randolph Caldecot Memorial Award for Illustration and two National Diplomas for Design, with one at additional level. The years at Art School had been much better than school. I'd worked hard and been rewarded for it. Now it was just a mater of time waiting for call up for National Service.

The waiting game is never easy so I would drift off to the farm at

Dodleston, doing a day or so working for Uncle Alf for a few things to take home for Mum when I really would have appreciated being paid.

Then, what a surprise, what an opportunity – I was asked to join a party of what had been fellow students to spend a week at the South Bank in London – the Festival of Britain. Mum and Dad funded me and so I was able to go.

One thing I forgot to mention was that from the age of eighteen I qualified for a grant from the Government of one pound a week.

At the Festival I had the privilege of meeting and sharing in the work of so many commercial artists that before I had only seen as names on illustrations in the Radio Times, in magazines and books. My idol and influence at art school was Abram Games. He designed the Festival symbol and those safety at work posters that Dad used to bring home for me from the aircraft factory.

The week passed and no sooner as it started I was returning home on the early morning milk train from London Euston. How different it was to be back in Chester. Mum was out when I got home. I let myself into an empty house and I was to find on the hall floor the brown manila envelope – 'On His Majesty's Service' – and enclosing the King's shilling.

Two years in the Royal Air Force was going to be a big change from being an art student and it was preventing me from starting my life as a commercial artist. In a way I was being robbed of two years.

I arrived late at Padgate and I was directed to the Airman's Mess. The food servery was closed, so I found my way to a long table where there were several soup plates containing jam, some with syrup. I was looking for bread. "Just go over there and knock on the hatch door and ask." It was opened by a young lady in a white jacket with three stripes on her arm. I asked 'Please can I have some bread.' All I got was "fu** off!" as she slammed the door down.

All kitted out with uniform, dentist, medicals and having injections for everything known to man I was on my way to Weeton for ten weeks square bashing. Fatigue week came and being an art student my job was painting the metal railings round the square!

Our flight was considered to be good at drill and what surprised me I became more than handy with a rifle. The firing range was way out by the perimeter fence overlooking open fields. I had a go with a Bren but it was the rifle I enjoyed; lying down, concentrating and letting a few shots off at a target. Then something I'd not experienced before, a sharp short whining sound followed by our Sergeant shouting, "Fu**ing hell – Rowland's shot a cow!" as it slumped to the ground. How they knew it was me I don't know. However, the cow didn't get up again. The fatigue squad's duty each day after firing was over was to riddle the sand free of bullets. Apparently this hadn't been done the day before we went on the range so it was thought to be a ricochet, so thankfully I wasn't in trouble.

End of square bashing I had an interview with an officer regarding a suitable trade for me in the RAF. He just looked at me saying, "I just don't know what we can do with you Rowland, you're the sort of chap that the RAF doesn't need." My response was, "Sir, I'm the sort of chap that doesn't need the RAF." He wished me well but I think I'd blotted my copy book.

I left RAF Weeton with a marksman's badge; nothing to do with the cow episode. My trade was going to be in signals as telegraphist/telephonist at RAF Wittering where I was to spend most of my time in the RAF.

I enjoyed being there; the sport, the football playing with the

Station Team. Pals were great and we had such fun times. Things we got up to and got into trouble for that has given me so much to look back on. All was going well. I'd got a few badges on my sleeve, a spark's badge and a single prop; (propeller).

The months were ticking by, fifteen - and I thought Wittering would see me through to demob. Then out of the blue a telephone call from Postings at H.Q. I knew the Corporal behind the desk. Looking up at me he just said, "It's Fazackerley." "Where's that?" I asked. "Canal Zone" was the reply. I was bound for Egypt! I stood there rooted to the floor in what I can only describe as prolonged silence. Then the Corporal started laughing, as did the rest of the office, and eventually he made mention of Fazackerley in Liverpool - the canal zone being the Leeds-Liverpool canal; one sadistic scouse Corporal. For him it would have been going home – for me it would be nearer home but I didn't want to leave Wittering.

I found RAF Fazackerley to be a sort of transit station and we left each day by coach according to what Watch we were on to RAF Blackbrook, North West Signals Unit, hidden amongst the slag heaps on a disused coal mine. Have I just blown the Official Secrets Act?

I was banded around from one posting to another before finding my way back to RAF Fazackerley awaiting demob. It was the time of the Queen's Coronation and they didn't want any demob-happy airmen on official parades, so I was tucked away along with a couple of pals in a transit hut all to ourselves. Me, Alan and Jim – no one else to share a demob party with. Not that anyone else would want to come to a demob party that still had time to do, so we decided to do something special. Not the usual 'boozy do;' we weren't really beer drinkers. Then Jim mentioned liqueurs. I would never have thought of liqueurs. So that was it, settled, and not a lot of volume, like pints, maybe more expensive but you're only demobbed once.

We talked about it for long enough and roughly the plan was to find our way to say Seaforth early evening and then calling in pubs along the Dock Road, ending up at the Pier Head where we knew we could get a Corporation bus back to Fazackerley. We'd not really thought about a meal but it would rob us of drinking time, so we decided on an early start with crisps on the way, and for the very last time the three of us would wear our best blues and flat hat. Did we work on getting ready, and I have to say on the night when we were ready for the off we were a credit to the RAF. Brass buttons and badges were brighter than they'd ever been and uniform pressed.

I don't think the Police Corporal on the gate had ever seen us in our best blues. He didn't seem to recognise us, but then he'd got used to seeing us in our working blues, a crumpled beret and no brass. He watched us go down the road with a confused look on his face.

Our intention was a round of liqueurs at each pub we came across, which Alan insisted on calling a hostelry, along the Dock Road and trying not to repeat the same liqueurs. We thought it was going to be on the tricky side as we had no idea of how many pubs there were on the Dock Road and weren't well up on liqueurs. I can't remember the name of the first pub; in fact I can't remember the name of any of the pubs, but we were to hear the activity from the first pub before we got sight of it. We were going to enjoy tonight and it was down to me to get the first round.

The noise intensified as I opened the door and made my way to what I thought was the direction of the bar through a crowd of smoking noisy Dockers. I felt uncomfortable to say the least, and out of place. I caught the eye of the Barman who I couldn't hear but I thought by his mouthing it was what I wanted by the way of drinks.

I've never been very good at mouth reading so I replied very loudly for his benefit. "Three crème de menthes please."

To my surprise the place became decidedly hushed and a few wind-ups were bantered about from the locals. This is when I noticed that Jim and Alan had found themselves a table tucked away in a corner whilst I had braved the flak and hostility. "Anything else, Sir? And would you like a tray?" Was he speaking to me? On the spur of the moment I could only think of potato crisps. "Only pork scratchings and salted peanuts" was the reply. Not having heard of pork scratchings, I thought, "Why not."

The pub settled down – we were made most welcome and managed the odd pint or two bought for us by the locals. I think we stayed too long. The pork scratchings and crème de menthes didn't seem to be compatible and we said our farewells to progress down the Dock Road.

The next pub was much the same, full of Dockers, but then it is on the Dock Road so it's going to be like this all the way. It was Jim that made the trip to the bar and Jim was a pretty lively and loud sort of person, but I knew he had made a mistake by the way he put it to the Barman. "Good evening landlord, three whisky things, Glava's and salted peanuts." There was the same remarks about being Brylcream boys in blue and army dodgers but again after they'd had their fun we were made most welcome.

We progressed along the Dock Road on liqueurs and snacks and several pickled eggs, none of which seemed to go with our refined choice of drinks. We had never anticipated the road being so long, so many pubs. I think we missed a few but we at last made the Pier Head and a double-decker Corporation bus back to Fazackerley. We got in a right mess on the stairs and decided after a lot of confusion to stay on the lower deck.

We slept soundly on getting back to Camp and believe it or not we were delayed the following day, overslept and missed breakfast!

All dressed in our civvies, our kit in packs and kit bag. It could be needed as we would be on reserve for two years. I had a farewell talk from the Adjutant and he asked if I had realised that I was one of a few privileged young men to have served under two Monarchs. I had nothing to say – I just wanted to be out.

It wasn't easy being back home after the routine of service life. I was at a loose end. I was spending time in the reference library reading newspapers and telephone directories in the hope of finding employment and all I could come up with was a Ticket and Showcard Writer in Watergate Street. I wandered down to have a look at the place and spent some time with him. He'd obviously got a nice little one man business going, but it wasn't for me.

With no opportunity of working as a Commercial Artist in Chester it was to a big city and Liverpool was the nearest. The alternative was Manchester and that was a non-starter after memories of that holiday with the Peacock's at Weaste. Another day spent in the reference library and from forty two names and addresses found in the Liverpool telephone directory I wrote asking for employment.

I was to go for several interviews, then back home to wait for confirmation of a job and it came from, believe it or not, Peacock's Advertising Agency in Leece Street. I'd got a job and I was going to earn four pounds and ten shillings a week. I'd only been at Peacock's three days when I got a letter from Littlewoods Mail Order Stores in Crosby offering me five pounds a week, another ten shillings. Without any hesitation I handed in my notice and arrived at Littlewoods the following Monday.

I was up early for the six thirty train to Birkenhead changing for the underground to Liverpool, and then the extra cost for a bus from Skelhorne Street out to Crosby. I was out of pocket for a few extra bob a week travelling, but it was worth it. It was a much nicer place to be than Peacock's.

The family were so pleased about me working for Littlewoods and Dad predicted that I would have a secure job for life and a gold watch when I retired. Then he mentioned a couple of provisos like my face fitting and keeping my nose clean. Dad's prediction wasn't going to be as I left Littlewoods after nine years.

In that time I'd married Bett and was living at her family home in Formby whilst we saved for a deposit on a house. There was freelance work to be had and one of the most interesting jobs was working on the 'Eagle' comic.

Dad became ill and I arrived back home to see him taken into the City hospital where sadly he died a week later.

Eventually the long awaited day came and we moved into our new semi detached house in Little Altcar. Most of it remained unfurnished for years. We had a bed and a whitewood kidney-shaped dressing table. It had three mirrors, a glass top and a curtain rail. Bett fitted some flowery curtains - a real oldie worldie looking thing but it was cheap and only in need of paint like the wardrobe.

A carpet fitter friend of father-in-law's from school days had some plain red carpet left over from fitting out a big store in Bold Street, Liverpool. This went in the living room with a bit left over for the stairs. Pale blue lino went into the hall, our bedroom and landing. A black background lino with a scatter of multi-coloured bits was on offer for the back kitchen. Again you might ask why? – it was cheap.

An annual pay rise each Christmas came in handy if your face had fitted and I assumed mine did as whenever the boss wanted to see me it was always, "send Jim Chester up." Or was it with keeping my nose clean? however it worked. I always got the full name, never just Jim; going to see Mr. Hubbard in his domain was always a bit scary – he was that sort of man.

Towards the end of a catalogue when it all got a bit hectic, there was plenty of overtime so we invested in an Ercol dining table and chairs from Waring and Gillow. Having a look around in the store across the road we recognised where our big red off-cut came from.

It was no longer just me and Bett. We are now three, our first born Deborah Jane.

Another first though not new, was an old banger of a car from Hatton's of Southport. It never made their posh showroom in Lord Street. I viewed it parked in the back street, a grey two-door Morris 1000, YKB8. The salesman said it was a good runner but thought the mileage had been tampered with. So we'd got a car.

With all its problems I loved that car. Turning the key and always hoping it would fire up the engine which it seldom did. Even if I got her going I knew she would conk out before I got her home. The engine seemed to burn a lot of oil, as we left a trail of thick smoke whenever we went out for a drive on a Sunday, not every Sunday as petrol was pretty pricey and so was oil. Was petrol four shillings a gallon? – sounds about right, five gallons for a pound!

It became a constant drain on the pocket, so many things done all to no avail. Then a neighbour suggested a garage in Crosby belonging to a friend of his. I left the car with him for the day with the idea of picking it up after work. Leaving the workshop he came across the forecourt to meet me. "Bad news I'm afraid Mr. Rowland - that engine's completely shot. Any attempt to fix it is only going to be money down the drain. That car's done a lot of mileage that doesn't bear any resemblance to what's on the clock." This I told him was mentioned by the salesman when I bought the car and that it had never recorded any mileage I'd done. His eyes looked up to heaven in despair. I could only think of 'scrap.'

Then he asked "had I considered having a reconditioned engine fitted. It would be well worth it. She's a nice little car and would give you years of trouble free motoring." That's what I wanted to hear, but could I afford it? A typed up estimate came in the post and it was for a lot of money. I couldn't see her scrapped and the only alternative I had was to go, as they say, cap in hand to borrow from the bank. I found the Manager was most understanding and I left with an overdraft. The shame of borrowing I kept to myself – no one else was ever to know.

The Morris Gold reconditioned engine was fitted along with a new clutch which they thought might as well be done whilst they had the engine out. I agreed; I was past caring. When I picked her up, her bonnet was off for all to see and the engine was gold, all gold. Was I pleased and I enjoyed signing the cheque. She went like a bird and was now going to last forever, but we became aware on one of our Sunday trips of the floor of the car being a bit on the whaffey side; something I thought I could fix. I made a floating floor of tongue and groove boarding and this is when I remembered some pieces of red carpet left in the loft. A bit of cutting and tacking and I'd fitted a carpet that complimented the aged red leather of the seats. We now had a car better colour-coordinated than the house.

Come the autumn, under-sealing the car was the thing to do in preparation for salted winter roads. Garages offered to spray on your old engine oil after a service. It wasn't too bad a job to do with a couple of coats of black bitumen paint, which most of us did.

Whenever we had a caller in the Studio this was engineered to become a talking point and I got to know what was coming. "Now Peter swears by a good couple of coats of fencing creosote." Then they would all fall about laughing except for the caller and me; then I would have to explain about the floating floor. Even then it wasn't funny for the caller or for me. I just got annoyed after a while which provided them with even more amusement.

The years at Littlewoods Studio were well spent. I was to see the catalogue progress from black and white photography enhanced by a lot of re-touching. Some merchandise was thought to be better hand drawn. There were some pages printed in two colours with just a few in full colour, and even they originated from a black and white photograph.

It was the floor coverings section. The work for the day would come in an A4 envelope. It would contain layout for two pages; a double page spread and the appropriate black and white photographs all one third larger than catalogue page size. I would then contact the respective buyer to provide merchandise samples. Then it was up to me to over-paint the photographs with the appropriate opaque designer's colours to match the samples and also to enhance the quality of the merchandise, then cut out and paste it all up as per the layout. Copy writing, type setting, proof reading, a final approval from the buying department and away for print.

The number of signatures of approval on the reverse of the artwork was mind blowing, mine was never asked for! The front cover was always taken from a coloured painting depicting a special occasion. The year I joined it was the Queen's Coronation.

We experimented a lot with airbrushing transparent colour over sepia tinted photographs. Then I think came the Metzo tint which was inconsistent and too time consuming. Then finally the big breakthrough, large format colour transparencies from Kodak.

We were no longer pasting up flat artwork on a drawing board – it was a new world, new skills to be learned. I was to work in a dark room at a light box. Colours on film didn't always match up with some of the merchandise, so we were again airbrushing, but this time with transparent photographic dyes before fitting them up into page form. But now pages were made up s/s, (same size), with no need to sharpen up by reduction; all to do with the improved quality in photography.

The Commercial Artist as I knew was becoming phased out. I was to acquire other skills, learning to adapt. I became quite accomplished at working with transparencies over the years and any problems would find the way to my desk. Somehow I missed the old way – it was so varied and so many materials to learn how to handle and always in the daylight of a Studio, not spending half the day in a darkroom.

Over the months several of my friends had left and I felt at a dead end and thinking it was time to move on. But I can't leave Littlewoods without a memory of my most pleasurable of days. It was a one off never to be repeated, just to disappear in time.

We had a works canteen at Littlewoods just open for lunch. Mid-mornings and afternoons a lady would come round with biscuits and hot drinks. It wasn't any different at Christmas but this year the Art Director, Mr. Hubbard who we knew affectionately as Reg, a tall, big man, the sort of man that you don't mess about with but have a lot of respect for, decided that we were going to have a Studio party before we finished for the day. Festive sandwiches, mince pies and an attempt at a Christmas cake appeared from the canteen.

Mr. Hubbard came down from his office wearing his paper hat and acting as though he was already in a party mood. We all tucked in, well plied with wine and it wasn't long before Mr. Hubbard took over with tales of his more youthful days – whether it was art college or university I don't know – but he was obviously impressed by a young man by the name of Bengie. Strange what comes out when you've had a drink or two.

He soon got us into shape and we were enjoying it. He spaced out three chairs on the floor and lay across them, his feet, head and bottom supported by chairs. This Bengie would then have three others sit across the length of his body. When Bengie gave the signal the centre chair bearing his bottom would be removed and he would support all three without a problem. It was hilarious listening to Mr. Hubbard shouting instructions to the three getting them all in the right place before the signal.

You could sense panic in his voice as he tensed his body ready to take the strain of the three. Then, "remove chair" and the language from Mr. Hubbard as he removed volunteers from the sit in was free and uncontrolled. There's some sinister pleasure in seeing your boss make a complete arse of something!

They say time is a great healer. The wine helped and shortly we were to have further exploits of Mr. Hubbard's teenage hero Bengie. A glass of wine in his hand (there was one of us handy with the bottle) he went on to tell us of Benjie's ability to run along the face of a wall. This one reduced the Studio staff to silence. The chair thing seemed feasible but running along the face of a wall was definitely a non-runner. We needed time to think about it.

It was obvious that he needed a lot of free space for this one. We were all ages clearing the Studio floor space of drawing boards, desks, filing cabinets, art work, racks and tables; it was surprising how much was on the walls. All Mr. Gillingwater's catalogue production charts gone for the memory of Bengie, but all of us were enjoying every minute of it.

I shuddered to think how long it was going to take us to get this Studio back, ready for work after Christmas. Not to worry. All was ready, the Studio cleared of everything, just like an airfield; one hell of a size when it's empty. Mr. Hubbard said Benjie insisted on at least a twenty foot clear run before going horizontal on his run along the face of the wall. This would probably be another five or six feet before he came back down to the floor. Then he'd need some sort of landing strip, maybe ten feet.

All ready to go was questionable whilst Mr. Hubbard plied himself with red wine, but somehow we all had faith in his ability to sort this one out. This was down to him – we were in no way involved; a solo performance. He was now straining on the leash. One, two, three ready steady go – he was off heading for the wall at the end of the Studio. All the forethought and stripping bare of the Studio was to no avail as no sooner had Mr. Hubbard left his run up he went straight through the wall with a resounding bang! All that remained of him in the Studio was his head and shoulders and outstretched arms which prevented him from ending up in the office next door. Luckily he wasn't hurt other than his pride and faith in the memory of Bengie.

He wasn't to know that in all probability Bengie had had the benefit of running along a solid brick wall, but he should have checked - our Studio wall was of partition quality, stud frame, clad with hardboard. How carefree one becomes after having had a few! A little too late we all went on to black coffee. This was to be the first and last of our Studio Christmas parties.

Three of us made the break from Littlewoods to start our own business – 'Studio Argent,' and I left with a much appreciated leaving card and a boxed pair of gold cuff links from the Studio staff that I still have. The years had been well spent working with so many talented people all with their own individual skills. They had accepted me as a new boy from art school and I had grown and benefited from their understanding and experience in the early years and I had left as one of them.

Studio Argent sounded rather grand and not at all like the disused shop we were working from in Waterloo. We were doing much the same mail order catalogue work as before. We knew it so well we couldn't go wrong and being ex-Littlewoods gave us an introduction into so many of the mail order houses throughout the country. Catalogue work is seasonal no matter who you are working with and we had to find work to fill the gaps between the catalogues. This was the work I enjoyed, being a change from mail order.

Our second daughter Sarah Ann was born.

At work it was out of the shop and into new premises over our bank, convenient but we hadn't room to expand and eventually moved to a purpose built unit on an industrial estate in Maghul.

As a family we had moved back to Formby to enable us to get Debbie into a school of our choice, St. Luke's Church of England School – Bett's old school, and still the same headmistress. Another new property, only this time it's a bungalow and it takes some getting used to being all on one floor. There were several large housing developments on the go in Formby and weekends became tempting times looking around show houses and the bungalow had served its purpose.

Norville Developments were building the type of houses we liked and we fancied something detached. A deposit secured us a choice of a corner plot which was to be number one, Greenloons Drive, and we were to see it built brick by brick as it was only down the road from our bungalow.

Mum died and my nephew John and family move into 5 Northway. House finished, the move went well but my working days weren't enjoyable any more. I'd become saturated with mail order. I suppose the safe option, but I'd had enough. It wasn't going to be as easy as the last time, but what to do. Ideally I wanted to get back into design and illustration, but where? I'd been at a loose end for months. Then one evening I was looking out of our living room window at the builder's site office still at the end of the road looking shabby. The site board was pretty naff as was the literature we had from the selling agents. I thought what a challenge that would be and I could do it.

I did a bit of delving into companies and found Norville Developments to be a subsidiary company of Norwest Construction, the head office being in Dunnings Bridge Road. I went and had a look at the place. I liked it and would enjoy working there. I designed them a new site sales board, changing the name to Norwest Housing in line with the holding company and with this enclosed a letter with suggestions to coordinate an overall image through advertising, brochures etc. and offering my services as an in-house graphic designer. This I sent to the Managing Director at Norwest Construction. An interview followed and I was given the job. I resigned my directorship at Studio Argent. A really nasty month followed but I was at last free of mail order and I was to start work with Norwest Holst.

I had an office of my own working within the newly established architects department. I was to work along with the Head Architect Dennis Walker and the Housing Sales Manager, Nick Coulson. My Director in overall charge was Donald Jackson. I couldn't have worked with three better people.

We were all new to Norwest Holst and had a free hand though there were lots of the old school still within that didn't want change. But how we changed it!

I established and coordinated a new corporate identity for Norwest Housing - a format for show houses. I introduced the first illustrated ads for house sales and industrial developments. I worked throughout the U.K., Ireland, France and Portugal. This was the most challenging and enjoyable job I had ever had. I won an award for a site logo from the Portuguese Tourist Board for literature and site presentation for our development on the Algarve. The Aldeia do Golf Vilamoura.

All this was over a period of around nine years and looking back it was about nine years at Littlewoods, about the same at Studio Argent and now it was about nine at Norwest Holst – but now it's all going pear-shaped. Asset strippers came in and within twelve months I became the last of the redundancies. I felt that I'd been sacked and how difficult it was handing in the company car key.

I found work on a day to day basis at advertising agencies in Liverpool whilst looking for work then I was offered work at Newage Kitchens designing kitchen layouts. They were a kitchen unit manufacturing company and I soon discovered this wasn't to do with design and preparing drawings for a client, it was how many units can be fitted in a kitchen. Design done with a calculator – it wasn't for me.

On one of our Sunday trips in the car we ventured out to Lancaster to have a look around Hornsea Pottery and Leisure Park. It hadn't been long opened; a modern architectural gem. What a place this would be to work I thought – might as well give it a go and I wrote a letter to the Managing Director including my C.V. and the possibility of employment. To my surprise I received a reply from Desmond Rawson, the Chairman of Hornsea Pottery in Yorkshire. He wanted to see me. He wanted to be called Desmond.

I spent a day with them and found they had two Design departments, one Ceramic Design within the factory and the Graphic Design Department in a large detached house, 'Whitestacks,' by the main gate to the Leisure Park. Much the same set-up as at Lancaster but well established. Desmond was impressed with my portfolio of work compiled from my days spent at Norwest Holst and he thought that my expertise and experience in construction would be of benefit to the Pottery, but unfortunately they had only recently appointed a Head Graphic Designer and how useful I would have been to them whilst the Pottery at Lancaster was being built.

My thoughts went back to the last year or so at Norwest Holst when I was hanging on but expecting redundancy and from what Desmond is saying there could have been a job in Hornsea.

We talked for a while and then he suggested "what about Special Projects Designer? We'd fit you in with an office at Whitestacks and you would be involved in trade shows, exhibitions, special editions, anything that disrupted the day-to-day routine of the Pottery. And there's still plenty to do over at Lancaster." After talking about a salary I was offered the job and I would have a few days to think about it.

We were invited as a family to spend a weekend at Hornsea staying in a hotel on the sea front to get a feel of the place and on returning home we decided we had no alternative other than to accept the job. I found lodgings in Hornsea and was working in Whitestacks sharing an office with the Estates Manager, Dick Robinson. What a character that man was.

After a few weeks in lodgings I found a very nice cottage to rent,

'Westgate Mews', owned by my newly found G.P. I moved in and got the place looking nice for Christmas with tree and decorations. It was time as a family to say farewell to Liverpool, a place and people we had learnt to love. A decision I have always regretted.

The Graphic Designer Terry Hird and I worked directly with the Chairman and he was looking for awards. They already had an award from the Design Council for the 'Contrast' range of tableware and wanted another for a range of tableware to be known as 'Concept.' Rumour had it that there were trial pieces already going through the kilns. This put the pressure on us at Whitestacks to go for an award for design management. I seem to remember that a crate of champagne was in the offing from Desmond which I assumed to be shared with Ceramics Design. We had two years before Desmond retired and Ceramics already had a start on us.

The work at Hornsea was very enjoyable and varied. I worked a bit with Graphics helping Terry out now and again and we would come together for the Trades Fair at Birmingham. It was as Desmond had said Special Projects.

I acquired quite a collection of mugs that I'd designed which always gave Ceramics a few problems as I wasn't really a Potter but we got on together. I designed a mini replica of a Victorian double-decker London bus that was made in Grimsby, not noted for its coach building. We moved it over to Lancaster as they had more roads to run on.

Work-wise it was fine. Bett was guiding visitors around the Pottery, we'd bought a lovely detached house with a Granny flat in Football Green with Bett's Mum in mind as she was now living alone back at Formby. Our purchase was much to the annoyance of a footballer by the name of Bremner who said he played for Leeds United. My response was that I worked for Hornsea Pottery which didn't appear to have any credibility whatsoever.

Debbie had finished with A-levels at Hornsea High School; had passed her exams to join the Cheshire Police and was to leave home for training at Bruche. She enjoyed the training and of all places a posting to Cheshire Police H.Q. at Chester.

It was strange that around this time I received a letter from Cheshire County Hall saying that I was on a short list of three to be interviewed for the position of Head of Graphic Design. I'd never applied for this but, Yes - I was interested. I went for interview and met a familiar face in the waiting room. He was the Designer at one of the new towns and second to go in. He was soon out and said to me, "I wouldn't bother – the guy from Nottingham's got the job." I did bother but I didn't get the job which was a disappointment as we could have been a complete family again at Chester and where better to be. How things go around in familiar circles.

Ceramics design won the Design Council Award for the range of 'Concept' tableware and we at Whitestacks were awarded the Presidential Award from the Royal Society of Arts for Design Management. Unfortunately the promised champagne never flowed probably because Desmond thought we'd never do it within two years. He brought forward his retirement plans and was to move cross-country to live at Glasson Dock, Lancaster where he could keep an eye on what they were doing at the Lancaster Pottery. I supposed being retired and no longer Chairman but couldn't let go.

Desmond was lost without designers around him and Terry and I were given the opportunity to move to Lancaster. I welcomed the move back to the west coast. We were going home. We moved into an apartment in Bolton-le-Sands, the owner being the daughter of

Albert Modley a famous Lancashire comedian. She was in the bathing beauty finals for Miss Great Britain at Morecambe, none of which I was aware of, and it didn't go down well.

The other temporary measure was that there was no room for us at the Pottery and Terry and I would be working from a spare room in Desmond's house whilst plans were drawn up for a purpose built design unit at the Pottery.

We found a good school for Sarah with Ripley Church of England in Lancaster, and Bett was asked to manage the seconds shop at Lancaster. We were settling in again as a family.

Hornsea were establishing a small pottery on the Isle of Man that Terry and I were involved in and designed most of the ceramics produced there. I was busy with the Rare Breeds Centre at Lancaster and enjoyed the celebrations of the opening by the Duchess of Devonshire; we as a family were introduced to her, except for Debbie who was away in Chester.

We moved to a nice family home at Oaklands Court, Aldcliffe.

The temporary measure proved to be longer and working in the confines of Desmond's house was getting more difficult by the day. I did have thoughts of leaving the company and it was around this time that I had a telephone call from the Financial Director at Hornsea. He wanted to see me and I met with him at a hotel in Lancaster. We discussed several issues. The Directors had never seen a viable need for an additional design unit at Lancaster. The bottom line was that Terry and I had served our purpose at Hornsea in achieving awards for Desmond and they wanted us out of Desmond's house and off their payroll.

We came to a compromise that I put to Terry and we agreed to part company with Desmond and Hornsea Pottery to establish a business of our own. We rented a floor over an architects practice in Dalton Square, Lancaster; we were in a good spot. I can't say I was sorry to leave Hornsea but we had a task on our hands.

Sarah leaves school and finds work at Atkinson's well established tea and coffee traders in China Street. That aroma when you entered the shop – and when they are roasting the coffee beans the smell wafts outside and around the street.

Debbie telephones me with the news that she's had enough of the Police. I met with her at a service station outside Chester. She wanted to go to University. I found her a suitable place at Lancaster University and she was coming home. We've got both the girls again.

Rowland and Hird, R&H, is progressing with a good client base, then one evening before tea, Bett tells me that she has a gentleman friend and will be leaving us the following morning for London, moving in with her brother Edward.

Thankfully I was left with my two girls. The evenings were difficult and we just talked of ups and downs, mainly downs, then Sarah, with a happy look on her face, came out with a gem, "and just think we won't have to have liver anymore." She does really hate liver. Financially it was a struggle establishing a business and keeping house and home together, but we coped. Debbie and Sarah were absolute gems.

Sarah was the first to leave the nest and married Steve, a friend from her early days at Ripley, who had almost become a resident at Oaklands Court. They seemed a happy pair and Bett came back for the wedding at The Priory Church. Sarah and Steve moved into a new house and I recall buying them a fridge freezer; how romantic can one get.

Another recall was of two lovely old ladies left stranded after the service and I asked if they had transport out to the Hampson House

Hotel where we were having the Reception. They hadn't, so I took them. They left the hotel thanking me for a most enjoyable day but they had a train to catch from Lancaster Station. Time was of the essence and I gave them a lift to the Station and saw them on the train. I had assumed they were Steve's relatives but no – they just happened to be around The Priory at the time of the wedding, so they had had an unexpected and enjoyable day!

All in all the planning and the day went well even though I had felt uncomfortable with Bett. It was nice being with Bett's sister Margot and Ron and their daughters Sylvia and Rhona. Somehow or other families don't seem the same anymore.

Another uncomfortable time, though less disturbing before the wedding was with Steve's dad, Jack Webster. Sarah decided that top hat and tails was a must for the men at a Priory Church wedding. When put to Jack his instant response was, "no one is going to see me 'poncing' around in a top hat and tails, Priory Church or no Priory Church." The situation dramatically changed when I offered to pay for the hire of his outfit. On the day he couldn't find me quick enough in his top hat and tails, "Who do I look like?" he asked. What a spot I was on, was it Les Dawson? Then Jack got fed up with waiting and with some excitement replied, "Stewart Grainger, don't you see – it's Stewart Grainger." They say that money is the root of all evil but it can give such a lot of pleasure.

I think Debbie must have thought it was about time I shook myself up as she got me to have a look at a nice light metallic blue Ford Capri. So the brown family Marina was traded in. I became a member of the Lancaster Fell Walking Club and enjoyed the company at weekends. I was to meet a young lady on one of my walks with the club; though Christine, she liked to be known as Chris.

Debbie had finished her time at the University. Sarah and I enjoyed her degree day. She looked great in her cap and gown. It wasn't long before she found a job with McEwan Younger at Chorley. Dear old Dad would have turned in his grave; a Rowland working for a brewery! She had a commute of a couple of hours a day and it wasn't long before she moved to a flat in Chorley. Oaklands Court wasn't the same any more.

The divorce settlement made it impossible for me to stay at Oaklands. The house went up for sale and I moved into a one-bedroom flat conveniently owned by a friend. How I missed my two girls – probably the saddest time of my life.

Bett's Mum died and I went to her funeral with my two girls – they both loved their Nan. Her brother Jim came over to thank me for going and thought it brave of me. We declined the offer to join the family gathering at Ron and Margot's home.

It is said that time heals over the years but I would argue the case. One has to move on and I had moved into a house, not of my choosing but out of necessity at Glasson Dock, overlooking the beautiful Lune estuary and the Pennines, which I was to share with Chris, the lady that I'd become friendly with when out with the fell walking club.

We both visited Sarah and baby Zoë in the Lancaster Hospital Maternity Wing. I was a Granddad. Debbie, after a spell working in Leeds, found her way to London.

I met with David for the first time when he quite casually found me in the front garden, fiddling around with plants and things, as you do. Debbie was parked down the road and he was asking for my approval of their marriage. Shock or surprise I don't know when one isn't prepared. But it all went well. Debbie vacated her parking spot and we established a happy threesome, which she wanted. They also wanted to be married in the Priory Church in Lancaster, just like Sarah. By this time, Zoë was three years old and she and her Mum were to be lovely bridesmaids.

We were both dressed up for the wedding and our day started from 21 Pennine. No sooner had we left in the white Rolls Royce and passing the school, than Debbie in a state of panic shouted "Bugger, I've left my bouquet in the house" much to the amusement of our chauffeur who reversed the car back to 21.

Chris was there with me to share the wedding and it was really a nice feeling – I was no longer alone. Sister-in-law Margot and Ron had had the opportunity to meet her. Most certainly Ron approved and thought she was lovely.

Other than the additions to my family, life just went along. Sarah gave birth to another girl, Samantha and Debbie broke the mould by giving birth to a son, Daniel; then followed Lydia, then Katherine.

Somewhere amidst all these births I married Chris. A quiet wedding in the Lancaster Registry Office witnessed by two of Chris's friends, and were on our way to a honeymoon in Ireland, a place neither of us had been to before. We stopped overnight in Chester, at – where else than at the Redland House, the home of the Hunter's on Hough Green. We sent all of our family a picture postcard from Ireland letting them know that we'd got wed. When we returned home, Zoë said to Chris, "I know you're not my Grandma but you're grandma material." What more could one ask.

This is when I inherited Chris's two daughters, Helen and Marianne. I don't like the words 'step daughters' – I prefer to see them as close friends.

Our design partnership had long since outgrown the top floor room in Dalton Square and moved to much larger premises across Town in the refurbished King's Arcade. We had a staff of five and looking to grow.

I suppose, all in all, families were going along as was the working day; though we always turned the key in the door on the late side. Life's like that when you're in business for yourself.

Then one morning, when I was leaving for work, my brother-in-law Eric telephoned to say that my sister Mary, wasn't well and in the Sue Ryder Hospice at Petersfield where she died peacefully. Chris and I were with her and we attended the funeral as did Debbie and Sarah. They were both very close to their Auntie Mary.

It wasn't long before I was considering retiring, not that I wanted to retire but the computer came along and I just loved everything that I performed with on the old drawing board. It was time to move on. I left one of the best graphic design practises in the North of England in good hands. I took staff, their wives and partners out for an evening meal at Well House, a local restaurant which was enjoyed by all. I turned the key in the door of R&H for the last time on the 26th March 1997.

What can I say about retirement other than it takes some getting used to. There is no need to strive to make good, to get on, to progress, but there's plenty to do if you have the will to find it. The first couple of years I spent doing all the DIY work in the house and garden. Chris, blessed by being ten years younger, left the house each morning for work as I waved her goodbye. Was it a plus being older? I don't know. I wasn't happy with this and Chris took early retirement to be at home which seemed to be a much better arrangement.

In our early days we'd been walking in Austria, Yugoslavia, Italy, and Madeira. Then something I'd always wanted to do – a holiday in the United State of America – the old pioneer's trail, cowboy country and wasn't it great!

Then I felt the need to draw again and paint. Chris went seriously into horticulture at Myerscough College – she just loves learning, whereas for me there had to be a purpose with an element of pressure, maybe withdrawal symptoms after a life on a drawing board – that's what I was missing.

I approached a friend from working days, Paul at the Lancaster Museum, about having a one-man show of paintings as a celebration of retirement. He went along with the idea. They had two galleries capable of hanging around seventy to eighty paintings. Two galleries would be pressure as I'd only got twelve months, so I went for the one gallery. I managed to exhibit thirty eight paintings and helped Paul with the hanging of them.

We had a most enjoyable evening private view with invited guests - both our families came, but Chris's Dad was missing. Paul had organised the event – there was plenty to snack on and more than a generous provision of wine – and people to busy around looking after our needs. The City Council had performed well. It just went too fast. By the end of the exhibition I had sold thirteen paintings. Unlucky? No – for me it was a buzz being a graphic designer now in an artist's world, so I continued to paint.

Galleries got a bit greedy for commission in my view, so I now paint for my own pleasure and pass some on to family apart from exhibiting in the one annual exhibition at Milnthorpe run by the Men's Forum where a percentage of sales go to charity. I exhibit three paintings – they usually sell and again we enjoy the preview evening.

When working both Chris and I ran a car. Then I had thoughts of, do we really need two? So I sold my car. It was soon missed and I remembered days past after demob from the RAF when I had missed out on a motor bike whilst saving to get married. How I wanted that BSA Bantam. Not that I didn't want a bigger BSA – I just couldn't afford one.

I found my way down to Wall & Sagar, the two-wheel specialists in Lancaster. I went home with an abundance of catalogues and without hesitation settled on a 125cc Peugeot dual- seater scooter in metallic blue. Enjoyed and sailed through the CBT test and two years of scootering, then my two girls got worried about their old Dad out on two wheels, even though I had all the protective kit and a mobile phone. I'd had my fun, sold the scooter, then what to do?

Chris suggested what about a two seater sports car? What else but a Mazda MX5 in bright red and not having a car to trade in I got a good deal and a few free extras. The salesman did, however, persuade me to invest in a set of alloys to increase the trade in value, which isn't going to happen. I love my car and it brings a smile from Chris when she has it for the day.

With her horticultural interest Chris just had to go to the Eden Project. We both got hooked on it and spent a week in Cornwall doing gardens. This was followed by Chris's dream holiday in Canada – Vancouver to the Rockies, which we flew over in a helicopter. It was fantastic.

We are now exploring on our doorstep in England and finding it much simpler – but Chris has a hankering for Spain. It's got to be this year (2011) as I'm getting a bit difficult and expensive to insure. Thankfully I'm never free of doing – there's not enough hours in the day – I'm always busy; so busy that I have a ridiculous low mileage on my MX5. DIY takes longer than you think it will. I don't do it only for ourselves, I'm in demand from family. I'm so busy and thankfully well enough to be so.

I suppose this brings me up to Christmas 2010 which we spent with Debbie, David and family at their home in Widdington, near Saffron Walden, Essex. Grandchildren, all three of them you could say, aren't children any more. It was a lovely Christmas and meeting with the grandchildren's boy friends and girl friend.

With Christmas past spent down in Essex and both of us having had a prolonged bout of 'flu' Chris mentioned that it's the first time we've been ill together and very inconvenient that was as neither of us are good at being ill. We just like to go away and hide which is difficult when both want to do the same thing. It didn't work.

With this delayed activity we had a late January celebration of Christmas taking Sarah and Sammie out to the Highwayman Restaurant at Burrow, near Kirkby Lonsdale, a first for them. Even though its not Christmas it's still very Christmas weather. We appreciated the warm welcome, the open fire, and we had an excellent meal. This was followed by an opening of presents back at Sarah's house amidst a lot of "Ooos" and "Ahs" and "You shouldn't haves." Yet another lovely time.

Now my thoughts go beyond the end of writing this book. One of the regrets I have is that I never thanked Mum and Dad enough for how they set me up at art school for a career that I was going to enjoy so much for the whole of my working life and into retirement.

I have constantly thought of my sister, Mary, who would have enjoyed going along with this book, to help and confirm my memories, though my brother-in-law Eric has been a great help with his writings of a Walsh and Rowland family tree which I have delved into from time to time.

My wife Chris has gone beyond the gem status with her patient editing and typing of my scrawls and Gary, one of my designers at

R&H for helping me on the road to print, something that I am now completely out of touch with.

I have enjoyed writing up my memories and they have been happy memories from 5 Northway, and beyond, though sometimes it's brought tears to my eyes when my thoughts have wandered.

Peter Rowland - 2011.